Writing across Cultures

A JOHN HOPE FRANKLIN CENTER BOOK

A book in the series
Latin America Otherwise
Languages, Empires, Nations

A series edited by
Walter D. Mignolo, Duke University
Irene Silverblatt, Duke University
Sonia Saldívar-Hull, University of Texas, San Antonio

Writing across Cultures

Narrative Transculturation
in Latin America

Ángel Rama

Edited and Translated by
David Frye

Duke University Press
Durham and London
2012

© 2012 Duke University Press
All rights reserved
Printed in the United States of America on acid-free paper ∞
Designed by Charles Ellertson
Typeset in Espinosa Nova by Tseng Information Systems, Inc.
Library of Congress Cataloging-in-Publication Data
appear on the last printed page of this book.

to Darcy Ribeiro and John V. Murra
Anthropologists of Our América

Contents

About the Series

Latin America Otherwise: Languages, Empires, Nations is a critical series. It aims to explore the emergence and consequences of concepts used to define "Latin America" while at the same time exploring the broad interplay of political, economic, and cultural practices that have shaped Latin American worlds. Latin America, at the crossroads of competing imperial designs and local responses, has been construed as a geocultural and geopolitical entity since the nineteenth century. This series provides a starting point to redefine Latin America as a configuration of political, linguistic, cultural, and economic intersections that demands a continuous reappraisal of the role of the Americas in history, and of the ongoing process of globalization and the relocation of people and cultures that have characterized Latin America's experience. *Latin America Otherwise: Languages, Empires, Nations* is a forum that confronts established geocultural constructions, rethinks area studies and disciplinary boundaries, assesses convictions of the academy and of public policy, and correspondingly demands that the practices through which we produce knowledge and understanding about and from Latin America be subject to rigorous and critical scrutiny.

Uruguayan Ángel Rama is one of three towering figures of Latin American literary and cultural criticism during the second half of the twentieth century, along with Peruvian Antonio Cornejo Polar, ten years younger than Rama (1936–97) and Brazilian Antonio Candido (1918–present), eight years older than Rama. The three of them constituted the pillar of radical ideas and criticism between 1960 and 1990. Candido established the links between literature and underdevelopment, Cornejo Polar is remembered for his concept of *heterogeneidad cultural y literaria* and Ángel Rama for *transculturación literaria y narrativa*. Rama took the concept from the Cuban intellectual Fernando Ortiz (1881–1969). Heterogeneidad cultural is not associated with a specific name, although it was Cornejo Polar who made it central to his intellectual pursuit. It is a natural term regarding Andean history and culture, where the concentration of indigenous people — those of European and of African descent — have been coexisting since the sixteenth century. Rama and Cornejo Polar shared one key example to theorize their respective concepts: the novels of the Peruvian bilingual and bicultural anthropologist and novelist José María Arguedas.

The reader not familiar with Rama's life and work will find in the superb introduction by his translator, David Frye, a clear and concise guide. Within Rama's narrative and arguments, the reader will little by little be introduced to a jungle of information, ideas, analysis, and insights, but he or she will never get lost. Rama's clear prose and arguments take the reader through the different facets and faces of narrative transculturation. Written a few years earlier than his acclaimed *The Lettered City*, and during the time when structuralism and poststructuralism were invading bookstores in Latin America, *Writing across Cultures* is a signal case of the power of Latin American imagination. Rama (as well as Candido and Cornejo Polar) was writing simultaneously with the boom of Latin American literature, which coexisted with the debates on dependency theory and the emergence of theology and philosophy of liberation. This book is, in other words, a key to entering three decades of Latin American social thoughts, cultural criticism, and literary imagination.

Introduction

DAVID FRYE

The book presented here for the first time in English, *Transculturación narrativa en América Latina* (1982), was the last one that Ángel Rama published before his unfortunate death at the age of fifty-seven. Together with *The Lettered City* (1984), published a year after Rama's death and until now the only one of Rama's more than two dozen books that was translated into English, *Narrative Transculturation* marks the culmination of a lifetime of omnivorous reading, deep study, and insightful analysis of history, anthropology, social theory, art, and above all, the literatures of the Americas. As in *The Lettered City*, Rama draws ideas and inspirations in this book from far-flung regions of Latin America and uses them to create a startling juxtaposition of ideas, revealing sudden flashes of insight into the hidden commonalities that underlie the continent's regional differences. (Here, I adopt Rama's habit, retained throughout this translation, of referring to all of Latin America—South and Central America, Mexico, and Caribbean—as "the continent" or simply "America." He specifies "North America" when he means the United States.) *Narrative Transculturation* also links his work on Spanish American Modernism, for which he is well known among students of literature from the continent, with his novel arguments about the strikingly innovative nature of regionalist literature. His conclusions— notably his persuasive position on the close relationship between literary movements such as modernism or regionalism and great world-spanning trends in social and economic development—and his insightful use of the Cuban anthropologist Fernando Ortiz's concept of "transculturation" to analyze the works of the Peruvian regionalist and *indigenista* novelist José María Arguedas have influenced an entire generation of Latin American literary and cultural critics.

Ángel Rama was born in 1926 in Montevideo, Uruguay, the largest city in one of the smallest countries in the Americas, and he was a son of immigrants from the impoverished region of Galicia in northwestern Spain. These facts arguably have some bearing on the course of his life and his life's work.

Montevideo is the capital city of Uruguay, and it is also a port city on the busy Río de la Plata waterway. When Rama was born, it was at its commercial apogee—a growing, bustling city of immigrants, vitally connected with international commerce, art, and ideas. Nevertheless, it remained the poor stepsister of the larger, more glamorous Buenos Aires just up river and across the Plata. Uruguay itself is a small country, and though it was rapidly urbanizing in the 1920s, it was still largely rural. It has one of the shortest histories among the Latin American republics, a product of the eighteenth-century jockeying for power between Spain and Portugal. (By the time Montevideo was founded in 1726, the well-established cities of the empire, such as Mexico City and Lima, already counted two centuries of colonial history.) Uruguay had an important and growing national literature of its own, but it was not large enough to satisfy a restless, searching mind (such as Rama's) forever—especially not when the broad, exciting literatures and languages of neighboring Argentina and Brazil beckoned, not to mention those of Peru, Mexico, Cuba, France, Britain, the United States, Germany, and more. Finally, Uruguay underwent a brutal coup and military dictatorship in 1973 that sent Rama into involuntary exile for the rest of his days.

Born into poverty, and striving for entrance into the middle classes, Rama's parents were sojourners who could just as easily have ended up in any other port or capital across the continent, such as Havana, Mexico City, Lima, or (like the Galician parents of Rama's second wife, Marta Traba) Buenos Aires. It is perhaps not too much to speculate that Rama, growing up in the small but cosmopolitan port city of Montevideo as the son of striving immigrants, and spending much of his later life in exile from Uruguay, was fated to move on, sooner rather than later, from the project of rethinking his own native country's national literature to a lifelong project of understanding it as part of something broader: a literature of the Americas. According to Rama's friend and colleague, the Argentine critic Noé Jitrik, Rama justified his obstinate and sometimes combative style in a roundtable discussion by proudly proclaiming it "a Galician and immigrant trait, a nameless and aimless tenaciousness: there were things that had to be done and so you did them, and twenty more things too, and you got into everything; Ángel," Jitrik concluded, "was the greatest Renaissance man I have ever known."[1]

Rama was the youngest charter member of what he called the "Critical Generation," the vibrant set of Uruguayan men and women of letters whom others termed the "Generation of 1945." In Rama's case, this latter designation is quite accurate, for he embarked on his public literary career in the "lettered city" in 1945 at the age of nineteen, writing on culture for the Montevideo newspaper *El País*, translating articles from French to Spanish for Agence France-Presse and taking classes in humanities at the Universidad de la República. However, Rama himself found the year less descriptive of his generation than it was of the "critical spirit" that pervaded the "cultural environment in which I was formed": "Parodying Graham Greene, I might say that 'Uruguay made me': the critical spirit that developed there during the exact historical period in which I happened to live was so dominant that I settled as a title for my book on Uruguayan literature from 1939 to 1968 on *La generación crítica*. Everyone—poets, fiction writers, essayists—was possessed by that critical spirit; all were inscribed by the times, by the urgency with which society had become embroiled in its self-scrutiny after a long period of carefree confidence, to such a degree that no other assessment was possible."[2]

From 1945 to the early 1960s, Rama played the role of the *letrado* to perfection. He founded or cofounded several small literary journals and publishing houses, beginning with the journal *Clinamen* in 1948. He worked, talked, dined, laughed, and argued with every member of his "critical generation," and in 1950 he married the prominent Uruguayan poet Ida Vitale, one of the cofounders of *Clinamen* and, like Rama, a charter member of the generation. He spent eighteen months in Paris on a fellowship from the French Embassy (1955–56); published two novels (1951, 1960) and two books of short stories (1958, 1966); and wrote and produced three plays (1958, 1959, 1961), which were presented to some acclaim by the Compañía Nacional de Comedia in Montevideo. All the while, he tirelessly wrote literary reviews, eventually publishing more than 1,400 during his lifetime.

Rama's primary focus during these years was the literature of Uruguay and Buenos Aires (in neighboring Argentina), but as he pursued a project of rethinking the connections between the history of *platense* letters and the political history of his country, he gradually expanded his scope to encompass a rethinking of regional literature within the broader currents of Latin America as a possible whole. As *Marcha*'s cultural editor from 1959 to 1968 (a position first held by the great Uruguayan novelist Juan Carlos Onetti), Rama deliberately expanded the spectrum of literature that the prominent Montevideo weekly published, introducing the broader literature of Spanish America and Brazil to his Uruguayan readers and, as the fame of *Marcha* spread, to a wider Latin American public. He was one of the first to bring writers such as Gabriel García Márquez of Colombia, Carlos Fuentes of Mexico, and Mario Vargas Llosa of Peru to the attention of readers beyond the boundaries of those writers' own countries. According to Mexican writer José Emilio Pacheco, "We largely owe to *Marcha* and to Rama our current idea of Latin American literature, in a part of the world where books, even those written in our own language, rarely circulate between one country and another unless they are published in the old colonial metropolis."[3]

With his career at *Marcha*, Rama embarked on the second phase of his literary career, swiftly becoming a transnational figure of Latin American letters. His home base remained Montevideo, where he was named professor and chair of the department of literature at the Universidad de la República in 1966, but he spent more time each year giving talks, attending conferences, and teaching university courses all across the continent. In 1973, when he was teaching Latin American literature as a visiting professor at the Universidad Central de Venezuela, his travel abroad unexpectedly became exile when a brutal military coup crushed the Uruguayan democracy. The dictators soon abolished *Marcha* and other symbols of freedom in the country. Clearly, return was impossible. Exile turned Rama's intellectual project of creating and defining "Latin America" (or, as he preferred to put it in terms drawn from José Martí, simply "América") into a personal quest to form a new, transnational homeland. The best symbol of this project was his primary role in creating the Biblioteca Ayacucho, a vast publishing project that Rama dreamed up and successfully proposed for funding to the president of Venezuela in 1974. Rama's vision for the Biblioteca Ayacucho was to have it create a framework for building a common Latin American culture by publishing a series of five hundred carefully selected books that would embody the literary, social, and political history of the continent and create a theoretical framework for understanding the unity of Latin America and its literatures within the diversity of its regions. The project was the perfect illustration of his expansive view of literature and the revolutionary power of "letters." As he wrote, "our cultural integration is a revolutionary effort, which, as such, intends to create a future, building the utopian vision of a continent and an ideal society."[4]

It was during this period that Rama wrote the articles that later became the scaffolding for this book. First came a lecture that he gave on "The Processes of Transculturation in Latin American Fiction" before a graduate seminar at the University of São Paulo in 1973, which he published the following year as an article in the journal of the University of Zulia, Venezuela.[5] In this article, which in revised and expanded form became part I of the present book, Rama placed the panorama of Spanish American and Brazilian literature within a framework of the structure of Latin America, as viewed through anthropological theory. He had, after all, studied history at the Sorbonne under Marcel Bataillon and Fernand Braudel, and he had worked closely with the brilliant Brazilian anthropologist Darcy Ribeiro, his colleague and collaborator at the Universidad de la República in Montevideo in the years following the Brazilian coup of 1964 and Ribeiro's own involuntary exile. In particular, Rama placed two Latin American literary anthropologists in posthumous dialogue with each other: the Cuban lawyer, folklorist, historian, and self-taught anthropologist Fernando Ortiz (1881–1969) and the Peruvian novelist, poet, indigenista, folklorist, and professor of anthropology José María Arguedas (1911–69). From Ortiz's foundational study of Cuban culture, *Cuban Counterpoint: Tobacco and Sugar*, Rama drew the concept of *transculturation*, which Ortiz introduced as a specifically Latin American replacement for the Anglo-American anthropological concept of *acculturation*.[6] The term *acculturation* was introduced during the 1930s to describe the process of cultural change observed in so-called primitive societies under the onslaught of colonial rule, but as Ortiz noted, the implication of the term seemed to be that the process of cultural change "consisted merely in acquiring another culture," as if the "primitive" were an empty vessel, immaculate of ideas and ready to receive enlightenment.[7] Transculturation, by contrast, emphasized the process of passing from one culture to another, and Ortiz further specified that this process included deculturation—"the loss or uprooting of a previous culture"—followed by neoculturation, "the consequent creation of new cultural phenomena," which would not be a simple replication of the colonizer's culture but would be a hybrid of two (or more) cultural traditions.[8] Ortiz's starting point for understanding Cuba was to insist that "the real history of Cuba is the history of its intermeshed transculturations."[9]

Ortiz's theory of transculturation made an immediate impact on Rama, who saw its applicability not only to Cuban culture but also to regional cultures across all of Latin America, where indigenous, African, and European cultures and societies had been intermeshing and forming kaleidoscopic new cultural arrangements for the better part of five centuries. In this regard, Rama was particularly struck by the manifesto-like declaration "Yo no soy un aculturado" (I am not an acculturated man), which José María Arguedas presented in 1968 on the occasion of his receiving the Inca Garcilaso de la Vega prize, Peru's highest literary honor.[10] For Rama, Arguedas's insistence that he partook equally of both Spanish and Quechua, the two major languages (and, by extension, cultures) of Peru, rather than of a homogenized, "acculturated" Spanish Peruvianness, immediately called to mind Ortiz's rejection of the terminology of acculturation to describe Cuban history and culture. Rama tirelessly promoted the literary genius of Arguedas, who until then had been considered a strictly regional writer of Andean Peru. By applying Ortiz's theory to Arguedas, Rama argued that it was precisely his immersion in local, transculturated sensibilities that allowed the Peruvian novelist to solve the problem of representing the underlying realities of his country, making him a major Latin American thinker and artist whose regionalist writing was illustrative of processes that had taken place all over the continent.

Arguedas had been born in the highlands of southern Peru, far distant (physically, culturally, and politically) from the political and intellectual capital, Lima. Though he came from a Spanish-speaking mestizo family (his father was a rural lawyer; his mother died when he was two years old), he grew up speaking the Quechua language of the family's indigenous servants. Moving to Lima at the age of twenty in 1931 to study literature and ethnology at the national university, he quickly felt the influence of *indigenismo*, the artistic and political movement promoted by Peru's most prominent intellectual of the era, José Carlos Mariátegui (1894–1930).[11] The positive evaluation of the long-suppressed indigenous cultures of Peru by Andean indigenistas, and the possibility they raised of building a new national consciousness for the country based on an appreciation of indigenous identity, made a deep impression on young Arguedas, who published his first short story in Quechua in 1933. His subsequent life was difficult, troubled by political repression (in 1937, his political activity landed him in prison for eight months), the familiar economic difficulties of forging an intellectual life in an impoverished country, and recurrent depression. Throughout, his steady attention to his intellectual project of understanding indigenous cultures on their own terms (in his role as folklorist and anthropologist) and to his parallel artistic project of reflecting the realities of Peruvian life as he knew them, in literary idioms that he invented to incorporate both Spanish and Quechua sensibilities, brought him growing recognition, culminating with a professorship in anthropology and the Inca Garcilaso prize, which he received one year before his final depression and suicide in late 1969.

Rama reminds us that Arguedas left behind an impressive body of literature, including novels—the best known being *Yawar Fiesta* (1941) and *Los ríos profundos* (*Deep Rivers*, 1958)—and short stories, books of poetry (he wrote all his poems in Quechua), and many scholarly studies of the folklore and ethnology of Peru. Indeed, during the very years that Rama was working through his ideas about narrative transculturation as a key to Latin American literature, he was also editing two posthumous compilations of Arguedas's anthropological essays.[12] Rama's prologues to those edited works, together with a third article inspired by his consideration of the anthropology of Latin America, form the early versions of the chapters presented here as part II. Then, a few years after this immersion in Arguedas's ethnological writing, Rama noted in his diary that he had picked up and begun rereading what he considered Arguedas's best novel, *Los ríos profundos*, and he was immediately struck with "amazement for its precise and rapid writing, for the lofty movement of the action, for the levels of construction that transform it into more of an 'opera' than a novel. The fabulous opera of the poor."[13] Looking over the articles he had written about the Peruvian writer, he realized that he would have enough material for "an ambitious book: 'The Narrative Transculturators—José María Arguedas,'" with the addition of two new essays that he was then writing.[14] These new essays form the chapters of part III, focusing on *Los ríos profundos* as the most accomplished example of narrative transculturation in Latin America, thus completing the circle that began with his general exploration of transculturation in Latin American fiction.

This reconsideration of Arguedas took place during the next phase of Rama's life—in reality, its final phase, one marked by a further expansion of his frame of vision. In 1979, Rama and his second wife, the novelist and art historian Marta Traba,[15] had begun teaching at the University of Maryland, where he received tenure in 1981. Fellowships from the university and the Guggenheim Memorial Foundation allowed Rama to undertake a broad-ranging study at the nearby Library of Congress for a book on "the building and structure of the Latin American culture."[16]

His work was interrupted, but not derailed, when he and Traba ran up against United States foreign policy. In July 1982, Immigration and Naturalization Service functionaries in the Reagan administration denied permanent working permits to the couple, largely in response to complaints about their work with the Havana literary institute Casa de las Américas since the early 1960s (even though they had already distanced themselves from the institute over the Cuban government's human rights record).[17] Forced once more into reluctant exile, the couple moved to Caracas, Bogotá, and Paris during the following year. Rama vigorously fought the visa denial, and in the long run he might have met with success, but an accident intervened. In November 1983, Rama and Traba were on their way to an international literary conference on Spanish American culture in Bogotá, together with their friends and colleagues, the novelists Jorge Ibargüengoitia of Mexico and Manuel Scorza of Peru. After leaving Paris, the plane crashed upon landing at a scheduled stopover in Madrid. There were no survivors.

Rama left us with plenty of work to consider, both published and not quite published yet. He had seen the first product of his new grand project, the Spanish version of *Transculturation*, into print in the same year he was forced from the United States, and he completed a draft of the second book of the project, *The Lettered City*, which was published posthumously in Spanish in 1984 and in an English translation in 1996. In the decades since his death, several newly edited collections of his writings on Latin American letters have been published, his concept of literary transculturation has entered the vocabulary of Latin Americanists, and new generations of readers continue to discover the comprehensive panorama that he constructed through his close and comparative reading of texts from across the Americas.

Sources

My main source for the basic facts of Rama's life is the "Cronología" and "Bibliografía," accredited to Fundación Internacional Ángel Rama, which appear as appendices to Ángel Rama, *La crítica de la cultura en América Latina* (Caracas: Biblioteca Ayacucho, 1985), 381–402. Other sources I found very useful, in alphabetical order, are the following:

Blixen, Carina, and Álvaro Barros Lemez. *Cronología y bibliografía de Ángel Rama.* Montevideo: Fundación Ángel Rama, 1986.
"Catch 28." *The Nation* (November 20, 1982): 515–16.
Correas de Zapata, Celia. "Marta Traba." In *Spanish American Women Writers: A*

Bio-Bibliographical Source Book, edited by Diane E. Marting, 513–21. Westport, Conn.: Greenwood Publishing, 1990.

Eloy Martínez, Tomás. "Ángel Rama, o el Placer de la Crítica." In *La crítica de la cultura en América Latina*, by Ángel Rama, xxv–xli. Caracas: Biblioteca Ayacucho, 1985.

Gale Chevigny, Bell. "A Latin American Odyssey Ends." *The Nation* (February 4, 1984): 126–28.

Jitrik, Noé. "Ángel Rama: Una imagen." *Texto Crítico*, no. 32–33 (1985): 101–8.

Migdal, Alicia. "Angel Rama: Un uruguayo renacentista." *El País Cultural* (December 31, 1993). http://letras-uruguay.espaciolatino.com/rama/angel_rama.htm.

Peyrou, Rosario. "Prólogo." In *Ángel Rama: Diario 1974–1983*, 5–30. Montevideo: Ediciones Trilce, 2001.

Rama, Ángel. "Prólogo." Prologue to *La novela en América Latina: Panoramas 1920–1980*, 9–19. Bogotá: Procultura, 1982.

Sánchez Lozano, Carlos. "Prólogo." In *Ángel Rama: Crítica literaria y utopía en América Latina*, edited by Carlos Sánchez Lozano, xi–xxxii. Antioquia, Colombia: Editorial Universidad de Antioquia, 2006.

Sosnowski, Saul. "Ángel Rama: Un sendero en el bosque de las palabras." Prologue to *La crítica de la cultura en América Latina*, by Ángel Rama, ix–xxiii. Caracas: Biblioteca Ayacucho, 1985.

Part I

CHAPTER ONE

Literature and Culture

Independence, Originality, Representation

A colonial society, violently imposed, gave birth to Latin American literature. In their blindness, the Spanish and Portuguese colonizers ignored the voices of their humanists who recognized and valued the "otherness" of the Americas, but their civilization was rich and diverse, encompassing the educated and the popular, and at its zenith it spanned the world. Theirs, too, were the splendid languages and sumptuous literatures of Spain and Portugal; these also gave birth to Latin American literature. Yet that literature has never been resigned to its colonial origins, nor has it ever reconciled itself with its Iberian past.

Latin American writers contributed enthusiastically to the Black Legend of Spanish cruelty—with reason enough—but they never seemed to realize that they were only spreading ideas created by thinkers from Spain itself, who were the first to indict Spanish cruelty. Almost from the beginning, Latin American writers avoided any hint of a direct connection with Spain and preferred to give themselves different cultural lineages: Italian and classical literature in colonial times; French and British after Independence (they never quite saw France and England as the new colonizing metropolitan centers that they really were); and most recently, North American letters, the current top dogs. Each and every time, Latin American writers were moved not only by a legitimate search for cultural enrichment but also by their desire to break free from their roots. Their slogan, from the late 1700s up to our days, might well have been: "Be independent!"[1]

Latin American letters fanned the demagogic zeal of the *criollos* ["Creoles," or Latin Americans of European descent who considered themselves as representing the "national cultures" of the American republics], who repeatedly called on a pair of themes—the destitute Indian, the cruelly punished black slave—as pretexts to justify their own bill of grievances against the colonizers. From the eighteenth century on, many grandsons of Spaniards and Europeans waved their rhetorical support for indigenous peoples as a battle flag. Of course, what these criollos actually did after Independence, once the time for keeping promises had come, didn't exactly do credit to their noble pretensions.

This persistent drive for independence led them to develop a literature that was flagrantly autonomous of Iberian letters—this, on a continent whose deepest and most enduring cultural markers keep it closely tied to Spain and Portugal. This was not because Latin American literature was some sort of unique invention with no known roots but because it always sought to tie itself to foreign, Western literatures to a far greater degree than the literatures of its mother countries have ever done. (One reason why the "burden of the past" has not been much of a formative presence in the literatures of Spain and Portugal is that those literatures reflect their societies, which haven't yet produced a modernizing dynamic in the modern era.)[2]

The originality of Latin American literature is driven by its restless and romantic yearning to be a part of international culture, but this masks another, more vigorous, more persistent source for Latin American writers: the distinctive cultural characteristics of the hinterlands of the Americas. In other words, the cultures that nourish Latin American literature are not the solitary work of a few literary elites but rather the massive efforts of vast societies to construct their symbolic languages.

The timing of Latin America's uneven independence bound its newly independent literatures to the bourgeois principles of Romanticism (rather than the Enlightenment, which had little influence on them). Romanticism stamped these literatures with the twin guiding lights from its dialectical axis of history: *being original* and *being representative*. Since these literatures arose in countries that had broken away from their mother lands and rebelled against their colonial past (which got the blame for everything), they had no choice but to be *original* in their sources. The theme of "European decadence" (to which the theme of "North American decadence" would be added a century later) came on stage and never exited. This became the underlying ethical principle of Latin American literatures and of the rejection of the foreign on which they were based; writers wasted little time reflecting on the fact that this ethical principle was itself foreign and already old, even outmoded, by European standards. Thus, Andrés Bello justified his "Alocución a la poesía" ["Address to Poetry," 1823] by asking the deified figure of Poetry to leave Europe:

> that region of light and poverty,
> in which your overweening
> rival, Dame Philosophy,
> who reckons virtue on a measured scale,
> usurps your cult among the mortals;
> where the crowned Hydra head does threaten
> to return once more to slavish thought
> the ancient night of barbarism and crime.[3]

The only way to attain the desired originality of literature, according to the views of Bello and his Romantic followers, was through literature's ability to represent the region that gave rise to it. For they perceived America as glaringly different from its mother societies, given its distinctive physical environment, its diverse ethnic makeup, and its difference in terms of development when compared to the only model of progress — Europe. Simón Rodríguez's slogan "we shall create or we shall fail" developed into Ignacio Altamirano's "patriotic mission" of making literature the tool for forging the nation. Ethics and national feeling were joined as one, and local themes became "raw materials," aping the incipient economic model of the Latin American republics. For Altamirano, writers were like the farmers and industrialists of the emerging nation, linked in a chain of production: "Oh! If there is anything rich in elements for the man of letters, it is this country, just as it is for the farmer and for the industrialist."[4]

Over the years that followed, despite the great changes that took place, Latin American literature did little to distance itself from the impulses that first molded it: *independence, originality, representation.* Inspired by the internationalism of the modernizing period (1870–1910), writers worked to transcend the restrictions of nineteenth-century nationalities and to reestablish the mythical common fatherland, which they called "Latin America," that had inspired Simón Bolívar during the war for independence (as in his "Amphictyonic Congress" of Panama, 1826). Rather than throwing out the representative principle, they translated it onto the same supranational level, demanding the representation of the entire Latin American region, beyond any localism. They restricted, though they did not discard, the Romantic view of what national affairs should cover (now limited to the country's events, characters, and landscapes), while they advocated for their right to set a story anywhere in the world—a thesis defended by Manuel Gutiérrez Nájera in terms that drew Altamirano's approval.[5] Originality was defended even more fiercely now than it had been during the nineteenth-century Romantic-realist period, but it was viewed as confined to individual talent—what Rubén Darío called the writer's "personal treasurehouse." The cosmopolitan thematics that framed this view placed less emphasis on "nature" and placed more on "the men" of the region and what made them special. The individualistic model adopted when the continent was integrated into the Western economic world had won its first battle, yet the guiding principles of the independence era that gave birth to the national literatures of Latin America were not dismissed. Witness the growing hunger for originality and the urge for independence (reverent nods toward internationalism aside), which saw language as its best guarantor. Given the modernizing dynamic at work, writers turned freely to the great trove of Iberian tradition without feeling crushed under its weight; this explains the modernists' vibrant Hispanism and the turn to medieval, Renaissance, and Baroque Iberian literatures that lay not far beneath their alleged "mental Gallicisms." At this new international juncture, language was once more the tool of independence.[6]

The criterion of representation was resurgent during the nationalist and social period (roughly 1910–40), pushed by the emerging middle classes, many of whom were people from the provinces who had recently moved to the booming cities. It was easier now than during the nineteenth-century Romantic era to visualize the place of literature in national or regional culture. Literature was now called upon to represent one social class—the middle class—at a moment when that class was fighting the top social strata for political dominance. Thus, writers again called for "local color," as the Romantics had once done, but now they were inwardly moved by the worldview (and especially by the interests) of a single social class. In keeping with the nature of their battle against the power of the old regime, middle-class writers adopted the demands of the lower strata as their own. *Criollismo*, nativism, regionalism, *indigenismo*, *negrismo*, not to mention urban *vanguardismo*, experimentalist modernization, and futurism:[7] all the literary trends of this period emphasized the representative principle, which was once more theorized as a necessary condition for originality and independence. The thinking on this point now owed much to the newly developing field of sociology, however. Sociology had gradually displaced and absorbed the Romantic concept of the nation, as can be seen among the founders of the field in Latin America, from Domingo Faustino Sarmiento and José María Samper to Eugenio de Hostos. It established the regionalist constraints that now characterized writing all over Latin America, according to Alberto Zum Felde: "The entire genre of the essay on the continent is, to a greater or lesser extent, linked to its sociological reality. The same is analogically true in the novel, which is also largely sociological; the differences between the two genres is often only their form, for in their common substance they are identical."[8]

It was now established as an implicit, though quite baseless, rule that the middle classes were the genuine interpreters of nationhood, and that they (and not the upper classes that held real power) drove the national spirit. This meant literature was now redefined according to the patriotic and social mission of the middle class, as legitimated by its representational status. This criterion was developed with great sophistication. Middle-class writers did not look for justifications of their representational status in the country's physical environment, in passing events, or even in national customs but rather in the "spirit" that inspired the nation, which they translated into forms of behavior that they could, in turn, record in writing. Here they went beyond the simplistic Romantic approach to the representative criterion, but the result was still more elementary or commonplace than the late nineteenth-century modernists' turn to language. In fact, in developing this point, they did not turn to the modernists but all the way back to the Romantics who shared their idealizing and ethical concept of literature. Middle-class writers, however, surpassed the Romantics in devising more finely tuned (though more instable) tools for defining nationality.

The "Mexican" reading that Pedro Henríquez Ureña (followed discreetly by Alfonso Reyes) gave to Juan Ruiz de Alarcón's works, which themselves contained no hints of a Mexican environment, was matched by the "Uruguayan" reading that the Guillet Muñoz brothers gave to Lautréamont's *Les chants de Maldoror* and by the "Peruvian" readings that José Carlos Mariátegui gave to the works of Ricardo Palma and that Ventura García Calderón gave to Alonso Carrió de la Vandera's book *El lazarillo de ciegos caminantes*.[9] In their analyses, nationality was confined to procedures, concepts of life, and sometimes to the literary sources that recurred throughout the long development of a literature. No matter how finely tuned these analyses were, they could not avoid certain pitfalls. On one hand, they posited the survival, sometimes over the course of centuries, of presumably national traits in the works they studied, a move that forced them to detect traits based on the country's unvarying geography rather than on its shifting history. On the other hand, the concept of nationhood that they used was defined by a single class in a single historical period, so their criterion was in fact shifting and historically contingent. This contradiction eroded the foundations of their new view of representativeness, though literary originality (and therefore independence) remained at the heart of it. Between the individual artist (on whom the modernizers of the twentieth century placed their bets) and society and/or nature (favored by nineteenth-century Romantics and twentieth-century regionalists), the latter won the day. Society and nature were seen as having greater potential, deeper molding capacity, and a stronger genetic framing than sheer individual creativity; however, it was not so much the abundant fertility of nature (which so many critics, even Menéndez Pelayo, had called on to explain what set Spanish American letters apart from other Spanish-language literatures) that gave them this potential but rather society and its inherent traits, for which the incipient field of anthropology had not yet come up with its definitive name: culture.[10]

The new perspective was taken up by the most perceptive literary critic of the period, Pedro Henríquez Ureña. Educated in the United States, where he first encountered Anglophone cultural anthropology, Henríquez Ureña aspired to incorporate the new field into a study of Latin American (or, to use his preferred term, Hispanic) characteristics, still in the service of the concept of the nation. The title of his 1928 book defines his project: *Seis ensayos en busca de nuestra expresión*, "Six Essays in Search of Our Means of Expression" (Buenos Aires: Babel, 1927). It was a well-documented, trailblazing investigation into the workings of a literature that had been born from the rejection of its roots, that had progressed due to the internationalism that gradually integrated it into the West, and that still sought autonomy in Latin America's cultural uniqueness. For the preceding two centuries, Latin American literature had swung like a pendulum between two poles—the foreign and the internal—not because writers deliberately resolved on swinging back and forth but because they were compelled first in one direction, then the other. These swings never paralyzed the persistent project of independence, originality, and representation, but they increased or decreased its intensity depending on changing circumstances, the productive forces at work, the trends moving society as a whole, the growing complexity of society itself, and the world period at the time. The result was that Latin

American culture never moved in a straight line toward progress, for there were setbacks, holdups, and jarring accelerations; above all, once the various Latin American societies attained a certain high degree of evolution, there was a power struggle among their social classes for the right to be considered the bearers of cultural forms.

Around 1940, a vast rethinking of the continent began, in which its writers and thinkers would become active participants. This rethinking began earlier in some parts (Argentina) and later in others (Brazil, Mexico). It seems to have come in response to a slowdown in the rise of the middle classes to power, the ebbing of their success, the self-criticism of their leaders, and the growing presence of the working class (even the peasantry) on the national stage, independent of the middle classes. This long period could be analyzed historically, sociologically, or politically. It could also be given a literary analysis—not simply by analyzing its authors, their works, worldviews, and artistic forms but, even better, by analyzing the particularities in their works as they responded to the basic norms that have governed Latin American literature from the beginning.

Proposing such an analysis today involves a hint of controversy. One group of literary critics, reacting against the clumsy content analysis that turned literary works into mere sociological documents—if not political manifestos—has turned toward an equally pernicious navel-gazing; focusing exclusively on the fine modulations of literature, these critics have divorced literature from its cultural context, ignored literature's search for representativeness, and ultimately turned their backs on the act of communication that is at the heart of any literary text. Placing literary works back in the cultural context of Latin American societies, while recognizing their daring construction of meaning and the enormous efforts they have undertaken to deal in a genuine way with the symbolic languages developed by the people of the Americas, is a means of reinforcing those bedrock concepts of independence, originality, and representation. Literary works do not stand outside of their cultures; they crown them. To the degree that those cultures are the inventions of masses of people over the course of centuries, they turn the writer into a laborer who toils with the products of innumerable others. An editor, Roa Bastos would have said. The most brilliant weaver in the vast historical sweatshop of American society.

In an era when the prestige of "modernization" has been severely diminished, and when the bedazzling technical contributions of the international avant-garde novel has led not only to great works of recognized brilliance (Borges, Cortázar, Fuentes) but also to the growth of a random series of mere experimental imitations that scarcely circulate even among their rarified coteries, it is worth examining the literary output of recent decades to see if there weren't any other sources that lent themselves to supporting a reinvention of the arts, aside from those that came over on ships from Europe. I have already studied this point in my essay on "La tecnificación narrativa" [The Technification of Fiction] (*Hispamérica* 30 [1981]: 29–82), but I did so from the angle of the diffusion of cosmopolitan literature in Latin America, rather than from that of searching for sources of Latin American literature in the cultures that had grown up organically on the continent itself. The latter is the theme of this book. It will only be when our internal cultural treasure troves can provide not merely "raw material" but a worldview, a language, a technique for producing literary works that the name of Latin America will cease to be taken in vain. There is nothing in this book that smacks of self-centered folklore studies — ridiculous in an internationalist age. It does, however, evince a push for spiritual decolonization through recognizing the abilities acquired by a continent with a long and fertile tradition of inventiveness, which has carried on a dogged struggle to become one of the richest sources of culture in the world.

Responses to the Conflict between Vanguardismo and Regionalism

During the 1930s, two avant-garde trends in writing fiction — a cosmopolitan approach and a critical-realist approach — developed organically in the great urban centers of Latin America, and particularly in Buenos Aires, the most advanced city in the region at the time. Both approaches spread through Latin America's distribution networks, which were based entirely in the same cities where these aesthetic projects originated; this fact alone meant the effective end of regionalism, which had been the most prominent literary movement on the continent since its emergence around 1910 as a transformation of *costumbrismo* and naturalism (as in the case of Mariano Azuela). Regionalism had been dominant everywhere, from the least educated areas of the continent to the most advanced, thanks to the wide success of novels in the 1920s such as *La vorágine* by Colombian writer José Eustasio Rivera (1924) and *Doña Bárbara* by Rómulo Gallegos of Venezuela (1929), whose broad distribution masked the growth of vanguardismo during the same period.[11]

At first, the regionalist movement adopted an aggressively defensive posture and went looking for a drastic confrontation with the avant-garde. The clash between regionalists and *vanguardistas* (or *modernistas*) opened with a text, "Ante el tribunal" [Before the Tribunal], published by the leading regionalist, Horacio Quiroga, in 1931: "My still-fresh battle wounds shall do me little good, for I fought against another past and against other errors just as viciously as they now fight against me. For twenty-five years I've struggled with all my might to win everything that's now being denied me. All an illusion. Today I must bow down before the court, confess my crimes, which I had thought virtues, and salvage at least some atom of my personhood from the abysm into which my name has been cast."[12]

Quiroga's lighthearted tone here cannot conceal his bitterness over fighting a losing battle in 1928 and 1929 through a series of texts on his narrative art and on the writers who served as his models, his Parnassus: Joseph Conrad, William Hudson, Bret Harte, José Eustasio Rivera, Chekhov, Kipling, Benito Lynch, and so forth.

This confrontation could perhaps be seen as just another conflict between generations. The same, however, could not be said of Gilberto Freyre's "Regionalism Manifesto" (1926), written for the regionalism conference he helped organize in Recife; his opposition to São Paulo-based *modernismo* was rooted in his disagreement with the writer Mário de Andrade, who was only seven years older than Freyre and therefore belonged to the same generation.[13]

Freyre's manifesto called for "a movement for the rehabilitation of regional and traditional values from this part of Brazil; a movement of which genuine masters such as the humanist João Ribeiro and the poet Manuel Bandeira are beginning to take notice." Regionalism should counter the foreign trends coming from Brazil's capital, Rio de Janeiro, and from other booming port cities such as São Paulo, and it should bring back a sense of regionhood, defined as follows: "what one might call the eternal sense — the regional, not merely provincial, way of being a person from one's own land — that is made manifest in a reality or expressed in matter that is perhaps more lyrical than geographic, and certainly more social than political."[14]

Even though the manifesto, with its anthropological orientation clearly drawn from the teachings of Franz Boas, paid more attention to the cuisine of Brazil's Northeast and to the architecture of its *mucambos* (peasant huts) than it did to literature, it was careful to emphasize how the spiritual formation of the intellectuals of the Northeast has been influenced by the idiosyncrasies of its culture, which are fully manifest in its common people, though Freyre avoided a vertical, classist definition of cultures and defends a horizontal, regional view of them:

> In the Northeast, anyone who goes to the people is going down to the roots and the source of regional life, culture, and art. Whoever approaches the people is going among the masters and becomes the apprentice, no matter how much of a Bachelor of Arts or Doctor of Medicine he might be. The strength of Joaquím Nabuco, Sílvio Romero, José de Alencar, Floriano, Padre Ibiapina, Telles Júnior, Capistrano, Augusto dos Anjos, Rosalvo Ribeiro, Augusto Severo, Auta de Sousa, and other great Northeastern conveyors of the culture or the spirit of Brazil, I see as coming primarily from the contact they had, as children on the sugar plantations or in the cities, or even as grown men, with the common people, with popular traditions, with the masses of the region, not merely with its rivers, trees, and animals.[15]

He did not want his regionalism to be mistaken "for separatism or *bairrismo* [exclusive or excessive interest in strictly local affairs]; for anti-internationalism, anti-universalism, or anti-nationalism." Right there, he demonstrated his fatal submission to Rio-based norms of national unity and thereby lost any momentum he might have had for aspiring to independence. Instead, he limited himself to attacking Rio's homogenizing function, arguing that the capital city used foreign cultural models while ignoring "the body of Brazil, victim since birth of the foreignisms that have been imposed on it without any regard for the particularities and inequalities of its physical and social configuration."[16] He mocked the modernized port cities for their symbolically significant adoption of Santa Claus, with his thick winter outfit and his snow-riding sleigh, whereas he found the culture of Pernambuco and of the Northeast in general second to none "for their wealth of illustrious traditions and brightness of character." With that, he refuted both the foreign discourse that was dismissive of the tropics and the anti-Portugal discourse of the modernizers who saw "in everything inherited from the Portuguese an evil to be despised."[17]

Though the conflict between regionalists and the avant-garde was most rigorously theorized in Brazil, it also raged in Spanish America. In the case of Peru, for example, José Carlos Mariátegui visualized it more from a social and class viewpoint than from a cultural one, hoping thereby to overcome the nineteenth-century contest between political centralism and regionalism, which led to administrative decentralization and only gave more power to rural Peru's *gamonales* [large landowners who monopolized politics in the countryside]. Mariátegui's social reappraisal of the conflict proposed joining indigenismo with a new kind of regionalism, which would be defined as follows: "This regionalism is no mere protest against the centralist regime. It is an expression of the sierra conscience and of the Andean sentiment. The new regionalists are, above all, indigenistas and they cannot be confused with the old-style anticentralists. [Cuzco-born historian and archaeologist Luis Eduardo] Valcárcel sees the roots of Inca society intact under the flimsy layer of colonialism. His work belongs to Cuzco, to the Indian, to the Quechua, not to a region. It is nourished on Indian sentiment and autochthonous tradition."[18]

Mariátegui's regionalism did not only meet opposition from official elites in the capital, whose view of national unity, based on international models, called for homogenizing the country. It also ran up against other unofficial, heterodox, and oppositional positions, for those, too, drew on internationalism to a substantial degree. Mariátegui's tendency to disregard the horizontal differences among regional cultures in the Andes is related to his alignment with a third ideological approach active in Latin American fiction during the era, which itself drew on the so-called social *indigenista* literature, from López Albújar to Jorge Icaza.[19]

This third approach was that of social narrative. Though related to the critical realist approach, social narrative displayed specific features that justified a separate category from the moment when César Vallejo inaugurated it with his social novel *El tungsteno* (1931), after which it spread throughout the bellicose "pink decade" of worldwide antifascism. Though social narrative derived from a less elaborate version of modernism, there are good reasons for considering it a modernist movement: it bore the stamp of the urbanization of literary sources; it adhered to ideologies imported from Stalinist-era Soviet socialist realism; and it translated the worldview of Communist party political cadres. Paradoxically, some of the ingredients that linked it to critical realism also tied it to the fantastic literature that was developed in Buenos Aires during the 1930s (the Jorge Luis Borges story "Tlön, Uqbar, Tertius Orbis" [1940] is a key work), which the social writers rejected over its identification with conservative thinkers. This third approach is what Alejo Carpentier was referring to when he wrote that "the 1930–1950 era is characterized, among us, by a certain stagnation in fictional techniques. Fiction becomes generally nativist. But a new element appears: denunciation.

And when you talk denunciation, you are talking politics."[20] It would have been more accurate to say that the narrative techniques of the social novel were very simple and were as opposed to those of the regionalist novel as they were to the fantastic, though less opposed to those of critical realism, because all of these approaches translated the perspectives of different social sectors, whether classes, groups, or the avant-garde, that had come into conflict with each other in ways that the economic crisis would only intensify.

There was indeed a literary war, though curious points of contact occasionally arose among the various approaches. Thus, for example, regionalism covered rural subjects, so it stayed in close contact with traditional and even archaic elements of Latin American life, many of them hailing from folklore. However, Carpentier, who helped develop the critical realist camp, was subtly appreciative of those same traditional elements, often handling them in the service of understanding the history of the Americas. Borges, for his part, in his reply to Américo Castro's book *La peculiaridad lingüística rioplatense* (1941), carried out a keen analysis of those same rural elements on the level of language, whereas Mário de Andrade used them directly in his modernist novel *Macunaíma* (1928).

Regionalism was the movement most challenged by the reinvention of literature. Taking up the challenge, regionalism protected an important set of literary values and local traditions, though in order to achieve this end, it had to transform itself and transfer those values and traditions into new literary structures—as radical as, yet not assimilable to, the new devices that inspired the various innovative trends in urban fiction. Regionalist writers saw that if the movement became stagnant in its debate with vanguardismo and critical realism, it would plunge into a death spiral. Losing their quiver of literary forms would be the least of their problems (considering that such forms are constantly being transformed in any case); more serious was the potential extinction of a broad swath of cultural content that only literature had brought to notice, even in the innovative urban centers—and hence the end to an effective way of uniting the national environment during a period of growing stratification and social fragmentation.

From the general structure of Latin American society, regionalism emphasized the cultural particularities that had taken shape in the hinterlands, helping to define their distinct profiles and at the same time admit them back into national culture, which more and more reflected urban norms. Therefore, regionalism tended to hold onto those elements of the past that had helped make the nation culturally unique, and it undertook the task of transmitting the resulting form to the future, as a way of resisting foreign innovations. Regionalism highlighted the component of tradition, one of the obligatory traits in any definition of culture, though it flagrantly overlooked the modifications that were already being progressively stamped on the traditional baggage of the past. As such, regionalist literary works tended to promote a historically crystallized version of tradition.

The result was the frail values of regionalism and the frailty of its expressive literary mechanisms as they came under assault from the foreign modernism that entered through the ports and capital cities. The first to succumb were the regionalists' literary structures. Changing times, of course, are revealed in such devices even before any changes can be detected in their underlying worldviews; literary structures endeavor to preserve the old values without overt change while in fact transferring them to a different cognitive perspective. Thus regionalism came to incorporate new literary articulations, which it sometimes set on the world stage but more often in urban Latin American settings close at hand. It was a matter of avoiding a drastic substitution of its bases and of trying instead to expand them to cover the entire national territory once more, if possible. To preserve its traditionalist message—easily transferred to the cities up until then, as they had grown through internal migration and incorporated a lot of rural culture—regionalism had to adjust that message to the aesthetic conditions forged in the cities. The cities' aesthetics, however, came from an urban evolution that absorbed foreign influences; this was what made them so responsive to the prestigious models marked "world culture," which in fact were produced in the metropolitan centers of the developed world. This was not just a problem for writers' specialized artistic activities; it formed part of a larger process of acculturation all over the continent, leading, under the combined impact of Europe and the United States, to a second modernizing period between the two world wars. The dynamic was quite evident in the modernizing urban enclaves of Latin America and their foreign-influenced cosmopolitan literature, but in this book we have chosen to analyze it in the traditionalist hinterlands of the continent, for in our view it was most significant there.

After the First World War, Latin America felt the effects of a new round of economic and cultural expansion from the metropolitan world centers. All the benefits of this expansion accrued to one sector of Latin American society, and they could not conceal the internal fragmentation and internal conflicts caused by the expansion itself; these effects only grew worse after the economic crash of 1929. One chapter in this history is that of the conflicts between hinterland regions and the modernization that was led by the capital and port cities and orchestrated by the urban ruling elites who wholeheartedly adopted the philosophy of progress.

The cities, with their foreign-based, modernized culture and their appropriation of the national social surplus, held sway over their hinterlands with the support of the new technological tools of the era. (This internal domination was actually just a displacement of the cities' own dependence on foreign cultural systems.) In cultural terms, the commercial and industrial hubs tolerated the folkloric conservatism of the rural hinterlands. The cities strained against rural conservatism, which made it harder for them to maintain their creativity and their obligatory cutting-edge status; modernization theory told them that this was just the first step toward the country's inevitable homogenization. For the hinterlands, with their multiple, diverse cultural configurations, the capital cities offered a fatal dilemma: either retreat and go into your death throes, or renounce your values and die outright.[21]

Regionalism was a response to this conflict. Basically, the regionalists wanted to keep national society from breaking apart while it was going through this unequal transformation. A halfway solution was the most common: pick up what modernity has new to offer, revise the contents of regional culture in that new light, and use both sources to cobble together a hybrid that can keep on transmitting the received heritage. It would be a reinvented heritage but still one that could be identified with its past. In the fine arts, regionalist groups emphasized the study of local traditions that had been growing stagnant in order to revitalize them. They could not renounce them, but they could update them in the light of modernist changes, selecting elements that were adaptable to the new system of the day.

Such adaptations were carried out in every artistic field during the 1920s and 1930s, most painstakingly in the various trends in fiction during that period. It is no coincidence that after Carpentier heard the dissonances of Stravinsky's music, he sharpened his ear to rediscover and appreciate the African rhythms that had been there to hear for centuries in the small black town of Regla across the bay from Havana; or that Miguel Ángel Asturias, dazzled by automatic writing, decided it would help rescue the lyrical poetry and philosophy of Guatemala's indigenous communities. Similarly, in an analysis of *Macunaíma*, Gilda de Mello e Souza put forward the perceptive hypothesis of a double source, expressed symbolically in one of the poet's verses ("I am a Tupi playing a lute"), in order to understand the work: "The interest of the book thus results in large measure from its 'simultaneous adherence to utterly heterogeneous terms,' or better put, to a curious satirical play that wavers incessantly between adopting the European model and appreciating the nation's difference."[22]

The impact of modernization caused the arts to withdraw, at first, into a defensive posture. Artists immersed themselves in protecting the mother culture. Withdrawal did not solve any of their problems, though, so in the second phase they critically studied their values and selected some of them after evaluating their distinguishing strong points and viability in the new era. It is instructive to compare Gilberto Freyre's 1926 *Manifesto regionalista* with his later forewords to new editions of it over the following decades. In those forewords, he redefined regionalism as "a Movement that is Regionalist, Traditionalist, and, *in its way, Modernist*," and he emphasized that "this movement, as modernist as it was traditionalist and regionalist, was a pioneer in initiating a revolution in Brazilian artistic norms," which Freyre illustrated with one of his characteristically generous lists of names. He was not so generous, however, as to include the *Semana de Arte Moderno* [Modern Art Week] of São Paulo, though on the other hand he managed to find a point of convergence with his old antagonist, Mário de Andrade: "From the outset he was also determined to investigate, to reinterpret, to appreciate inspirations arising from the earthy, traditional, oral, popular, folkloric, at times even anthropologically intuitive roots of our own culture. Everyday, spontaneous, rustic things, dismissed by those who are sensitive only to the distilled and the erudite in the arts or culture."[23]

Here, he was pointing toward the third phase, in which regional cultures absorbed the impact of modernization. After the regionalists' evaluative self-study and selection of their cultures' fittest elements, they went on to rediscover cultural traits in this third phase that, though drawn from the stores of tradition, had never before been noticed or systematically utilized by writers but whose expressive possibilities became apparent when viewed from a modernizing perspective.

Lanternari's distinction between the three responses to acculturation can also be applied to regionalist literature: there too we find "cultural vulnerability" (accepting foreign notions and giving up one's own notions almost without a struggle), "cultural rigidity" (barricading oneself drastically behind the objects and values that constitute one's own culture while rejecting any new contributions), and "cultural plasticity" (deftly aiming to incorporate new things, not just as objects to be absorbed by a cultural complex but above all as fermenting agents to inspire the traditional cultural structure, which is thus capable of inventive responses, drawing from its own component elements).[24] Especially relevant to this "cultural plasticity" are the artists who do not limit themselves to a syncretic composition by merely adding contributions from first one culture and then the other, but who, perceiving that each culture has its own autonomous structure, understand that their incorporation of foreign elements must go hand in hand with a total rearticulation of the cultural structure, which means calling on new focal points within it.

To carry this out, they must immerse themselves again in the sources of their culture. This can lead to intensifying certain elements of the traditional cultural structure that seem to come from even more primitive strata than those recognized previously. The signifying power of these strata makes them invulnerable to the corrosive effects of modernization; witness the terse syntax of César Vallejo and later of Juan Rulfo or, on another plane, of Graciliano Ramos. For a writer, these are mere artistic solutions; however, they emerge from actions that take place in the heart of the culture by reviving elements that are real yet previously unrecognized and that become revitalized when faced with the aggressive forces of modernization.

Transculturation and Fictional Genre

The processes of acculturation are as old as the history of contact between human societies. These processes have been studied under various labels in all the key ancient cultures: Crete, Greece, Alexandria, Rome. The anthropological concept of acculturation, however, is as recent as the discipline that developed it.[25] Given anthropology's relation to European (and particularly British) colonialism and twentieth-century decolonization, the acculturation concept has been dogged by ideological inferences that cannot be dismissed, especially when dealing with its application to the arts and literature.

Latin American anthropology has questioned the term *acculturation* but not the transformations that it denotes, and has tried to refine its meaning. In 1940, the Cuban writer Fernando Ortiz proposed replacing it with the term *transculturation* while extolling the importance of the process it denotes, which in his words was "fundamental and indispensable for an understanding of the history of Cuba, and, for analogous reasons, of that of America in general." Fernando Ortiz reasoned as follows: "I am of the opinion that the word *transculturation* better expresses the different phases of the process of transition from one culture to another because this does not consist merely in acquiring another culture, which is what the English word *acculturation* really implies, but the process also necessarily involves the loss or uprooting of a previous culture, which could be defined as a deculturation. In addition it carries the idea of the consequent creation of new cultural phenomena, which could be called neoculturation."[26]

This concept of transformations (enthusiastically endorsed by Bronislaw Malinowski in his introduction to Ortiz's book)[27] clearly translates a Latin American perspective, including the incorrect interpretations it might encompass.[28] It resists considering the country's own traditional culture as if it were passive, inferior to the foreign culture that would modify it, destined for great losses, and lacking any means to respond creatively. To the contrary, the concept is developed on a double set of proofs: on one hand, it notes that the current culture of the Latin American community (which itself is a product of long-term transculturation and in constant evolution) is composed of idiosyncratic values that can be identified as having been active since the remote past; on the other hand, it corroborates the creative energy that propels it forward, making it quite distinct from a simple aggregate of norms, behaviors, beliefs, and cultural objects, for it is a force that acts with facility on situations arising from its own development as well as on contributions coming from elsewhere. It is precisely this capacity for creative originality, even under trying historical circumstances, that shows that it is the culture of a lively, creative society; such traits can be found throughout the cultural area, though they are found in their most complex forms at the deepest layers of the hinterlands.

These hinterland cultures can be exposed directly to the influence of foreign metropolitan centers. Such was the case in several rural areas of the Caribbean basin where companies exploiting tropical crops established a presence during the first third of the twentieth century. This was the history told from a patrician viewpoint in *La hojarasca* [by Colombian novelist Gabriel García Márquez, 1955] and from a social realist viewpoint in *Mamita Yunai* [by Costa Rican novelist Carlos Luis Fallas, 1941]. It could also be told through a number of other literary systems by turning to their original sources and making sure to correlate the three essential elements: event, worldview, and literary form.

More often, however, hinterland cultures receive transculturative influences from the national capital or whatever area is most closely tied to the outside world; many different types of clashes result. If the capital, which typically directs the country's educational and cultural systems, happens to fall behind in modernization compared with one of its hinterland regions, we find the regional intellectuals passing judgment on those in the capital. This has been going on in Colombia for several decades now. The most noteworthy cultural event in Colombia has been the cultural insurrection of the Caribbean coastal zone (Barranquilla, Cartagena) against the norms of the national capital in the central highlands, Bogotá, which can be followed in the articles that a young Gabriel García Márquez wrote for *El Heraldo* of Barranquilla in the 1950s. In them, García Márquez not only contrasted his region's loose lifestyle with the circumspection and constriction of life in the capital, but he took advantage of the Caribbean coast's more rapid modernization. Speaking about "The Problems of the Novel" in Colombia, he noted the absence of the great innovative trends from world literature, using terms that were clearly meant to provoke:

> The Colombian novel has still not been written that is indisputably and fortunately influenced by writers like Joyce, Faulkner, or Virginia Woolf. I say "fortunately" because I do not believe that we Colombians can, for the time being, remain exceptions to the play of influences. In her foreword to *Orlando*, Virginia admits to her influences. Faulkner himself cannot deny the influence that Joyce has exercised over him. There is some connection—especially in the handling of time—between Huxley and, once more, Virginia Woolf. Franz Kafka and Proust range freely all over modern literature. If we Colombians are to choose wisely, we should inevitably join this trend. The regrettable thing is that it hasn't already happened, nor does one detect the slightest signs that it might ever take place.[29]

Similarly, around the same time this article appeared, García Márquez considered the charges of provincialism aimed at him and directed them right back at the capital in a picturesque and humorous attack on the traditionalism that had overtaken Bogotá at a time when modernization characterized the Caribbean coast of Colombia. "An intelligent friend warned me that my position on some of the literary guilds in Bogotá was typically provincial. Nevertheless, my well-known and very provincial modesty allows me, I think, to state that in this regard the true cosmopolitans are those whose thoughts agree with this journalist on the parochial exclusivity of the capital's standard bearers. Literary provincialism in Colombia begins at 2,500 meters above sea level."[30] His position was well grounded not only because "La Cueva" [The Cave, a Barranquilla-based group of writers during the 1950s] introduced an unmistakable modernism into Colombian fiction (only hinted at in Eduardo Zalamea Borda's 1934 novel, *4 años a bordo de mí mismo*) but also because the coastal region had long been distinguished by its openness to world culture and had acted on that openness with an intensity never glimpsed in the capital. The Bogotá literary movement called "Los Nuevos" [The New Ones] of the 1920s never displayed the sort of interest in new literary trends that Ramón Vinyes's journal *Voces* [published in Barranquilla] had shown a decade earlier. The reinvention of the arts in Colombia would come about through a variety of personal ventures (León De Greiff, José Félix Fuenmayor, Arturo Vidales), with most contributions coming from the hinterlands that had felt the impact of modernization defended by García Márquez, but they incorporated it like a fermenting agent to spur their own regional cultures' expansive responses.

Nevertheless, it is more common for the hinterlands to be influenced by the country's more modernized regions. Thus, two transcultural processes typically occur in succession: first is one undergone by the capital city (or, more often, by its main port), taking advantage of its resources, though this is where foreign pressure wins its greatest battles; second is one undergone by regional culture in the hinterlands, under the impact of transculturation transmitted there from the capital. These two processes were often resolved into a single one due to the migration of most young provincial writers to the major cities, where they often gathered with writers who were equally provincial in their own way, though born in the capital. These groups of writers came up with aesthetic solutions that combined modernizing impulses and localist traditions in various proportions, sometimes yielding picturesque results. In the south, Pedro Leandro Ipuche coined the term *cosmic nativism* as a metaphor for this crossing of cultures, which had Borges's initial approval. The unique handling of world culture seen in José Lezama Lima's essays justifies Edmundo Desnoes's description of it as "the lucubrations of a brilliant small-town druggist."[31]

Fernando Ortiz's definition of transculturation would have pleased the Peruvian writer José María Arguedas, who, like Ortiz, was an anthropologist and equally suspicious of foreign academics' evaluations of the transformative processes in American culture. In the talk he delivered when he received the Inca Garcilaso de la Vega literary prize in 1968, Arguedas belligerently rejected the label of "acculturated" for himself, given what he took the word to mean: losing your own culture and accepting the colonizer's in its place, with no possibility of ever again expressing your singular tradition, the one you grew up in:

> The encircling wall could have and should have been destroyed; the copious streams (of wisdom and art) from the two nations could have and should have been united. And there was no reason why the route followed had to be, nor was it possible that it should solely be, the one imperiously demanded by the plundering conquerors, that is: that the conquered nation should renounce its soul (even if only formally appearing to do so) and take on the soul of the conquerors, that is to say, that it should become acculturated. I am not an acculturated man: I am a Peruvian who, like a cheerful demon, proudly speaks in Christian and in Indian, in Spanish and in Quechua.[32]

Some adjustments have to be made to Fernando Ortiz's concept of transculturation before it can be applied to literary works. His notion is geometric, with three moments. The first moment involves varying degrees of "partial deculturation," which can affect different aspects of both culture and literary production, though it always entails a loss of elements considered obsolete. The second involves the incorporation of elements from the foreign culture. In the third, there is an effort at mending culture, using both surviving elements from the original culture and elements from outside it. This schema pays insufficient attention to the criteria of selection and inventiveness that must always be part of the mix in any case of cultural plasticity, for such a state testifies to the energy and creativity of a cultural community. If the community is alive, it will carry out that act of selection, both on itself and on the introduced foreign elements, and it will necessarily invent new things through a combinatory system that matches the cultural system's own autonomy. The "stripping down process," to which George M. Foster has called attention in his book on the Spanish colonization of the Americas,[33] corresponds to selections that the donor culture introduces into its contributions in order to make them as viable as they can be. The same selectivity is found in the receiving culture in every case where a predetermined norm or product is not strictly forced on it, allowing the culture to choose from a rich range of foreign contributions, or to search for other contributions from among the hidden elements of the dominant culture. The transculturing impact of Europe between the wars did not include Marxism in its repertoire, yet that was precisely what many groups of university students chose throughout America, extracting it from what Toynbee would have called the heterodox forces of the original European culture. Moreover, the tendency supporting independence—which we have singled out as the leading element in the cultural process of Latin America—has always tended to choose the rejected elements from the metropolitan centers of the European and North American system, ripping them out of context and appropriating them in a dangerously abstract way. Thus, in recent decades, Latin American theater has not accepted the North American musical comedy, but it has appropriated the off-Broadway spectacle *Hair*. The critical message that this show communicates can be adapted to the material limitations of many theater groups and their dedication to social critique.

This selective capability is directed not only at the foreign culture but also particularly at the community's own culture, vast parts of which are destroyed or lost. This task of selecting traditions is carried out during the investigation mentioned above, the one that can lead to a rediscovery of primitive values that have almost been forgotten in the community's own culture. In effect, this is a search for resistant values that can stand up to the damaging impact of transculturation; it can thus be seen as a creative task, part of what Fernando Ortiz called neoculturation—working on both contact cultures simultaneously.

There will, then, be losses, selections, rediscoveries, and incorporations. All four are concomitant; all occur as part of the general restructuring of the cultural system, the highest creative function that the transculturation process will accomplish. Tools, norms, objects, beliefs, and customs: these exist only in living, dynamic articulation, which is precisely what the functional structure of culture seeks to design.

Language

Just as in the modernism of the late nineteenth century, language once more became a defensive stronghold for Latin American writers and proof of their independence during the second assault of modernization during the interwar years. Language behaviors were decisive in the case of writers, whose choice of "linguistic series" provided their raw material and determined their artistic production. Modernism established two models: first, a purist reconstruction of the Spanish language, most fit for historical themes (*La gloria de Don Ramiro* by Argentine novelist Enrique Larreta [1908] or the Mexican historical novel set in colonial times); second, a strictly literary language created by restructuring the syntactic forms of American Spanish along learned lines. Underneath the layer of modernism, a Romantic costumbrismo spread in what came to be known as criollo forms, which began to collect idioms in regional dialect. This was the trend that won out when the regionalists appeared on the scene around 1910, during the waning years of modernism. They came up with a dual system in their writing, with the learned literary language of modernism alternating with the dialectal register of their mainly rural characters who supplied the realism for their settings. The dialectal language of their characters was not simply a phonetic register; it was a reconstruction that emerged from the novelists' handling of their entire lexicon, its dialectal phonetic changes, and to a lesser degree, the local syntactic constructions. This language, as Rosenblat has observed,[34] was placed on a secondary level, set off from the narrator's learned, modernist language, and even condemned within the works themselves — see the lessons that Santos Luzardo incessantly gives Marisela in *Doña Bárbara*; the use of stigmatizing quotation marks for the American usages that appear in these texts (a practice begun by early Romantic novelists such as Esteban Echeverría [Argentina, 1805–51]); and the glossaries of terms not listed in the Dictionary of the Spanish Royal Academy, which are added as appendices to novels. These literary solutions were characterized by their linguistic ambiguity, which faithfully reflected the social structure and the writer's higher position in it. Though the writer descended to the lower strata, he never failed to confirm his higher status linguistically, given his education and his knowledge of the language norms that distanced him from the common people.

The heirs of the regionalist writers transformed this approach to language under the influence of modernism. They used less dialect and less American vocabulary, got rid of the phonetic spellings of popular speech, and made up for these changes by using their own American speech with new confidence. They cut out the glossaries, reasoning that regional words expressed their meaning perfectly well within the linguistic context of their writing, even if readers were previously unfamiliar with them. Crucially, they diminished the distance between the language of the narrator/writer and the speech of their characters, viewing linguistic duality as contrary to the rule of artistic unity. In the case of characters who use one of the indigenous American languages, they worked to find an equivalent in Spanish, creating an artificial literary language (Arguedas, Roa Bastos, Manuel Scorza) that let them register the speech difference without fracturing the unitary tone of the work. These are some of the ways writers unified their literary texts linguistically in response to a clearly more modern concept of artistic organicity, with the aid of a very new, impetuous confidence in their own American language, the speech these writers used as a matter of course day in and day out. With predictable variations, this trend guided all literary production after 1940. It can be seen at work in one of the best examples of literary cosmopolitanism: Julio Cortázar, who unified the speech of all the characters, Argentines and foreigners alike, in his novel *Rayuela* (1963), by using the spoken language of Buenos Aires and its typical words *vos* [you] and *che* [hey] and minimally distancing the characters' speech from the writer's own language. Such a linguistic solution could have been considered drastic, coming as it did after Argentine authorities had set school norms to combat those same dialectal forms, even though they had been in common use in the country for at least two centuries.

For regionalist writers who were caught up in the transculturation process themselves, the lexicon, prosody, and morphosyntax of the regional language became their favorite means of expanding the concepts of originality and representation and, at the same time, of solving the question of the unitary composition of the literary text, which their modernizing norms recommended. What for earlier writers had been the language of lower-class characters, contrasted in the text itself with that of the writer or narrator, was hierarchically inverted. Instead of being the exception and singling out the character placed under the writer's scrutiny, it became the narrating voice, thus covering the totality of the text and taking the narrator's place, displaying his view of the world. However, it was not a mere imitation of dialect; instead, it used the writers' own syntax and lexicon to form a polished version of the colloquial language characteristic of their regional version of American Spanish. The difference between these two literary (rather than linguistic) behaviors can be seen by comparing two excellent stories: "Doña Santitos" (1930) by Chilean author Marta Brunet, the last representative of regionalism, and "Luvina" (1953) by Juan Rulfo, who already represents the ongoing transculturation of fiction.

The author rejoined his linguistic community and spoke from inside it, using all its idiomatic resources freely. If, as was frequently the case, this community was rural, even bordering on indigenous, the writer would work from its linguistic system, not trying to imitate regional speech from the outside but rather to polish it from within, with artistic aims. From the moment the writer stopped seeing himself as an outsider to that language and started to recognize it, without shame or belittlement, as his own, he no longer traced out its irregularities, its variances from some foreign academic norm, with calligraphic care. Instead, he began to investigate the possibilities it presented for building a specific literary language within its bounds. This was a case of neoculturation, in Ortiz's term. The principles of textual unity and construction of a literary language for exclusively aesthetic invention may derive from the rationalizing spirit of modernity, but when these writers took up those principles, their linguistic perspective helped revive a regional view of the world, extend its useful life in an even richer and more intimate form than before, and thus expand the original worldview in a way that was better adjusted, genuine, artistically worthy, and indeed modernized, yet without destroying its identity.

Literary Structure

This linguistic solution to the impact of modernization from abroad subtly restructured a tradition and went on to produce works now considered classics of Latin American literature, including *Pedro Páramo* (1955) by Juan Rulfo. All things considered, the problems stemming from the new circumstances of modernization were less difficult on the linguistic level than on the level of literary structure. There, the distance between traditional forms and their modern, foreign counterparts was much wider. The regional novel had been modeled on nineteenth-century naturalist fiction, shaping that model to fit its own expressive needs. Now it faced a panoply of avant-garde devices, which were quickly absorbed by poetry and soon afterwards enriched critical realist fiction, basically giving rise to cosmopolitan fiction and, particularly, the literature of the fantastic. The new devices endowed those genres with greater imaginative agility, a more restless perception of reality, and more pervasive emotionality, but they also stamped them with a fractured worldview. If one recalls that regionalism was a response to a rigidly rationalizing ideology—offspring of the sociologism and psychologism of the nineteenth century, superficially updated in the twentieth—one may imagine the difficulty it had in adapting to the new structures of the avant-garde novel.

At this level, too, drawing from the wellspring of traditionalist culture yielded solutions, and so regionalism delved even deeper in search of local literary mechanisms that could be adapted to their new circumstances and could resist the corrosive power of modernization. The singularity of this response consisted in a subtle opposition to modernizing projects. Thus, it countered fragmentary "stream-of-consciousness" narration—ubiquitous in the modern novel from James Joyce to Virginia Woolf—by reconstructing the hoary discursive monologue technique (as in *Grande sertão: Veredas* [1956] by João Guimarães Rosa), whose sources derive not only from classic literature but also, vividly, from the oral sources of popular narrative. The compartmentalized tale, in which isolated pieces of a narrative are juxtaposed (John Dos Passos, Aldous Huxley), was countered by the scattered discourses of the "village gossips" who intermingle their whispered voices (as Rulfo does in *Pedro Páramo*). Both of these solutions arose from reclaiming oral and popular narrative structures. Perhaps the finest example can be found in the problems García Márquez faced in writing *A Hundred Years of Solitude*, where he had to find a stylistic solution to juxtaposing the plane of credible history and the magical plane through which his characters viewed those real events. It is worth reading the author's explanation in which he points to the oral sources of his fiction and, beyond that, to the worldview that rules its particular stylistic choices by evoking the habits of one of his aunts:

> Once she was sitting in the hallway doing her embroidery when a girl came in carrying a very odd chicken egg, a chicken egg with a large bump. For some reason that house was like some sort of information desk for all the town's mysteries. Whenever there was something that nobody could understand, they'd go to the house and ask, and usually that lady, my aunt, always had the answer. What I loved was the naturalness with which she resolved these things. Going back to the girl with the egg, she asked, "Please look at this, why does this egg have a bump?" So my aunt looked at it and said, "Ah, it's because it's a basilisk egg. Light a fire in the patio." They lit a big fire and burned up the egg like it was the most natural thing. That naturalness, I think, was what gave me the key to *A Hundred Years of Solitude*, where people tell the most shocking things, the most extraordinary stories, with the same deadpan expression my aunt had when she told them to go to the patio and burn the basilisk's egg, and I never found out what a basilisk was.[35]

Still, the literary losses on this level of narrative structure were extensive. A large part of the regionalists' repertoire came tumbling down, surviving only in the work of a few latter-day imitators and, curiously, in the post-1930 line of social fiction. Writers occasionally made up for these losses by adopting avant-garde narrative structures (the García Márquez who discovered the spot-on stylistic solution of *A Hundred Years of Solitude* was the same who took Faulkner and Woolf as models for the series of alternating monologues in *La hojarasca*), but those sorts of imitative solutions did not yield as many artistic dividends as a return to the literary structures of oral traditions could produce, especially because they didn't draw the old oral structures they used from the lined notebooks of folklorists but rather from other, older, more real, more obscure currents.

These two levels (language and literary structure) became of capital importance in another writer who both continued and transformed regionalism: the Brazilian novelist Guimarães Rosa. In the words of Alfredo Bosi, "Regionalism, which gave us some of the loosest structures in writing (the chronicle, the folkloric tale, the journalistic report), was fated to undergo, in the hands of an artist-demiurge, the metamorphosis that would make it the centerpiece of Brazilian fiction."[36]

On both levels, his literary operation was the same: he started off with popular language and a popular narrative structure, both well rooted in the life of the *sertão* [the arid backlands of northeastern Brazil]; deepened them through systematic research, which explains the compilation of so many archaic words and the discovery of the varied viewpoints through which the narrator spins the interpretive text of his reality; and, finally, projected both levels onto a recipient/producer (Guimarães Rosa) who mediates between two disconnected cultural worlds—the interior/regional and the foreign/universal. The main mediator is introduced in the novel itself: the character Riobaldo in *Grande sertão* is both a *jagunço* [a somewhat pejorative term for a person from the backlands] and an educated man; the same role is played by Grivo in Guimarães Rosa's novella *Cara-de-Bronze* (1956), who brings the names of things to his room-bound master. This is the origin of the unusual genre of Riobaldo's tale, which Roberto Schwarz has categorized as speech arising in response to a silent interlocutor,[37] in what Unamuno astutely defined as a monodialogue. Likewise, Grivo's interlocutor, who never speaks but without whose existence Grivo's monologue could not take shape, contributes the modernizing inducement (something we've become familiar with in literary journalism) to research a culture that is basically illiterate and continues to be transmitted orally. From one end of Guimarães Rosa's writings to the other, we find his testimony on how he undertook this process to collect information and study the narrative forms and language of a cattle-raising culture—in 1947, it was the text *Com o Vaqueiro Mariano*, published the same year as his short story collection *Sagarana*; in 1962, it was "A Estória do Homen do Pinguelo," which also reconstructs the original scene of a rural informant being judged by the writer while he spins his discourse.[38] In the first example, Mariano's narrative about his oxen is being observed by his interlocutor who writes down the information while adding references to Mariano's style and words ("He reflected before answering me in a colloquial mixture of *quasca* and *mineiro*" [two regional dialects of Brazilian Portuguese]; "A few words—intense, different—open up vast spaces where reality steals from fables") before he acknowledges at last that this narrative system is what constructs the person, the character, of the narrator: "His stories, as well, scarcely let go of the narrator: they perform him; to tell a tale is to resist."[39] To put it another way: what undergirds the resistance of a culture that is undergoing modernization, even more than the survival of its lexicon, is its narrative systems, a higher level that gives us an insight into its ways of thinking. When we transcribe the message, we simultaneously reveal the code that developed it—the two being inseparable, as Bosi suggests, citing Lucien Sebag. As such, the task is to construct a totality from which the forms of rural storytelling can be recovered—disjointed, dispersed, but fit for a unification deriving from the modernizing impact. This task is itself a transcultural one, for to carry it out, the writer must draw on a traditional means of expression (spoken discourse) and spread it evenly across the entire story. Walnice Nogueira Galvão has rightly observed that "speech is also the great stylistic unifier, overriding the proliferation of narrative techniques; the narrator's varying persona, letters, dialogues, other monologues, even the other characters in the plot: all speak through Riobaldo's voice."[40] Within speech in the novel, as Nogueira Galvão has also observed, there is a higher unification at work via a matrix model in which the author aligns his code with that of the narrator.

Worldview

There is still a third level of transculturation for us to consider: the central, focal level of worldview, which generates meaning. It was on this level that the artistic heirs of regionalism yielded their best results. This is the intimate realm where values abide and where ideologies are put on display; by the same token, it is the most difficult one to hand over to the process of homogenizing modernization along foreign patterns. As we have emphasized, the modernizing movements of the interwar years (called modernismo in Brazil and vanguardismo in Spanish America) affected all of the different literary trends, imprinting almost all of them with the same mark, though the intensity of the phenomenon differed substantially among these trends, and, in particular, the way each responded signaled the place it occupied in the diverse Latin American cultural scene of the era.

Vanguardismo called into question the logical/rational discourse that had driven literature since its bourgeois origins in the nineteenth century. Three literary trends had relied on this discourse, either through their referential, denotative language or through their symbolic, mechanical designs: the regional novel, the social novel, and the critical realist novel. Faced with vanguardismo, the social novel responded by clinging to its didactic logicism and its nineteenth-century bourgeois model but inverting its value hierarchy and developing an antibourgeois message. The critical realist novel (in the widest sense, which encompasses Juan Carlos Onetti, Graciliano Ramos, and Alejo Carpentier) made use of avant-garde suggestions for structuring the novel and, particularly, for innovative writing styles. We have discussed how the regionalist novel responded, but the trend that adapted most quickly to the impact of the avant-garde, the one that actually came into existence under its influence, was what we are calling the cosmopolitan narrative (with an eye to its most important practitioner, Jorge Luis Borges, and the definition of his work by René Etiemble).[41] This trend included a few different groups, each of which developed mainly in Buenos Aires. One, the literature of the fantastic, boasted an open structure and was guided by unconscious, subterranean currents, opening it up to multiple meanings (though Julio Cortázar, its most authentic representative, noted that it could become as rigid and logic-bound as any social novel).[42] Another was what Jorge Rivera termed the literature of ambiguity,[43] thinking of the works of José Bianco, though his definition also fits many of the works of Juan Carlos Onetti.

This is not the place to examine the causes, traits, and consequences of the European irrationalist movement that pervaded every realm of intellectual activity. It turned up in both philosophy and political thought, which explains why Georg Lukács condemned them jointly in his book *The Destruction of Reason* (1954); it deeply influenced the centers of artistic reinvention, from German Expressionism and French Surrealism to Italian Futurism, and had its greatest impact on Dadaism; and it pervaded the philosophy of living, through the various and diverging existentialisms. Even fields that were basically alien to the movement, such as anthropology and psychoanalysis, made contributions that were taken up by those who rejected reason. Of these contributions, none was more vividly incorporated into contemporary culture than the new view of myth, which, in some of its expressions, seemed like it might be a substitute for the religions that had undergone a deep crisis during the nineteenth century. Emerging from the revisionist views of British anthropology (Edward Tylor, James Frazer), this concept of myth was taken up by twentieth-century psychoanalysts (Sigmund Freud, Otto Rank, Sándor Ferenczi, Carl Jung) and scholars of religion (Georges Dumézil, Mircea Eliade), and it became ubiquitous during the twentieth century. By 1962, Mircea Eliade observed that this change had taken place "more than half a century ago" in the academic world. "Unlike their predecessors, who treated myth in the usual meaning of the word, that is, as 'fable,' 'invention,' 'fiction,' they have accepted it as it was understood in archaic societies, where, on the contrary, 'myth' means a 'true story' and, beyond that, a story that is a most precious possession because it is sacred, exemplary, significant."[44]

One of the most important centers that reestablished this concept of myth and rediscovered it as a living, active presence in rationalized societies was pre-Hitlerian Germany, where Ernst Cassirer produced his key works. Another was France, where Lucien Lévy-Bruhl taught; his book *Primitive Mentality* (1922), considered authoritative up until its devastating critique by Claude Lévi-Strauss and his structural anthropology, provided a theoretical basis for the development of Surrealism, which was taking place at the same time. The Spanish Americans living in Europe during the interwar period (our "lost generation") and the intellectual circles of Spain (*Revista de Occidente*) imported this brand-new "object" of internationalized culture to Latin America—probably with less of a delay than Pierre Chaunu has hypothesized in the many examples he gives of Spanish American "backwardness" in adopting European inventions. "Another sign of this long-term intellectual displacement: the conquest, between 1940 and 1950, of the major Spanish American universities—Mexico, then Buenos Aires—by German thought from the first two decades of the twentieth century. On the surface, this was a consequence of the American diaspora of intellectuals from the Spanish Republic, whose cadres, drawn from the lower and middle bourgeoisie, like Ortega y Gasset, drank from the springs of early twentieth-century German philosophy as a reaction against the Francophile high bourgeoisie and aristocracy."[45]

Here, Chaunu is referring to the translations from German put out by the Mexican scholarly publishing house Fondo de Cultura Económica (such as the works of Wilhelm Dilthey, translated by Eugenio Ímaz) and to the incorporation of idealist stylistics (Karl Vossler, Leo Spitzer), all of which coincided with the introduction of French thought and Surrealist art, whose mythic underpinnings were appropriated by writers as diverse as Miguel Ángel Asturias, Alejo Carpentier, and Jorge Luis Borges, and which were explored in the early essays of Julio Cortázar (especially "Para una poética," 1954). Myth (for Asturias) and archetype (for Carpentier) were seen as valid categories for interpreting the distinctive traits of Latin America, in sui generis combinations with sociological schemes, but not even these writers' frank and resolute appeal to surviving popular beliefs among indigenous or African communities in the Americas was able to mask the origins and intellectual basis of their interpretive system. Some of the misunderstandings of magical realist fiction derive from this double origin (subject matter from inside the culture, meaning from outside). Indeed, the coherence of Jorge Luis Borges's fiction is due to its frankly cosmopolitan and universal setting. After his story "Tlön, Uqbar, Orbis Tertius" (1938), myth became a bibliographic dream, made up of the books that comprised his Library of Babel, and which completed the symmetric inversion that Horkheimer and Adorno detected in their observation that, when enlightenment became myth during the irrationalism that dominated the twentieth century, it was a turnabout of the original transmutation of myth into enlightenment, these being the twin fulcrums of bourgeois civilization.[46]

The deculturation induced in regionalist cultures by incorporating this ideological corpus must have been extreme, but it paradoxically served to open up new routes for enriching those same cultures. The literary discourse of the regionalist novel basically corresponded to the cognitive structures of the European bourgeoisie. It was therefore as distant from its subject matter as the narrator's voice was from his characters' popular language. This linguistic contradiction replicated the contradiction between discursive structure and subject matter. In both cases, a distorting imposition was at work. When logical/rational discourse was called into question, the regionalists delved back into their inspiration—local sources—and began to study the forms of those cultures in the words of their traditional practitioners. Theirs was a search for replenishing and survival, drawing forth contributions from their cultural heritage that would be binding and permanent.

Delving like this put regionalist writers back in fertile contact with the living sources of culture: the inextinguishable sources of mythic inventiveness, which exist in every human society but are most awake in rural communities. The writers rediscovered the energy that had been reined in by the narrative systems regionalism had been employing; they recognized the potential of rural speech and popular story structures.

They took part, thus, in recognizing a diffuse world of free associations, of incessant inventions correlating ideas and things, and of particular ambiguity and fluctuations. It had existed all along, but it had remained hidden under the rigid literary rules that came from the scientific and sociological thinking derived from positivism. To the degree that positivistic thinking was incapable of appreciating a protoplasmic, discursive imaginary tied to an immediate reality that gave sustenance to its oppositional schemes, it preferred to force such seemingly errant material into the systematic logic that had its sources in Spencer, Comte, or Taine. The breakup of this logical system freed the real material from the hinterland cultures of Latin America and allowed their other dimensions to be appreciated.

A sentence by Riobaldo, the narrator of *Grande sertão*, in which he reflects on the world of the Brazilian backlands, encapsulates the instability at the heart of the novel: "The sertão is like that, you know: everything uncertain, everything certain."[47] The extraordinary fluidity and constant displacement of lives and events, the transformations of reality, and the unsteadiness of values, then, knit together the substrate on which the interpretive discourse will unfold. In much the same way, in Rulfo's story "La cuesta de las comadres," the main character's instable discourse is built on the scattering and contradictions of its constituent elements. The narrator, in each case, becomes a mediator building on scattered elements to construct what will be an equally problematic meaning. The structure of the story is replicated by the structure of its discourse; the forms taken by its dramatic crises add up to its narrative form. Benedito Nunes notes these two superimposed journeys in *Cara-de-Bronze* and argues that the mediating function plays a role characteristic of myth: "This bifocal view of the work fits the ambiguous, mediating nature of Grivo, a character ultimately based on the mythical figure of the Child, one of the archetypes of the Sacred, which dominates Guimarães Rosa's fiction even more than other important avatars such as Diadorim and Miguilim."[48] The correlation between the two planes in this novella is blatant, given that its theme is the search for the word. Walnice Nogueira Galvão has made the same observation with regard to *Grande sertão*, drawing on two leitmotivs of the novel: "Living is a very dangerous business"; "Telling something is a very, very difficult business."[49]

This is why the transculturators eventually discovered something even beyond myth. Unlike the cosmopolitan fiction of their time, which revisited the literary form of myths in light of the era's irrationalism and subjected them to new refractions and universal settings, the transculturators began spinning new mythic tales, drawing forth precise and enigmatic inventions from the ambiguous, powerful trove of regional culture. Nothing could be more vain than to force the tales of Comala into the fixed models of Greek and Latin mythology; though Rulfo's inventions certainly touch on—better said, muddy—the classical myths, their significance lies elsewhere. They emerge from other flames, seek other dangers, and issue spontaneously from an unknown cultural background that our methods of knowing can only clumsily handle.[50]

Even more important than recovering these constantly emerging cognitive structures was the research into the mental mechanisms that generate myth, the ascent to the operations that make these mechanisms. We find this second level in the paradigmatic case of José María Arguedas, an anthropologist who collected and studied Indian myths. With Arguedas, it was not only the novel's narrator but also the author himself who built upon these operations, working on indigenous tradition and Western modernization, indiscriminately associated with one another in an exercise in "mythic thinking."

So the response of avant-garde irrationalism to deculturation, on this level of worldview and the search for meaning, only appeared to harmonize with the modernizing project. In reality, it superseded it with unexpected richness such as few modernist writers could produce: to the manipulation of "literary myths," it countered with "mythical thinking." We will analyze this process concretely in the literature of José María Arguedas.

On any of these three levels (language, literary structure, worldview), we find that the works resulting from modernizing culture contact are not equivalent to the urban creations of the cosmopolitan area, but neither are they equivalent to the regionalist works that preceded them. We note that the inventions of the transculturators were broadly facilitated by the existence of the continent's own particular cultural forms, which had come about through a long process of adopting foreign messages and "creolizing" them. Direct contact between the regional cultures of the Latin American hinterland and modernization would probably have been fatal to the former, given the distance between the two, which in cases such as that of the European-indigenous polarity was vast. Mediation came about through the cultural forms that had grown in the course of centuries-long efforts of accumulation and elaboration: in the case of Brazil, the organic national culture; in the case of Spanish America, the development of a fruitful intercommunication among its disparate regions. Therefore, the dialogue between regionalism and modernism took place through a broad literary system, a field of integration and mediation, that was functional and self-regulating. The most important contribution of the "modernization period" (1870–1910) was to pave the way for this eventuality by creating a common literary system in Spanish America.

CHAPTER TWO

Regions, Cultures, and Literatures

Regional and Class Subcultures

The unity of Latin America has long been a project of Latin American intellectuals, and it has long been recognized by international consensus. There are persuasive reasons for supporting it, and there are real, powerful unifying forces behind it. Most of these reasons — ranging from a common history to a common language and similar modes of behavior — are rooted in the past and have deeply molded the lives of the peoples in the region. Other, more contemporary reasons, though fewer in number, have great potential, for they have developed in response to the worldwide economic and political pressures that led to the expansion of the world's dominant civilizations. As real as this unity is as a project and as real as the bases of its support are, beneath it one finds an inner diversity that defines the continent more precisely. Unity and diversity is the formula preferred by analysts from many fields for understanding Latin America.[1]

The diversity of Latin America is governed, first, by the diversity of the countries that comprise it; some have made nations of themselves because of the unifying factors that they enjoy, but other countries have not yet done so. Second, a more robust and enduring proof of this diversity can be found in the existence of cultural regions. In the largest Latin American countries, these regions are extensive and well defined — the regional map of Brazil looks like the multicolored mosaic of independent countries that is Spanish America as a whole — but such regions exist even in the smallest countries. Anthropologists have documented such regions in as small an island country as Puerto Rico.[2] The division of any country into regions has a multiplier effect, which in extreme cases can destroy national unity. The same can be said of the very large regions within some countries, which can be subdivided into subregions that have the same disintegrating effect, as Guimarães Rosa discovered when he wrote a profile of his native state of Minas Gerais.[3]

Some regions straddle two or more countries; others designate areas with common features within a single country. The regional map of Latin America, then, does not coincide with the map of its independent countries. This second map of Latin America is truer than the official one, whose borders were drawn, for the most part, following old colonial administrative divisions, as reworked by the vicissitudes of national and international politics. On this second map, the Brazilian state of Rio Grande do Sul is seen to have closer ties to Uruguay and the Argentine Pampas than to Matto Grosso or other states in Brazil itself. The Andean region of western Venezuela is more closely related to the Andean zone of Colombia than to the central Caribbean zone of Venezuela. Countering these similarities are national norms, which dominate the hinterlands of each country and impose the national language, educational system, economic development, social system, and so forth upon them. The impact of these national norms on cultural formation is not insignificant, so we cannot ignore the boundaries of the independent republics when we look at the overall division of Latin America into cultural regions.

The relationship between Latin American unity and these two levels (national and regional) is repeated on the strictly regional level of cultural macroregions and miniregions, the proposed limits of which usually depend on the needs of the researcher who defines them. On the largest scale, the anthropologist Charles Wagley divides all of Latin America into three great regions: Afro-America (Atlantic coast, lowlands, plantation agriculture, slavery, significant contributions from black culture and correspondingly less from indigenous culture, feudalism), Indo-America (Andes, temperate and cold zones, heavily indigenous population, economy based on agriculture and mining, Spanish domination, Catholic religion), and Ibero-America (temperate South America, late colonization, heavy European migration, little influence from African and indigenous cultures, economy based on livestock and agriculture, middle-class political economy).[4] A similar outline is drawn by Darcy Ribeiro, who pays special attention to the processes of transcultural mestizo formation: Witness Peoples (Mesoamericans and Andeans), New

Peoples (Brazilians, Grand Colombians, Antilleans, and Chileans), and Transplanted Peoples (River Plate).[5]

This is the broadest possible sketch—a translation, as it were, of Latin American unity into its three basic components. Although the unity of Latin America is based on its systematic differentiation from foreign cultures—from the cultures of the mother countries, Spain and Portugal, too, but especially from those of the Anglo region (United States and Canada), which served as the defining contrast for the first people to call themselves Latin Americans—these macroregions involve internal differentiation through a corresponding set of contrasts, based on cultural anthropology with the backing of history and the current economy.

Given the complexity of the continent and the demands made by concrete studies of countries and even smaller areas within Latin America, more attention has been paid of late to defining microregions, as in the research on Puerto Rico by Julian Steward and his students [see note 2]. Brazil has been a logical place to carry out this kind of study, since its size, varied ecological zones, ethnic composition, history, and diverse economy have fostered the independent development of internal cultures. Skilled anthropologists, both Brazilian and foreign, have contributed perhaps more studies of this type for Brazil than for any other country in Latin America, and their studies have yielded a variety of taxonomies. Thus, Wagley first proposed that Brazil be divided into six major regions, each of which represented a subculture within what he regarded as the country's advanced cultural unity: Amazon, Northeast Coast, arid Northeast, extreme South, industrial Middle States, and Far West frontier.[6] For his part, Manuel Diegues Júnior, a student of Gilberto Freyre, sketched nine cultural regions in Brazil: the Northeastern Coastal agricultural zone, the Mediterranean Livestock zone, Amazonia, the High Plains Mining zone, West Central, the Livestock-raising Far South, the Foreign Colonizing zone, the Coffee Production zone, and the Urban-Industrial Belt, as well as three others that revolve about salt production, cacao, and fishing.[7]

These classifications are based on methodological reflections such as this one by Wagley: "I find it useful to think of Latin America in terms of regions, each of which has a different type of physical environment, a population composed of different ethnicities, and a distinct variation on Latin American culture."[8] Wagley looks at the physical environment, the ethnic composition of the population, the dominant form of economic production and the social system that derives from it, and the cultural components that these frameworks mold and pass down. Above all, though, he privileges the horizontal spread of subcultures (a necessary concept for discussing regions), recognizing that a regional subculture establishes the behaviors, values, and habits—and generates the products—that correspond to the generalized consensus of the people living in the region, regardless of their position in its social structure. He looks at the culinary habits, linguistic behaviors, and basic beliefs that affect everyone in the community equally, allowing them to see themselves as members of a regional subculture and to set themselves apart from, or in opposition to, other regions.

This basically culturalist view has gradually given way to what Strickon calls an "evolutionist typology" that pays greater attention to the economy and social structure: "The criteria were economic and structural. Their theory held that the interplay between technology, environment, and economy was central to an understanding of society and culture."[9] The example of the Puerto Rican regional taxonomy established by Steward, based on observing the effects of different systems of production (tobacco, sugarcane, coffee) on cultural configurations, has helped demonstrate the links between culture and external forces, all within the transculturating field of modernity/traditionalism upon which the entire dynamic of Latin America rests. This approach would allow us to group the various regions, regardless of where they are located in Latin America, according to their structural types, which, as Strickon writes, "were seen as emergent societies resulting from the changing structure of the great commercial and industrial centers of the Western world."[10] A systematic example is the typology established by Charles Wagley and Marvin Harris; drawing a distinction between society and culture, they rank nine types of subculture, which can be reorganized into six broad groups: Tribal Indian; Modern Indian; Peasant; Engenho Plantation (family-owned) and Usina Plantation (modern corporation-owned); Town; and urban (Metropolitan Upper Class, Metropolitan Middle Class, and Urban Proletariat).[11] As the authors recognize, several of these subcultures overlap due to the criteria (racial, social) used to define them, so new subtypes will have to be elaborated, whereas other types will have to be recognized, such as the culture of livestock ranches and the incorporation in the urban centers of marginal wage earners who do not fully participate either in the urban proletariat or in the rural culture from which they migrated.

The economic and sociological criteria introduced by Wagley and Harris complement the notion of a subculture as basically horizontal.

They give the concept depth and verticality. Even if we presuppose that the region is the fundamental community that shares a subculture, these criteria establish the existence of strata superimposed on that space; the differences between social sectors become important. This is especially apparent in cities, which are smaller in area than rural regions and correspondingly more vertical, as seen in class, occupation, income, and education differentials, with concomitant variations in culture. Though spatial distribution is important in cities (neighborhoods, shantytowns, central city, suburbs, residential zones, industrial zones, and so on), vertical distribution is still more so, and it is the vertical dimension that forces us to acknowledge the differences among multiple strata. The sociological classifications of these strata derive from economic criteria and their place on the social pyramid and much less from the cultural criteria proposed by anthropologists. Even though all urban strata participate equally in the strict, homogenized norms imparted by education, the benefit system, and the domination of the ruling class, we can still detect important differences in the way the different strata use this general cultural framework, which is as much as to say that we can recognize the existence of different subcultures within the same space. Beliefs, behaviors, interests, tastes and choices, activities, and habits are markedly different among the various groups — management, landlords, middle-class office workers, industrial workers, small business owners, university students, the poor, and so on. These differences can be seen in the cultural products they use, in their means of communication and the messages they form with them, and even in their lexicons. Our pioneering dialectology used the horizontal criteria of anthropology to create linguistic maps of the Americas (Pedro Henríquez Ureña), but it has had to give way to sociolinguistics (Basil Bernstein, Joshua Fishman), for which cities are ideal research sites, allowing for studies that link speech to social groups. As Theodore Caplow has pointed out, "there is more cultural variation within the Latin American city than within most cities of the United States or Europe."[12] This tendency dates all the way back to the foundation of Latin American cities by the Spanish conquerors (this was less true of the Portuguese), who put a civilizing plan into practice to dampen the variation that was taking root in the fortified heart of the cities and spreading beyond their walls. This plan, which José Luis Romero has termed "the ideological city," is what deeply stamped the continent with its Hispanic culture; in an inversion of the usual practice that had formed medieval towns, the Latin American city was given the task of molding the space around it, based on a centralizing, authoritarian ideology. The city did not emerge from its ecological environment; the city was imposed on the environment, transmitting norms that did not even arise spontaneously from the culture of the conquering nations but was instead a project carried out by an absolutist monarchy. Romero notes that "the assumption that the ideological city had the potential ability to mold reality was based on two premises. One was the inert, amorphous character of preexisting reality. The other was the decision that this reality, arising from a preconceived plan, would not—should not—develop in an autonomous, spontaneous way."[13] If it actually did develop on its own, creating the powerful regional cultures of Latin America, that was due to the fact that the city was incapable in practice of exercising dominion over so vast a hinterland. This does not mean, however, that it ever—in colonial times or after independence, under Spanish administrators or the rule of the *criollos* who succeeded them—abandoned its project of imposition and domination. The centralist project began to mature only at the end of the nineteenth century, and to succeed in the twentieth;[14] this is what has led modernization, centered now on imperial capitals other than Madrid, to collide with the traditional cultures of the hinterlands.

This modernization has had an even harder impact on the heterogeneous cultural elements in the cities, where it has imposed a rigid hierarchy. To consolidate their sway over the field of culture, the intellectual elite turned to the aristocratic pattern that has been so influential in Latin American cultures throughout their history. The intellectual elite—what I have elsewhere called the "lettered city"—already enjoyed disproportionate importance in the colonial era, and they have continued to do so up to the present, despite the vicissitudes of life in the Americas. They took over the exercise of literature with confiscatory snobbishness, imposing the rules that defined literature and thereby deciding who could practice it. Except during a handful of historical moments (independence, the Mexican Revolution, the abrupt wave of immigration to the Southern Cone, the recent massive rural migration to the cities), the "lettered city" has kept an iron grip on intellectual and artistic life, controlled the educational system, and decided who the cultural heroes of the Latin American countries should be, in accordance with its own cultural values.

The growth of the cities, along with the social upheavals mentioned above, rapidly expanded the size of the lower social strata and weighed against the attempts of the "lettered city" to homogenize urban society. The growth of criollo theater in Southern Cone cities during the late nineteenth century and the growth of the Mexican revolutionary novel during the late 1920s and 1930s signal defiance of the norms that had once dictated the rules of literature. More recently, we see this in the classification of the middlebrow music of recently urbanized sectors (tangos, boleros) as literature. Yet the "lettered city" has not disappeared. In some cases, it has adapted; in others, it has kept up the fight and stuck to its norms, aided by its control over the educational system and its close relationship with the centers of global power. Perhaps nothing demonstrates this better than its ability to keep indigenous languages from being taught in the public schools, despite continual protests, or to keep characteristically American forms of Spanish out of grade school classrooms. However, it is also the case that the social strata and their particular subcultures have now become visible.

If vertical structuring became overt in the cities, there is no reason to suppose it was not also at work in rural regions, the preferred terrain of the regionalists. Indeed, the same sort of classes appeared there, albeit in paternalistic, neofeudal forms that tried to eliminate, or rather paper over, the social pyramid and its cruelties. Only by introducing this perspective can we accurately reconstruct the functioning of regional society, for the common values that pervade it over its long evolution are complicated by class and group differentials that indicate the existence of subcultures within a subculture. This is something that anthropologists have also studied recently (see the work of Ricardo Pozas in Mexico). It can be precisely measured in the admiring but critical evaluation by Darcy Ribeiro of the monumental work of Gilberto Freyre, which was fundamental to legitimating the existence of Brazil's mulatto culture but was also affected, as Ribeiro says in his foreword, by Freyre's "gentlemanly myopia."[15] For an example of paying attention to both the horizontal and the vertical coordinates in an analysis of a regional subculture, see the work of the Peruvian author José María Arguedas, who was both an ethnologist and a novelist. In his novel *Todas las sangres*, he aimed to offer a complete panorama not only of all the social classes in the Andean highlands but also of the cultural forms within which his characters acted. However, even the excellent example of Arguedas demonstrates that the integrating power of regional culture is incomparably stronger than anything that might bind the diverse classes of an urban culture together. After all, regional cultures have developed over the course of many years, even centuries, in communities with very little social mobility and in which patterns of behavior have been internalized, validated, and accepted, passing on from parents to children, generation after generation. Only a catastrophe or the abrupt incursion of modernization seems capable of making people conscious of the rigid stratification that undergirds a region's social structure.

Such wake-up calls disturbed the peace of several hinterland regions in Latin America during the period between the world wars. Some regions, such as in Peru's southern highlands, were in a frozen state, sidelined from the slow but steady innovations that were taking place elsewhere in the country—including other hinterland regions of Peru. (In 1922, a poet from the northwestern city of Trujillo, César Vallejo, published *Trilce* and shook up intellectual life all over the nation.) The intellectual interpretation of modernization was carried out in Peru by a generation of young men who took up the cause of *indigenismo* (Víctor Raúl Haya de la Torre, José Carlos Mariátegui, Luis Alberto Sánchez, César Vallejo, José Sabogal) and endowed regionalism with an aggressive social consciousness, as seen in Mariátegui's critique of the older version of regionalism in Peru. It is significant that these intellectuals were exact contemporaries of the modernization movement that began to spread from the capital, transmitting its economic system to the provinces, attempting to achieve the long-postponed unification of all Peru under its aegis, and consequentially subverting the same cultural values that the *Amauta* group would endlessly idealize.[16] Thirty years after Mariátegui's programmatic texts, José María Arguedas noted that "the *Amauta* movement coincided with the opening of Peru's first highways,"[17] the domineering roads that symbolized the country's modernity—though not necessarily its harmonious regional progress.[18]

Paradoxically, then, regionalism returned to prominence in Latin America because modernization had begun to penetrate regions that were isolated, paralyzed, or in decline after one of the continent's typical boom-and-bust economic cycles. Though we cannot trace the economic sequence in detail here, there are two reliable indices of this process, strictly from the intellectual sphere. The first is the defensive reaction displayed by hinterland regions toward a given country's capital or most dynamic city, which can only be explained by the aggression against their traditional values that was coming from those economic centers, as perceived by the people living in the hinterland. The second derives concomitantly from the first, for such a defensive reaction would not have been possible if the hinterland did not already have a group of highly educated intellectuals ready and able to take up the challenge and oppose modernization by debating it on an equal intellectual level. In the theorizing of Peru's *indigenistas* or the contemporary *négritude* writers in the Caribbean area (the works of Fernando Ortiz, but also the literature of Palés Matos, Nicolás Guillén, and others), as well as in Freyre's First Conference on Regionalism in Recife, we see the development of autonomous forces working to oppose the homogenizing domination of the dynamic cities and their foreign protectors (treated as two sides of the same coin), though not to fan separatist tendencies, which could only be permitted in modernized zones. In areas that had seemed hopeless, destined to be erased by acculturation, there arose teams of researchers, artists, and writers to reclaim their place and oppose the indiscriminate submission that was demanded of them. José María Arguedas raised essentially the same protest in Peru as José Lins do Rego and the Recife group did in Brazil, much as their art differed.

The advent of these intellectuals points to a certain level of regional development (with overtones of neoculturation), leading to a sufficient "surplus" to support a social stratum of educated specialists. It also points to intensifying conflicts with the modernized capital cities. This duality should be noted. In the works that Gilberto Freyre wrote at the time, as well as in his later recollections of this period,[19] one clearly sees the environment of international modernism in which he moved, the ties to the wider intellectual world that he ingenuously coveted, and his appropriation of a modern intellectual system (Boas) in order to have some chance of success in the debate he was engaging. The same was true of García Márquez's readings of fiction, more radically avant-garde than the Russian and Scandinavian literature that allowed Juan Rulfo to find his own path—though García Márquez and Rulfo concurred about one great North American writer, William Faulkner, who not coincidentally hailed from a cultural area that Wagley defined as belonging to "Plantation America," which included both the U.S. South and parts of Latin America (particularly the Caribbean). One could say that not only these groups of intellectuals but also entire hinterland regions were shocked by the modernizing process, and in reaction to their shock they developed their defensive discourse. At the same time, it should be recognized that intellectuals in the capital cities were also making rapid advances, helped along by their growing incorporation into a foreign system and favored by their use of mass media technology, which gave them greater influence and therefore greater dominance. It was in this era that radio first appeared and film distribution networks continued to expand. The acceleration of the modernizing process and the ceaseless imbalances it created are illustrated in Claude Lévi-Strauss's story of the construction of Brazil's telegraph line to Cuiabá, which was completed after unbelievable feats of engineering in 1922, precisely when the invention of wireless radio rendered it obsolete.[20]

This was, then, a conflict-ridden panorama. It also wasn't the first; the interwar conflict mirrored the struggles from the last third of the nineteenth century and from the so-called independence period of the late eighteenth century before that, but never before was the response so vigorous and coherent. The regions boasted skilled teams of intellectuals who could interpret the conflict both in their theorizing and in their artistic creations. This forestalled the politics of scorched-earth acculturation that the Spanish and Portuguese conquests had practiced during the sixteenth century. In fact, it is significant that in the course of this twentieth-century resistance, we find valuable contributions that reexamine the sixteenth-century conquest and colonization and recover the intellectual opposition that at the time had been presented by Indian intellectuals, which had long gone unrecognized. At the same time, reflective European researchers were working to visualize the "otherness" that some of the sixteenth-century evangelizers had glimpsed in the midst of the trauma of conquest; these researchers proceeded to correct the Eurocentrist perspective of earlier accounts.[21]

It is important to keep both of these evaluations in mind, because they simultaneously define permanence and change. This was not a new conflict, for it evoked a series that began with the conflict par excellence: the imposition of Hispanic culture on the indigenous Americas, followed by the creolized and regionalized conflict that gave us the domination of the urban liberal oligarchy over rural communities after independence. Nevertheless, it was a conflict that had a distinctly different resolution — one that did not lead to overwhelming subjugation but one in which the regions could express and assert themselves in spite of the gains made by the forces of national unification. One may conclude that this new outcome shows a strengthening of what we can call the continent's hinterland cultures, not to the degree that they held rigidly to their old traditions but to the degree that they transculturated without giving up their souls, as Arguedas would have said. In so doing, they made their national cultures more robust (and thereby the project of a Latin American culture as well) by providing them with materials and energy to avoid simply giving in to the impact of modernization from abroad and demonstrating their utter vulnerability. Modernity cannot be renounced, and refusing it would be suicide — as would be renouncing yourself in order to accept modernity.

Conflicts between Regionalism and Modernization

This age-old conflict has gone by many names throughout Latin American history. At first, it was Catholic religion and morality versus indigenous paganism and savagery. Then came other labels: free trade versus colonial monopoly, republican independence versus imperial colonialism, the European principle versus the American principle (Sarmiento), liberalism versus conservatism, positivist progress versus religious obscurantism and indigenous backwardness, and revolutionary social thought versus retrograde oligarchic thought. For the past two decades, it has been the conflict between modernization and traditionalism but also between center and periphery and between dependence and autonomy.

The dualism of modernity and tradition is no more ambiguous than any of the earlier conflicts, nor does it entail any less virtue—or any less harm. On the other hand, none of the ambiguities are exact replicas of what came before; indeed, there is no way that the same person could consistently take the same position in all the many dichotomies, which are marked by curious shifts. Religion started off on the side of the bellicose foreigners; by the nineteenth century, it was with the home side, helping them stand up against ideologies that they now saw as "foreign." The same holds for liberalism today, just two centuries after it was codified. Each new dualism reappears on a new level of development for each side—on the internal side, after its idiosyncratic potential has grown markedly, and on the foreign side, after technologically developed societies have intensified and expanded.

This historical sequence leads to the persistent transculturation of the internal camp and to an extreme compartmentalization and stratification that transforms the conflict between the internal and the foreign into an entirely internal one, so that both the internal and the foreign sides are represented by Latin Americans. This American bipolarity is symbolized by the distance between the consumer societies at the heart of the capital cities and the impoverished rural societies. The transculturing process, for its part, is manifested in the shifts that occur in doctrinal canons over a long period of creolization after they have entered from abroad. Their transformation in this creolizing process, after which they become thoroughly identified with the nation or region, is perfectly illustrated by Catholicism, the foreign doctrine that has been present for the longest time in Latin America and has penetrated popular culture most deeply. During the last third of the nineteenth century—the era of positivist modernization—Catholicism became the expressive medium for rural resistance to the violent acculturation suffered by the people of the hinterlands, as seen in the tragic incident of Canudos, which was recounted by Euclides da Cunha in *Os sertões* (1902).

To view the process schematically, foreign pressure was constantly present, but over time it went from intense bursts to periods of greater calm, each new burst of activity offering up a new and innovative set of intellectual and technical tools. Latin America's traditional regional cultures developed in a less dynamic way, but the overall effect was equally evolutionary. In this evolution, the interplay between resistance and neoculturation led the way. This development of regional cultures bore the stamp of the general cultural patterns of Latin America and its three basic components; nevertheless, for a long time these regional cultures did not achieve the compact unity that they appear about to attain now at the end of the twentieth century. This is because it was precisely those fragments of America—its diverse regional cultures—that held out, independently, against foreign modernizing pressures. They were the ones that went through the three stages of reaction to those pressures: resistance, a return to roots, and neoculturation. This regional fragmentation (very marked in the case of island cultures) was one of the causes of the weakness—in some cases, the extreme fragility—of the opposition to transculturation, for the regional cultures were up against powerful forces that could level them entirely. The loss of indigenous languages is an index of this conflict in the Caribbean, which has been subjected to repeated and diverse colonizations, but holding onto Spanish has also been an index of the strength of resistance in Puerto Rico, the only country in Latin America that has a holiday dedicated to celebrating the Spanish language.

In contrast to the fragmentation of regional cultures (which mirrors the fragmentation of countries and the isolation of large expanses within them over long periods of time), the pressure of modernization has been backed by the unifying norms of the European cultures that directed modernization, especially over the past two centuries—which is to say, the years when Latin America has been independent and when industrial and imperialist capitalism has developed and tried to take over the world. Darcy Ribeiro has used his concepts of "reflex modernization" and "historical incorporation" to analyze the varied junctures of all these forces.[22]

We have recognized a basic unity in modernization, deriving from the technical and industrial development that has given it its great power and has led to a specific cultural form and ideology. Nevertheless, the ways modernization has been applied in Latin America and the resulting effects have varied widely, depending on the independent variables in each case: the different historical periods, how intensely it was imposed, how long the pressure lasted, how well modernity adapted to the regional circumstances, how much resistance it met, what kind of neoculturating dynamic it favored, and so on.

We have also recognized a basic unity in Latin American culture, for its three main component cultures have been strongly molded by Iberian (Spanish and Portuguese) cultural patterns. Nevertheless, its regions with their extreme fragmentation and consequent multitude of particular cultural forms offer many different responses to the impact of modernization. The original island cultures of the Caribbean, as we have noted, gave way under foreign pressure, often backed by military force. Foreign demand for raw materials (saltpeter, guano, natural rubber, and so on) produced partial economic booms, which in turn gave rise to abrupt but fleeting modernizing processes, but these tended to do the most damage in the very same extractive zones that received the fewest benefits. The more isolated the regions or subcultures exposed to modernizing pressure, the greater their acculturations were, for such regions had fewer defenses on which they could rely and were less able to adapt. By the same token, the more integrated the nation and the more developed its own cultural trends, the less harmful the process was, allowing for harmonious progress that kept traditions and identity alive, adapting them to the new circumstances.

Without trying to establish a typology of cultural conflicts in Latin America (something beyond the scope of this book), we outline a few examples in the following sections, focusing in particular on contemporary cases that provide the cultural background for recent original contributions in fiction. Our aim is to note successful efforts at creating a literary discourse based on a writer's own strong traditions, using examples of transcultural plasticity that have not yielded to modernity but rather used it to their own ends. If transculturation is the norm all over the continent — as much on the cosmopolitan side as on what we specifically term the transculturated side — it is the latter that has accomplished an even greater feat than the cosmopolitans, in our judgment, for they have maintained the historical continuity of cultural forms that were profoundly elaborated by the social masses, adjusting it with the least possible loss of identity to the new conditions determined by the international setting of the time.

Indigenous Cultures Frozen in Time

The most serious and intractable conflict stems from the stagnant old compartmentalization between indigenous Indian cultures and those that date to the beginnings of the Iberian conquest and colonization, followed in later centuries by the transfer of modernizing to other metropolitan centers (France, Britain, and the United States, especially). This division is most inflexible in the Andean region (Peru, Bolivia, Ecuador), but it also exists in other zones with a strong indigenous presence (Mexico, Guatemala, Paraguay). In the Andean case, "cultural rigidity" was a factor in each of the opposing camps, frustrating any attempts at integration and condemning the indigenous and dominant Spanish cultures alike to mutually independent self-sufficiency, a fact that, as we will see, made them each more outdated and hindered their creative growth. This case, being the oldest and most serious, is the one we will analyze in detail later in this book, analyzing the cultural components of the Andean region, the appearance of contact brokers (the mestizos), and the differing views of the conflict offered by the two sides, and concluding with a study of the fiction of José María Arguedas as a paradigm of transcultural solutions, for in the construction of his major novel *Los ríos profundos* [*Deep Rivers*], we find (1) examples of deculturation; (2) examples of how he selected foreign ideas, for the most part, from heterodoxies that rejected European modernization; (3) his search for and discovery of internal cultural elements that could stand up to modernization; and (4) the literary neoculturation that he brought about by juggling all these components, but especially by his whole-scale restructuring of the forces behind a particular culture.

However, to give some examples of this conflict for the purposes of this chapter, let us turn now to a less prestigious and less studied region in the heart of South America: the Indian cultures of the northern Amazonian rainforest in the border region between Brazil, Colombia, and Venezuela, home to tribes from many diverse linguistic and cultural families, some of them still little known. These tribes, especially those from Colombia's Vaupés-Caquetá region and the upper reaches of the Rio Negro and its tributaries in Brazil, have diverse origins. The earliest stratum in the region, represented by today's Makú, Waiká, and Xirianá, was overlaid by migratory waves of Arawaks from the north (today's Baré, Manao, Warekêna, and Baníwa) and of members of the large Tukâno family from the west, which heavily infiltrated the area and, according to some anthropologists (Curt Nimuendajú), gave rise to the cultures that survive in two wings of the region: the western zone of tribes along the Napo and Putumayo rivers, and the eastern zone of Brazilian tropical jungle along the Rio Negro, with the largest concentration at São Gabriel da Cachoeira.

Following up on monographs by researchers earlier in the twentieth century (Theodor Koch-Grünberg, Curt Nimuendajú, Irving Goldman, Julian Steward),[23] the past decade has witnessed considerable growth in the number of studies on Tukâno culture, most notably those by Gerardo Reichel-Dolmatoff, Stephen and Christine Hugh-Jones, and Robin M. Wright. A singular point of reference for each of these recent writers has been the publication in Brazil of *Antes o mundo não existía*, a book by two Desâna Indians—Umúsin Panlõn Kumu and Tolamãn Kenhíri—in a Portuguese translation created with the help of the anthropologist Berta Ribeiro. In her introduction, Ribeiro notes, "This is the first time in the history of Brazilian anthropology that indigenous protagonists have written and signed their own mythology. Tolamãn Kenhíri, a Desâna Indian from the clan of the same name, and his father, Umúsin Panlõn Kumu, 33 and 53 years old respectively, decided to write this book in order to pass on their tribe's mythic legacy to their descendents, convinced that it would otherwise become lost or corrupted."[24]

Her observation recalls a distinction that José Carlos Mariátegui drew in 1928 with regard to the indigenista literature of his era: "It is still a mestizo literature and as such is called indigenist rather than indigenous. If an indigenous literature finally appears, it will be when the Indians themselves are able to produce it."[25] The Desâna book was produced by Indians, and the radical significance of this event is evidenced by the myths and legends it recounts, which are more radically Indian than the many books that were published in indigenous languages by culturally mestizo Indians after Mariátegui's pronouncement. (One example is the poetry book *Taki parwa* by Kilku Waraka, a pseudonym of Andrés Alencastre, whom José María Arguedas praised for his knowledge of Quechua, which he found comparable to that of the author of *Ollantay*: "We thought that such mastery was no longer attainable by modern Quechua speakers."[26]) In the end, predictably, the most common way for Indians to communicate their own genuine ideas has been by writing in American Spanish about social, political, and literary themes that replicate the general currents of criollo national culture. The most visible and productive of these writers has been the Aymara writer Fausto Reinaga, a leader of the Partido Indio of Bolivia, who has been deeply influenced by the model of the revolutionary Andean indigenista.[27]

The practice of the two Amazonian Indian writers is quite different. Theirs is a defensive line of cultural resistance, yet one that also bears witness to the profound transculturation they have already experienced. Before we analyze their book, we should note that they live in one of the largest and most sparsely inhabited zones of the three countries where their Tukâno culture is based.[28] The tribes are settled along the rivers, concentrating at the rapids (*cachoeiras*), with loose ties among the lodges (*malocas*) in which they live. Their numbers have steadily declined, to the point that there now seem to be no more than a thousand individuals who speak Desâna. They have long been in contact with Western cultures. Contacts intensified after a Salesian mission settled in their territory in 1926; they intensified yet more, and became dangerously corrosive, when Brazil began planning a northern perimeter highway.

The region had a period of ephemeral luxury during the late nineteenth and early twentieth century, when the rubber boom led, in literature, to a series of reports by Euclides da Cunha and the images of the "green hell" that Arturo Cova traversed in José Eustasio Rivera's novel *La vorágine*. One marginal portion of this region, belonging to the part of the Marañón basin whose capital is Iquitos, Peru, entered literature through Mario Vargas Llosa's novel *La casa verde* (1965). More recently, the Brazilian Amazon, long the subject of books by writers from other regions of the country, has produced more of its own literary activity, aimed at preserving and promoting its local traditions.

No one better exemplifies this trend than Márcio Souza (born in Manaus, 1946), beginning with his 1976 novel *Galves, imperador do Acre*, and no one else has done more to ground his attitude toward the region in a historical and theoretical discourse that has revived Brazil's cultural regionalist perspective from the 1920s. In his novels, Souza uses feuilleton-style narrative techniques such as those occasionally employed by García Márquez. What makes Souza's literary work stand out is his distinctive mix of traditional forms (Indian rituals and settings, musical and dramatic compositions modeled after popular operas) and modern communication techniques (especially film, which he studied during his college days in São Paulo, where he majored in social sciences). The result is a dissonant, baroque complex, with old-fashioned overtones, yet it is highly sophisticated.

In his book *A expressão amazonense: Do colonialismo ao neocolonialismo*, Souza asserts that "Amazonian history is the most official, the most deformed, embedded in the most backward, the most superficial, the most bureaucratic tradition in all of Brazilian historiography,"[29] and he attacks this situation from the point of view of a very modern writer who creatively handles Marxist categories and the latest aesthetic theories: "Art is a dangerous text, an exercise in counter-massacre, fighting on terrain occupied by the language of silence; repressive and castrating."[30]

Writing about the systematic ethnocide practiced by Western civilization on its global march, Souza notes its technological failure in the tropics, which went hand-in-hand with the failure of Western intellectuals: "The same thing occurred with the 'civilized' artists, who never solved the enigmas of language in the region."[31] These observations lead him back to the anti-Eurocentric discourse of the Americas, which over the course of at least the past two centuries has turned again and again to indigenous nativism for support: "A more detailed knowledge of indigenous cultures is enough to knock down the old ethnocentric pretensions. How can you call cultures barbarous when they have produced literature of the quality collected by Nunes Pereira in *Moronguetá, um Decameron indígena?* How can you call a civilization primitive when it is able to unite the Dionysian and the Apollonian in a single creative force? Among the Indians there is no separation between manual and intellectual labor, between poet and philosopher, between living and being."[32] The book by Umúsin Panlõn Kumu and Tolamãn Kenhíri points toward this greater knowledge of indigenous cultures and their survival over the ages, as well as their gradual mestizo transformation. The book belongs to the deepest, innermost layer of Latin American literature — because it is linked to an Indian language, because it seeks to recover a culture's mythic vision and insert it in an alien contemporary society, and because it is not a mere archaic remnant consigned to a chapter on pre-Columbian literature. Rather, it is a contemporary work resulting from the second trauma of ongoing modernization, which (as in Freudian theory) returns the first, original trauma to consciousness.

In his description of the Amazon, Manuel Diegues emphasizes the cultural unity of Amazonian men, despite the wide and diverse range of their activities. This approach effectively puts the criollo process of becoming mestizo, governed by Portuguese norms even if it is infused by a native substrate, at the heart of the region's cultural configuration. The past half-century of anthropological research, however, has demonstrated that Indian society has survived in important ways and cannot be reduced to Amazonian mestizos (so-called *caboclos*), who are in effect the only people Diegues describes when it comes to indigenous Amazonia. And Indian society gives access to the root sources of the Amazon's cultural uniqueness. Even Diegues recognizes this ("the Amazon is thus fundamentally indigenous, and this is what characterizes it most strongly as a cultural region").[33] This centuries-long cultural continuity is not what interests him the most, though. He is more drawn to the products of miscegenation with the Portuguese and the people from Brazil's Northeast; the extractive industries (rubber); the adoption of indigenous cuisine; and the way in which all of these things were mixed and molded together, following the same Western cultural patterns that have molded all of Brazil.

Nevertheless, this vast, sparsely populated jungle region is not only one of the habitats least touched in the world by the West but also home to a society that is extremely protective of its social, economic, and cultural traditions. To understand the literary products that emerge from this deep layer of American culture, we must first take a brief look at its characteristics.

The overview of the tribes of the Vaupés-Caquetá region by Irving Goldman (author of the most comprehensive report on the Cubeo Indians)[34] argued that they descended from three sources: Tukânos, Arawaks, and Caribs. The largest of these groups were the Tukânos, with at least eighteen tribes spread over the region bounded by four rivers—the Guaviare in the north, the Rio Negro and the Guiainía in the east, the Caquetá in the south—and in the west by the Andes. Here is Goldman's synthesis of the regional cultural traits across the area:

> Among the distinctive cultural features of this area, to which will be noted numerous exceptions, may be listed the following: Primary emphasis upon bitter manioc cultivation and fishing, with hunting of secondary importance; the use of large multifamily houses, each constituting a local kinship group, rather than villages; a complex of men's rites associated with an ancestor cult, inadequately referred to in the literature as yurupary; the existence of patrilineal sibs; painted bark-cloth masks, unevenly distributed in the area; frequent and prolonged chicha drinking, with intoxication common; chewing of powdered coca mixed with leaf ash and use of vision-inducing lianas; shamanism associated with the jaguar; and striking emphasis upon sorcery. Tribal organization is either weak or absent, with authority vested in the leader of the sib or local kin group.[35]

Subsequent studies have generally supported this overview. The Desânas, who live along the banks of the Papurí and the Tiquié, right at the equator, reside in scattered *malocas* in family groups of twenty to one hundred and are characterized by exogamy with virilocal residence, strengthening the ties among the many Tukâno tribes. Our best evidence to date on their culture comes from the excellent book by Gerardo Reichel-Dolmatoff,[36] thanks to his Desâna informant of Colombian nationality, Antonio Guzmán, who recounted the cosmology and myths of the Vaupés tribe to which he belonged and who kept up the long interexchange with Reichel-Dolmatoff that allowed the latter to form an intelligent reading of their particular cultural forms.

The texts that Reichel-Dolmatoff transcribed are few, recorded on consecutive working sessions and edited to form a single coherent discourse. They are very unlike the ones we find in the book by Tolamãn Kenhíri, who wrote the texts himself in the Desâna language and translated them himself into Portuguese with assistance from Berta Ribeiro. Whereas Guzmán had moved to Bogota and received the education he needed to hold teaching positions, Tolamãn Kenhíri (his Portuguese name is Luis Lana) lives in the village of São João on the Tiquié River and learned Portuguese in the Salesian mission where, we infer, he also learned to write Desâna. His book *Antes o mundo não existia* was published jointly under his name and that of his father, Umúsin Panlõn Kumu (Portuguese: Firmiano Lana Arantes). The father, who decided never to learn Portuguese even though he allowed his children to do so, acts the part of informant to his son and takes advantage of the knowledge he holds as *kumu* to his tribe—a spiritual teacher similar to the *payé*, which is described in Reichel-Dolmatoff's book as the highest authority on myths, granting him a wisdom (*mahsí-doári*) that allows the deepest understanding of the meaning of what, for most of the tribe, were no longer anything but rituals.[37] Berta Ribeiro notes in her introduction that Tolamãn Kenhíri is the most attached of all of his father's children to the traditions that his father represents, to the point that he has gone through the apprenticeship needed to inherit the post of kumu.

The reasons that led him to write the book are interesting: on the one hand, a desire to save the traditions that were being lost during the acculturation process that the area was undergoing; on the other, a feeling that the appearance of tape recorders now allowed "even sixteen-year-old boys" to start recording the knowledge of the ancients, creating a danger that "everybody will get our history wrong, it'll all come out in a jumble."[38] His solution, then, was to write himself what his father agreed to dictate to him, in the little ruled notebooks that Father Casemiro Beksta of the Salesian mission had given him. This gave him a pride of authorship, of being the author of a book, which Berta Ribeiro recognized when she met father and son and encountered their resistance to becoming her informants: "They both would argue that we, we anthropologists, go to their villages, collect their legends, study their traditions, and then publish our books in Brazil and the United States, while they, the bearers of those traditions, earn a few paltry presents."[39] This recognition led Berta Ribeiro to decide instead to help them publish their book under their own names and to make sure that they retained copyright.

We see here their consciousness of the categories of *book* and *author*, which obviously do not derive from their tribe's cultural traditions but from Brazilian cultural practice. They have predictably learned these categories through schooling; though they embrace them, they use them against the impositions of Brazilian culture. The authors' ambition centered on bringing the book back to the tribe, where it could be read by young people who are losing their ties to the region's own culture, and it could serve as a counterbalance to an education that, as Berta Ribeira notes, teaches them more about ancient Greece and Rome and the political history of Rio de Janeiro than about the concrete realities of Desâna life and its past. The other thing we see here is the existence of a model of the intellectual, represented by the anthropologist—a typical agent of cultural contact. In recent decades, through the work of a youthful generation shaped by movements such as those of 1968, anthropologists have moved away from neutral data collection for the purpose of academic study, opting instead for greater participation in the destiny of disintegrating Indian societies. Their positive reappraisal of the cultural heritage of archaic societies has served as a model for the emergence of what can only be called the Indian intellectual, the Indian writer. The production of Indian intellectuals is infinitely more interesting and valuable than anything created by any other educational influences on the Indians, such as those emanating from religious missions. Despite their progress in perceiving the Indian cultural problem, the missions can only erode the Indians' worldview, seeking to replace it with Western religion and with worldviews from the same political and social groups that are actively seeking to erode Indian views in precisely this way, in order to replace a mythical view with the classist or social view that goes with whichever doctrine they uphold.

Using anthropological studies as a model, the authors achieve a form of cultural resistance—of identity preservation—reminiscent of what the millenarian Franciscans vainly and tragically attempted to preserve when they tried forging an isolationist fantasy during the first century of colonization (Gerónimo de Mendieta's missionary work in New Spain).

To the degree that these Indian intellectuals remain immersed in their living cultural roots and draw on that experience in their work, they layer their work beneath a series of social masks; for all that, however, their work still displays a great deal of transculturation.[40]

The flame of cultural resistance that enlivens their book had to pass through a new educational system (and, by the same token, a new socio-cultural system); through the use of writing; and through media which, however prestigious they might seem to us in modern societies, are quite impoverished in comparison with the traditional media of archaic societies. Traditionally, creation myths and explanatory myths about everyday life were passed on in Desâna *malocas* during two collective celebrations (*dabucurí* and *cachirí*), in which every inhabitant in the group of neighboring malocas took part. People went to these celebrations with ceremonial paintings and musical instruments and dressed in special clothing. They carried out a prescribed ritual, drank, danced, and recited the myths with the help of the kumus and the payés, generally the tribal elders. The community feeling was heightened by consuming drugs, particularly *yajé*.[41] In place of this organic community—which tied everyone to a collectivity, attaining their spiritual, physical, and social participation and which handled the multiplicity of emotional and rational energies of the human beings who belonged to it—there is now one man who no longer speaks directly to another man but instead writes and writes, in solitude, with his pencil and paper, hoping that other equally distant and solitary men might read his writing and seek to reconstruct through their imaginations the complex codes that were set in motion at community celebrations. The appalling impoverishment that writing implies—the principles of grammatology, with its system of graphic symbols stripped of voice and skin—are plainly visible in this leap that has allowed an Indian to enter the modern cultural systems.

In our own culture, when it comes to theater (a privileged literary genre, with deep roots in religious ritual and set above all others since the time of Aristotle), we are aware of the huge gap that separates the spectacle of drama from the text. We can measure the extreme technical difficulty that the playwright faces in trying to introduce, on the grammatological level, the presence of the many codes that constitute the stage (gestures, intonations, lights, costumes, and so on). We have the text of Juan José Podestá's stage adaptation of the pantomime version of *Juan Moreira*, which he based not on Eduardo Gutiérrez's original feuilleton novel but on his realist pantomime play. Our historical knowledge of how this drama was staged allows us to measure the enormous distance that separates it from the written text and the extreme poverty of expression that it displays.[42] Something similar can be inferred about Tolamãn Kenhíri's book, in relation to the models we know through anthropological writings. There is also a second impoverishment that we can derive from Basil Bernstein's observations about the popular use in language of "restricted codes," "condensed symbols," and "collective roles," which cannot be separated from their context and in fact presume their context, even if they do not set it down in writing.[43]

In this transformation of a drama once shared and experienced by all of its participants, whose historical model was the dithyramb—precursor to classical Greek tragedy (and whose contemporary model in the Brazilian Amazon can be found in plays by Márcio Souza based on indigenous models, such as *Tem piranha no piraruco* and *As folias do látex*)[44]—now reconstructed as a written text, we find that the anthropological monograph has unconsciously remained our guide, underlining the dominance of denotative and referential levels of the text, given our inability to translate the connotative and richly symbolic multiple dimensions of the original drama into text. This said, it should be recognized that the cosmology related by Tolamãn Kenhíri is more subtle, complex, and suggestive than the one that Antonio Guzmán passed on to Reichel-Dolmatoff, which by comparison seems like a more advanced stage of rationalization and a stricter adaptation to the anthropological monograph model.

We have not even mentioned yet the most important aspect of the book *Antes o mundo não existía*, though to do so we will first have to insist on a crucial change in the way we usually deal with literary concepts. Because of a slippage resulting from the increasing specialization and technification of historiographical discourse—which, like other scientific (or allegedly scientific) disciplines, is characterized by its constant negation of earlier discourses that have been displaced by newer and better grounded models—literature has been taking on a lot of materials that have jumped their original disciplinary channels and flowed into new frames that give them meaning and survival value. There is nothing new about this in the annals of culture. Latin American literature has long embraced huge numbers of chronicles from the conquest and colonial era; it is now beginning to include an even greater accumulation of hagiographies, catechisms, sermons, and religious histories. It has also embraced indigenous religious, ritual, and historiographical discourse (the *Popol Vuh*, the books of Chilam Balam, and so on) and, due to their foundational prestige, incorporated them into literature very early on.

This enhanced receptivity to the heterogeneous works of the past has not been matched by any such receptivity to the even greater number of works that anthropology has produced over the past century. The monumental corpus of myths and legends collected by anthropologists has scarcely been touched by literature, nor has it piqued the interest of contemporary scholars, not even those who propose updating the concept of literature while they continue to study what have traditionally been accorded the title of "literary works" by the learned rules of the ineradicable "lettered city," which has governed the continent from the dawn of colonialism to the present.

Antes o mundo não existía is a literary work that belongs entirely to the bookish orbit, even in terms of the transculturation it underwent by adopting the book format as a means of communication, taking up a model drawn from the existing intellectual discourses of modernity. By transforming a ritual celebration into a textbook and by using two main languages (both Desâna and Portuguese) to ensure widespread communication that is national in scope, it fully entered Brazilian literature, within the bounds that limit the depth of a literary product during any era. It had been a work in an Indian language, transmitted orally and therefore fixed by community censorship, located inside and outside of history, belonging to a mix of genres (words, rhythms, beliefs, dances, pictures, smells, sex, skin) and meant to regulate the life of the community; now it is a text by individual authors, in Portuguese, in the mythical story genre, that has acquired marked features of the current (Western) definition of literature.

The vast array of literary materials that are usually called anthropological (a myth is a tale, Barthes says)[45] is clearly mediated by the intellectual filters of the times and by the primitive filters of anthropologists. Just compare one collection with another, even from the same community; just compare two distant periods in the same collection. In the latter cases, the cultural filters of each era in the West become clear, just as one sees with literary works only a few decades after they are published. In the former cases, we can establish a typology according to famous brand names: Frazer, Boas, Lévy-Bruhl, Malinowski, Whorf, Lévi-Strauss, and so on. These filters are modified when it is an Indian telling the story, but they do not disappear, given the impact that cultural patterns have on any individual they govern.

These filters all aim to create an objective report that strings together a cohesive discourse. Even though these impositions of what we might call anthropological genres usually vary by era, individual, and doctrine, they nevertheless all are guilty of neglecting the strictly literary aspects of the message—what Jakobson would call its poetic aspects—because they are interested only in the communication of meanings, which they can then subject to a symbolic reading, in a sort of Euhemerism. This emphasis on meanings (translatable ones, at that) has been legitimated by Lévi-Strauss, and it no doubt increases the effectiveness of the kind of logical/structural analysis that he has used to study fundamental categories, but it has also hampered his ability to make literary judgments and thus capture meaning holistically.[46] The distinction between literature and myth that Lévi-Strauss has tenaciously maintained—insisting that myth is translatable so that he can base his analysis on bundles of meanings that he discovers in the text itself—is not obviously convincing, nor does it square with any linguistic notion of what a message is. It is impossible to think of a text in which signifiers play no role and have no impact on the production of meaning. Reaching such a level of interpretation seems overly ambitious for now, when we have just begun to identify the codes based on which messages are constructed. Altogether, we have slowly progressed in our understanding of the mental operations that govern the construction of messages—operations that we have learned about through the contributions of rhetoric over the years.

Reichel-Dolmatoff's research tries to take these problems into account. His reading uses the usual methods of interpreting symbols with a markedly Freudian bent, but by paying attention to tropes as well, he is able to study their incorporation of metaphor and metonym.[47] His starting point is to look for acts of repression—a necessary component of culture—and to observe their effects on the production of messages—that is, their chains of analogies and their displacements onto adjacent elements. To do this, he first had to build up a fine-grained knowledge of the habitat in order to parse the meaning of texts with a high degree of implicit contextuality. His reading is persuasive and has been praised by Lévi-Strauss. Its limitations come from the almost insuperable problem of language, both for the texts and for the area in which they are produced, which can be measured by the difficulties Berta Ribeiro describes in translating Tolamãn Kenhíri's original into Portuguese.

Desâna, let us recall, is a disappearing language, with no more than a thousand speakers living in dispersed malocas along the Tiquié and Papurí rivers. It belongs (says Goldman) to the Tukâno language family, which encompasses no fewer than eighteen tribes in the area, where it serves as the lingua franca. It is joined by several other language families (Arawak, Carib, Witoto) spoken by scattered tribes, and the widespread Nheengatú or Lingua Geral, the common indigenous language of Brazil that missionaries created in the eighteenth century based on the Tupi language found on Brazil's Atlantic coast, to which various Amazonian tribes have become acculturated (in this region, the Warekêna). It seems like a linguistic hodge-podge, further complicated by the exogamous practice that has women moving into their husbands' residences, and it is even further complicated because it is a border area where two official languages — Spanish and Portuguese — meet and mix. As the dominant languages, Spanish and Portuguese have become the vehicles through which we have received most indigenous literary production; thus, Tolamãn Kenhíri wrote his book in Desâna and then translated it into Portuguese, although the mythical text provided by Antonio Guzmán was translated into Spanish.

Berta Ribeiro lays out the problem perfectly when she describes how she collaborated on translating the Desâna text into Portuguese. She opted for a strictly literal, word-for-word translation of passages that the author, Tolamãn Kenhíri, had left in Desâna in his own translation. "The literal translation allows us, I argue, to deduce the Tucâno's thought structure and the symbolic meaning of expressions such as 'Kenhíri Tolamãn ponlãn,' the clan to which the authors belong. 'Tolamãn' = personal name; 'Kenhíri' = flowers or pictures that appear in dreams; 'ponlãn' = offspring. Earlier translation had rendered this term as 'children of the dream flowers.'"[48] We will find the same problem in Arguedas's critical essay on Quechua poetry and popular songs, where he describes linguistic translation as an inescapable zone of cultural encounter. His essay points to the same difficulties that Ribeiro experienced when, as she goes on to say, "He refused to give me translations for certain ceremonial words that are considered secret, or whose equivalent in Portuguese he did not know."

What the translation barrier reveals is our ignorance of the cultural codes that frame indigenous texts, codes that embody meaning in the strict linguistic operations through which thought and feeling are expressed. The Indian literary works that are part of the cultural resistance movement are the ones that mark the outer limits of literature in Latin America, for they, more than any other linguistic communication, reveal cultural otherness. By the same token, they set out new functions for literature, which would include integrating these discourses into a homogeneous framework. Literature has served many functions on the continent (and in the world). In colonial times, it formed the basis for Westernization; after independence, it formed the basis for nationhood. In this century, it might well become the basis for cultural messages, endowing them with the homogeneity of its discourse. We have already noted that literature has gobbled up other disciplines that are much more distant from it than anthropological monographs, which are created by transcribing oral literatures and are therefore given to freer constructions of the imaginary.

Regions Steeped in Isolation

The peculiarities of the conquest and colonization of Latin America gave rise to the many regions that slowly developed there with few ties to their colonial capitals. The markedly separatist, or at least isolationist, tendencies of these regions led them to develop cultural patterns of their own, which were often quite archaic and frequently the product of unique syncretisms. These patterns, in turn, served as a basis for strong localist tendencies. The immense territory of the Americas was subjugated in just half a century, but colonial dominion was consolidated in cities that ruled in turn, and only with difficulty, over their own neighboring hinterlands. This left almost untouched vast stretches where colonization was confined to extractive exploitation and the growing haciendas. This was especially the case during the seventeenth and eighteenth centuries up to the Bourbon and Pombaline reforms—the long incubation period of regionalism and separatism. In several cases, the colonial administrative divisions (the Audiencias) served to consolidate regions and even forge the future nationalities of Spanish America.[49] Even within these Audiencias, we find rivalries of the same sort that set their own capital cities against the capitals of the Viceroyalties; smaller regions were using the Audiencias' own examples of pursuing autonomy to consolidate themselves, helped along by the great difficulties in transportation that had relegated their rule to the Audiencia cities to begin with.

The map of Latin America is based on regions and miniregions, which over the course of centuries became accustomed to developing their own autonomous and endogamous practices, based on their ethnic and cultural makeup, the economic activities from which their people lived, their sometime grudging adaptation to their geographic settings, and their lax acceptance of the supraregional order. The actual domination of the entire territory and its subjugation to the administrative centers would only be rigorously enforced during the last third of the nineteenth century as part of the modernizing project. Even so, well into the twentieth century, many regions would still cling to the isolation and cultural distinctiveness that they had formed over the course of several centuries after the conquest.

In some cases, these historically based conditions were exacerbated by the modern-day country's size and geography; Brazil, Colombia, Mexico, and Bolivia are still defined by their regions. Indeed, the other countries of Latin America all have sharp regional divisions as well, even the smallest ones. Many indices can be used to define a region (geographic, economic, historical, ethnic, social), but they all agree on the importance of cultural differences in the ways in which the inhabitants of the region are educated, especially during the decisive period of childhood and adolescence. This is so true that most people who leave their regions as young adults and move to urban centers or the country's capital never lose the deep imprint of having been molded by the regional culture, even if that imprint was later mixed with other influences and practices. This is the norm for writers who are absorbed by the capital cities in which they often carry out their adult literary work yet who, for all that, never break ties to their roots and the cultural patterns that formed them. This can be clearly seen in the writers we call narrators of transculturation; João Guimarães Rosa cannot be separated from his roots in Minas Gerais any more than García Márquez can be from Colombia's Caribbean coast or Juan Rulfo can be from Jalisco. This is not to say that they conform to any stereotypes about their regions of origin—to suggest as much would be to deny the productive and inventive nature of their artistic creations, which, as we have noted, set out to recover forms that have sometimes been neglected but that belong to their regions' cultural configurations, which they have reworked under the circumstances arising from the modernizing conflict.

To speak of this is simply to speak of history, and this is what is special about the new regionalism in Latin America: it came into being at a historical moment when the traditional values and behaviors that defined regional cultures were deeply shaken. The modernizing conflict started a movement against permanence, but its pressure was not felt on objects or values imported from abroad; rather, it afflicted those that were steeped in regional culture. It set in motion the formerly static, traditional culture of the self-contained region, challenged its secret potential by demanding answers, and shook up rigid patterns by extracting new, nonhackneyed meanings from them and using them to construct messages that would be useful under new circumstances. The literature that arose from regionalism during this era of conflict was, therefore, neither traditional *costumbrista* discourse (the result of simple acquiescence to the fact of being a subjugated minority, which turns one into mere subject matter and picturesqueness for the eyes of outsiders) nor modernist discourse (another kind of submissive acquiescence, this time at the expense of looking picturesque to the eyes of insiders); rather, it was an original invention, a neoculturation based on regional culture as it was laid down when history and modernization ran over it. To the degree that culture tends to become second nature for the human group that creates it—so that it comes to define their being—the literature that emerges in such a transitional moment straddles nature and history. Even more, this kind of literature joins nature and history together in an artistic structure that aims to integrate and balance them, and in so doing to give them meaning and help them to survive. The meaning of history becomes accessible through the use of cultural forces that are specific to the regional community, and these forces enter the future that history predicts for them, aspiring to persist without losing their intimate texture.

The historical factor played a remarkably similar role in hinterland regions all across Latin America, for it reflected the era's worldwide pressures and the measures taken by foreign imperial centers to achieve global penetration. The regional cultures, by contrast, displayed such specificity and particularity that they could scarcely be confined within the taxonomies proposed by sociologists or economists. Most regions had pronounced rural traits and were associated, in some of the more refined typologies (Wagley), with relative good fortune, but not even a recognition of the traits that they had in common with other Third World regions would suffice to dissolve the irreducible components of their ethnic origins, languages, traditions, and the always singular and original circumstances of their development. We can trace relationships between Jalisco and Minas Gerais (in Mexico and Brazil, respectively) that mirror relationships we might deduce from the works of Juan Rulfo and Guimarães Rosa. We can find similar literary operations and exercises common to a certain sort of popular imaginary, but we could never strictly equate them. What is original about each culture is its own originality itself, the impossibility of reducing this culture to any other culture, no matter how many fundamentals they have in common. This is how they differ from the historical factor of modernization, which lacks that stubborn, inner, persistent trait found in regional cultures, even when one is critical of them. For Juan Rulfo, one of the worst aspects of regional cultures is that they make the people of a region "feel like they are absolute lords and masters," but he based his novel on that value: "They were opposed to any force that seemed like it might threaten their property. Hence the atmosphere of stubbornness, of resentment that had built up over the centuries, which is sort of like the air that my character Pedro Páramo breathed, from his childhood on."[50]

The vigor and constancy of these traditional cultural components is what made the novelists of transculturation pay attention to the archetypes of power in regional society and what often drew their unconscious and unwanted attraction to the vestiges of aristocracy. A patrician vision underlies the inventions of José María Arguedas, Gabriel García Márquez, Juan Rulfo, and João Guimarães Rosa. It operates on a diametric opposition between past and present, where the just demands of the present fail to tarnish the admiration shown toward the remnants of an idealized aristocratic conception of the world. Critics have described this attitude in Gilberto Freyre's monumental *Casa grande e senzala*, one of the major products of twentieth-century regional neoculture, but it has also been expressed in concrete and artistic ways by almost all the writers we have cited. We see it in the feudal world of warlords that Riobaldo joins in *Grande sertão*, the tessitura of which is related to the imaginary developed in Brazil's traditional *cordel* literature. This relationship between the world of popular literary fiction and the world of men who actually carry out such actions gave rise to Ariano Suassuna's novel *A pedra do reino*. The same world of the idealized past feeds into the patrician vision in which García Márquez's narrative emerges, creating a whole series of austere colonels for Colombia's Thousand Days War, each of whom is forced to witness the breakdown of the values on which he has built his worldview, after the appearance of "the whirlwind" (*la hojarasca*), which economic desires or the predatory political and material interests of village social groups easily shift from one side to the other.

This is no classist view, pitting the patrician class against the vulgar mob, but a cultural choice that replicates the one that had been famously taken during the late nineteenth-century modernization of Latin America, when those same patricians were seen confronting unscrupulous merchants. However, it does contain a culturalist view that defends local traditions, local value systems, a past that shaped the people of the region, all the things highlighted by the economic ruin in which those people found themselves, and the close ties they were able to develop with the common people with whom they shared a culture.

This attention to the regional upper class (the *señores*) can also be seen in the works of Rulfo and Arguedas, albeit within more modern and finely drawn social parameters. In Rulfo's novel *Pedro Páramo* and in Arguedas's *Todas las sangres* (as well as in his earlier *Diamantes y pedernales*), the señores are capable of greatness and even generosity, derived entirely from the basic cultural components in which they have been educated. These are examples of the resistance that Guimarães Rosa spoke of, a resistance that not only builds patrician points of view but also moves the writers' pens. The señores may be condemned by the ideological frames of these works, but they can only be admired for something that is beyond their own power or personality, which is the cultural system they represent.

These characters represent one pole in a schema of forces; the other pole is the story's narrator—often one of the characters but sometimes an outside figure to whom the narration is being addressed. This narrator (or addressee) plays the role of mediator in the tale, one of the characteristic roles of the transculturation process. He becomes the guardian of a cultural heritage, and an entire scaffolding is built on him in order to transmit a new example of development, now modernized. It is the writer who holds the position of mediator because that is his primary role in the process, and it is he who returns that role to the story itself through characters who carry out the task of the mediator within the text. The long discourse by Riobaldo is not a monologue but rather a disclosure to a *senhor* who, by the same token, is present in the text—Riobaldo can appeal to his knowledge of the cultural environment with confidence—yet remains outside the text in that borderland that defines the mediating role. He is both inside and outside the message; he straddles that second nature of culture and the emergence of modernizing history. The vagueness with which the mediator is sometimes designed points to his own ambiguity, his dual behavior, and his vacillation between one territory and the other. We will see this in the role of Ernesto in Arguedas's novel *Deep Rivers*, where Arguedas has good reason for making his character a child, for that excuses his imbalances (such as between imagination and operativity) and gives him the plasticity necessary to move back and forth between opposing forces.

The narrator is introduced into the story as one of two polar forces that are indispensable for elucidating the pattern of changes that the texts postulate. In Juan Rulfo's novel, this bipolarity is constitutive of the narrative structure from the moment we have two linked and contrasting principal narrators: the personal narrator, Juan Preciado, recounting from his grave the story of his return to Comala, and the impersonal narrator, focusing on the story of Pedro Páramo and his infatuation with Susana San Juan. Although the two narrations alternate and interweave, their distribution throughout the novel does not hide their conflicting and contrasting positions; one opens the novel, dominating the whole first part, and the other grows within that first narration like an echo or a rumble, coming to dominate the second half and closing the book with the ritual of parricide.

The bipolarity that organizes this text is accompanied and highlighted by a number of literary devices, which are layered on top of the basic literary articulation that is established by the grammatical opposition between personal and impersonal. On the surface level of the text, this opposition defines the narrators' bipolarity, but it is duplicated on the level of content, where the object of each statement is seen to be the son/father opposition—the key signifier in all of Rulfo's writings. The leap from a personal to an impersonal account is, as Benveniste has observed, a leap over a fundamental heterogeneity masked by our grammatical habits, by what we call our linguistic laws, which mimic the laws of society and force upon us a homogeneity that is no such thing, for the so-called third person actually has the status of a non-person. "In order not to imply any person, I can use any subject at all, or no subject all, and this subject, whether expressed or not, is never established as a person."[51]

The novel thus sets up an opposition between person and non-person in the field of narrators; meanwhile, in the field of subjects, it also contrasts two distinct people with distinct names: Juan Preciado and Pedro Páramo. Despite their different surnames, these two are in fact father and son. Therefore, the structure of grammatical narrators, as well as the structure of statements about first one and then the other subject, reproduce an equally discordant structure in which homogeneity of blood cannot conceal the true heterogeneity of people, and this is nothing less than the father/son relationship. This is a relationship that harshly dominates Rulfo's fiction (as in his short stories "¡Diles que no me maten!" and "No oyes ladrar los perros"), based on his observations of difference and rupture, which become most apparent only when they happen to people who are closely tied to one another—and no tie is greater than the blood tie of father and child, from which Rulfo persistently excludes the maternal link ("La herencia de Matilde Arcángel"). Juan Preciado is Pedro Páramo's son, the son who comes to seek the father he never knew. His first meeting, however, is with Abundio, another of Pedro Páramo's sons who also does not bear his father's surname (symbolic in this text of the blood link) and who undertakes the father's ritual murder at the end of the novel. Continuity and rupture are thus juggled simultaneously. The same schema is repeated isotopically on every level into which the text can be subdivided: derived continuity versus rupture, seeming homo-geneity versus deep heterogeneity, and efforts to rebuild family ties ver-sus the impossibility of restoring them. This schema underscores the par-ticular cultural situation into which Rulfo tried to insert the mediating function. In its drama and frustration, Rulfo's work can be linked to that of Arguedas, but it differs from the solutions reached by Guimarães Rosa and García Márquez.

For his part, García Márquez—who, let us recall, came from a region that modernized before its own national capital did—privileged the me-diator's function of writing things down, which he contrasted with the ceaseless memory loss that dooms one to ceaseless repetition. This is the role he gave to Melquíades and his system of coded writing, which leads Aureliano to decipher his writing and create literary discourse as some-thing that absorbs and negates all the cultural past. It was also for this role that García Márquez joined the circle of young writers known as La Cueva and personally took on the role of mediator—one who believes in the reality of the legend that crumbles into memories and who therefore resurrects the old traditions of a culture and gives them new life through a modernized system that is foreign to their practices: writing a book.

The role of mediator is similar to that of a contact agent between dif-ferent cultures. This is how we view the novelists we call transcultur-ators, while recognizing that, beyond their personal gifts, they have been strongly affected by the specific situation of the cultures to which they belong and the patterns by which those cultures modernize. Though we will mainly analyze this point by focusing on Arguedas's ideas and cre-ations, let us give a brief example of this original neoculturation here, drawn from an area very distinct from highland southern Peru. The re-gion is central-western Mexico, which encompasses the states of Michoa-cán, Jalisco, Colima, and parts of Guanajuato, Aguascalientes, Zacatecas, and Nayarit. This region experienced a long historical period of isolation during which it became organized autonomously as a region centered on the Audiencia of Nueva Galicia, whose history has been detailed by José López Portillo y Weber[52] and whose economic and social develop-ment paralleled the nearly autarkic development of the great colonial haciendas.[53]

In contrast to the Peruvian highlands, the Mexican region centered on the state of Jalisco is characterized by the absence of a large Indian population; instead, contingents of Spaniards created a rural culture there under conditions of isolation. "Its most notable feature, the one that distinguishes this region of Mexico, is its absence of an indigenous tradition, even though one finds food or clothing customs here and there that are conceptualized as indigenous," said Jean Meyer.[54] Luis González y González, in his splendid book on San José de Gracia, adds a note of conscious pride to this apparent racial purity: "There is no reason to believe that they thought of themselves as part of the Mexican nation; their feeling of race was stronger than any sense of patriotism. Although their way of life differed very little from that of the Indians of Mazamitla, they took pride in their Spanish blood."[55] Finally, Juan Rulfo expressed a negative interpretation of this conviction of their own superiority in an unconscious economy of spirit: "But the fact of having exterminated the indigenous population lent them a very special characteristic, that rather reactionary attitude of *criollos*, aiming to conserve their vested interests."[56]

This region, though only marginally linked to one of the key components of Mexican nationality—the Indian—has nevertheless given the nation some of its defining behaviors. Studying the region, Jean Meyer said that if he dared offer his most outlandish hypotheses, he would consider "Jalisco a paradigm of 'Mexicanness': *charros*, bulls, machismo, a soccer team on which no foreigner has ever played (Guadalajara), religiosity, big weddings, Francophiles, and so on."[57] This stereotype is obviously the one portrayed in songs such as "¡Ay Jalisco, no te rajes!" (1941), and it is subject to serious correction. Over the past half-century, this same region has provided Mexican literature with some of its most ingenious innovators in fiction—Agustín Yáñez, Juan José Arreola, Juan Rulfo. More than a vision, what they have proposed is a thorough revision of this stereotype; without rejecting it, they have subverted it and given it a new meaning. They have delved into its inner workings, rediscovered the exclusive functions it has that suit the new historical circumstances, gone on to analyze it critically, and yet, curiously, they have only strengthened it. Luis González y González himself acknowledged the debt he owed, by dedicating his book "to Agustín Yáñez for his *Al filo del agua* [The Edge of the Storm] and *Las tierras flacas* [The Lean Lands], to Juan José Arreola for *La feria* [The Fair], and to Juan Rulfo for *El llano en llamas* [The Burning Plain] and *Pedro Páramo*."[58] For his part, Jean Meyer preferred the contributions of popular literature, which he found portrayed the regional character traits better than works of high literature, and he put forward a curious comparison between Rulfo and Arreola, exact contemporaries who participated jointly (together with Antonio Alatorre) in their very first literary adventure, the journal *Pan*. He found that they were marked not by their common cultural background in Jalisco but by their contrasting social locations within that complex:

Juan Rulfo was born into one of the richest families in the town of San Gabriel (Venustiano Carranza), Jalisco. He has externalized the pessimism of the landowning social group that was ruined by the Revolution and further impoverished by the particular history of San Gabriel, which has never recovered from the damage caused by the Cristero War. Arreola, from a humble family in Zapotlán el Grande (Ciudad Guzmán), for his part partakes of the optimism of anyone who has experienced upward social mobility and has lived in a dynamic small city. And then, Rulfo lives in Mexico City, while Arreola spends as much time as he can on his native soil.[59]

Based on Meyer's premises, one could draw a different interpretation, however, even within the limits of literary sociology by pointing out how each of these writers received the message of modernization differently. That is, one could emphasize the choices each made from the broad range of foreign literature that modernism offered them—choices that could even link them to their particular situations of rising or falling within their social groups of origin. Let us toss out the categories of optimism and pessimism, which, despite the naive prestige in which they are held by members of the modernizing political class, have not proved very helpful for judging the artistry of world literature, especially given that the frequent pessimism of certain works and writers has actually been borne out by subsequent history. The writers' choice of literary models matters more, for it is genetically guided by their cultural patterns and social positions. Arreola clearly trusts the arguments of the European avant-garde, as critics noted in reviews of his early books *Varia invención* (1949), *Confabulario* (1952), and *Confabulario total* (1962), recognizing the influence of French author Marcel Schwob, whose writing was so admired by Borges in the south.[60] In those subtle exercises in the life of the spirit, so elegantly placed in human and universal settings, one sees a carefree confidence in the intellectual propositions of modernization, whose supposedly universalist basis is taken for granted without any misgivings. Given the same set of literary choices, Juan Rulfo leaned toward works from the Nordic fringe of Europe (Norway, Sweden, Denmark, Finland, and Iceland) produced during two periods: the late nineteenth–early twentieth century and the interwar years. Similarly, his taste in North American letters centered on the southern periphery, as represented by Faulkner, to the detriment of the more urbanized and industrialized New York trends that gave us avant-garde writing and Hemingway's fiction. Within French letters, the writers he preferred were not the widely known ones who taught Latin Americans about the avant-garde (Valéry, Gide, Malraux, Celine, Proust, Breton); they were the narrators of the earth, full of poetic inspiration and social concern: the Swiss writer Charles-Ferdinand Ramuz and the poet of Manosque, Jean Giono. The writer who, in the opinion of many, was the founder of Mexican avant-garde narrative did not turn to the major figures of the European avant-garde who were so important in the tremendous output of Latin American cosmopolitan writing (Joyce, Woolf, Kafka, Musil) but rather to representatives of a European periphery who, half a century before Spanish Americans, experienced an intrusion of modernity from the great metropolitan centers. Not enough attention has been paid to this unusual yet highly significant behavior, and it is worthwhile compiling various statements by Rulfo on the subject of his literary influences, which generally make the same point.

In 1959, he admitted to José Emilio Pacheco, "The turn-of-the-century German and Nordic school—which created a reality, a special perspective, based on flights of the imagination—has given me one of my favorite pleasures. I have read Sillanpää, Bjørnson, Ian Mail, Hauptmann, and the early Hamsun. Through them I discovered how to find the foundations of my literary faith. Their successor, the 'heir to their way of telling,' is Halldór Laxness. Laxness has rebuilt the Icelandic saga, created the *Kalevala* for our times."[61]

In 1974, he was more explicit in his answer to Joseph Sommers's question about the chaotic readings of his youth:

Among them, the works of Knut Hamsun, which I read—or rather, absorbed—at a young age. I was about 14 or 15 when I discovered this writer, who really impressed me, carrying me off to places I had never known before. To a misty world, the Nordic world, right? But at the same time, he got me out of this light-filled place where we live, this bright country, where the light is so intense. Maybe because of a certain tendency I had to look precisely for something foggy, something nuanced, not as hard and sharp-edged as the environment one lives in here. Then among the Nordic authors—Knut Hamsun was actually the first, but then I continued to seek them out, reading them all until I finished the few authors that were known at that time, such as Bjørnson, Jens Peter Jacobsen, Selma Lagerlöf. For me, Halldór Laxness was a true discovery— that was long before he got the Nobel prize. So I felt a kind of sympathy with these authors. They gave me an impression that seemed fairer, or better put, more optimistic, than the rather harsh world we lived in.[62]

In 1966, he repeated the same list of names, in addition to the Russian writers Leonid Andreyev and Vladimir Korolenko, to Luis Harss and admitted, "I once held to the theory that literature was born in Scandinavia, in the northern reaches of Europe, and that it later descended to the center, from which it moved off into other places."[63]

It is a literary catalogue that may surprise the modern-day reader, for it includes names that have disappeared from our reading lists, and I suspect few of us have developed a taste for them. (It is possible to think of other names that are missing on his lists, such as Jensen and Strindberg; it is possible to add the masters of literature of the earth, such as Wladyslaw Reymont, Ivo Andric, Nikos Kazantzakis, and Panait Istrati; and it is strange that, despite the hedonism of these readings, they do not include Kierkegaard, at least the fraudulent edition of *Diary of a Seducer*.) It was the literature of the 1920s and 1930s, whose authors would win endless Nobel Prizes until the avant-garde writers began to take their places and condemn them to temporary oblivion, from which they have now begun to emerge. It was the literature of the European periphery, from the time when it was beginning to feel the impact of modernization emanating from Paris, London, Vienna, and Berlin. If I had to characterize the features they have in common, I would say they are fundamentally about rural life in insignificant villages and forsaken regions, where an intense spiritual life nonetheless arises (the trajectory of Olafur Kárason in Laxness's tetralogy, *World Light*). They are tense personalities placed in impossible situations that the writer has constructed, at times overworking the heartbreaking or the absurd, as in Hamsun's first four novels: *Hunger*, *Mysteries*, *Pan*, and *Victoria*. They are rhapsodic landscapes brought to life and made to pulse in unison with the characters of the novels, as in Selma Lagerlöf's *The Story of Gösta Berling*. They are elusive, laconic, difficult, misty (Rulfo's term) relationships and love affairs, immersed in the life of nature, as in two remarkable novels by Jens Peter Jacobsen, *Maria Grubbe* and *Niels Lyhne*. They are exceedingly hard human relationships that put the unexpected irrationality of temperaments on full display as they struggle against the extraordinarily rigid forms of social life, as in August Strindberg's or Bjørnstjerne Bjørnson's novels. They are clear concepts of social justice and clear rebellions against the oppressive order of rural life in which harsh, archaic hierarchies cling to power, just as Laxness showed them in his novels and theorized them in his essays. They are, often, ardent responses to the modernization in progress, viewed through scientific paradigms (Jacobsen's Darwinism), naturalist theories, or socialist dogmas (Ramuz), but at the same time they assiduously defend regional life, its people, affairs, and environments as the only genuine things. They are works of radical realism, constructed for the most part around real events in real settings that are familiar to the authors, written in the already outmoded French school of naturalist realism but imbued with a powerful lyrical momentum that could carry off characters and situations and confuse them with the runaway forces of nature in a single rhapsodic motion—in a way that could perhaps be described by the well-known commentary on Rulfo that Alí Chumacero wrote in 1955, in which he spoke of the "adverse encounter between a preponderantly realist style and an imagination given to the unreal."[64] They are also works in which the regional language itself acquires de facto citizenship and in which it is even flaunted aggressively in opposition to internationalized forms as a kind of rite of passage to adulthood for the community, as illustrated by the adoption of Nynorsk by the Norwegian writers of the nineteenth century.

Even more important than working out where Rulfo's fiction fits within the framework of these great influences (something that has not even been attempted yet) is the recognition that these Scandinavian writers emerged from cultural situations that were very similar to those experienced by a Mexican writer born in Jalisco in 1918 and subjected to the process of adapting to city life (first in Guadalajara, then in Mexico City) in the 1940s and 1950s while building his literary personality and narrative, a process that he underwent together with a huge rural population. As Hélène Riviere d'Arc points out, the demographic growth of Guadalajara outpaced that of many other Mexican cities: "From 229,335 inhabitants in 1940, the capital of Jalisco grew to 738,800 in 1960 and an estimated 1,400,000 by 1970. While in 1900 it contained 29% of the urban population of Jalisco, according to the national census, by 1960 it accounted for 51% of urban dwellers."[65] Jean Meyer adds that this migration from the countryside to the cities, which was compelled by poverty and left behind the abandoned villages that literature has described, did not necessarily mean radical cultural changes because of the extreme forms "of resistance, of rootedness" that tied the new urban population nostalgically to their origins: "More than just nostalgia, it is a matter of a fond commitment to their land that forms part of their collective mentality."[66] It is not surprising that Rulfo should also have continued to cling tenaciously to the world he came from and should endeavor to pattern his literary material on it.

Many of the themes and characters and much of the atmospherics in Rulfo's work had appeared earlier in Agustín Yáñez's novel, *Al filo del agua* [The Edge of the Storm], which itself was published at the outset of the boom in new Mexican literature, yet there was no artistic common ground between them. Yáñez gave us a bland, sententious description of a rural society that he observed clear-sightedly but for which he found no equivalence in his narrative structure. The two authors were separated by a period that some might measure as the difference between two generations (fifteen years); more than that, what separated them was their conception of literature. Yáñez preached perceptively about a world; Rulfo constructed a world literarily. Yáñez's own resolve to reconstruct the closed, obscurantist, constrained, hard life of a pueblo before 1910 impeded him from rendering an account of the revolutionary storm that had flattened the foundations of that society and that had continued for far too long in central-western Mexico, and particularly in Jalisco, because of the Cristero War that broke out when Rulfo was an infant. Rulfo was the child of another society, another historical time that suddenly set traditional cultural patterns spinning. It convulsed them and set them on edge; better yet, it ripped off their appearances and plainly revealed the bridled power that they had repressed or kept in check. This was the foreseeable effect of a modernization whose earlier transformative actions can be followed in economic, sociological, political, or demographic studies. Those were simply indicators of a transformation with deep repercussions in the field of culture, where it produced the greatest noise and the greatest surprises. The parsimonious account of the Cristero War by Jean Meyer is as illustrative of this cultural upheaval as the two books by Luis González y González.[67]

Rulfo's main innovation, carried out with recourse to what must be seen as a reactionary turn compared with Arreola (in the sense that it took him back to his cultural roots and tied him to them thematically, literarily, and spiritually), has been described many times by the author himself and by his critics. What he did was to recover popular speech and use it as a substitute for educated bourgeois writing and to go back to the use of the narrative structures of popular tales. His fundamental difference with Yáñez was, thus, evicting the author from his intellectual background and having him take up in its stead a view of the world drawn from cultural forms shared by members of a particular tradition, under the particular historical circumstances that overthrew that tradition.

Juan Rulfo pulled off this trick so neatly that he went on to join a category that younger generations are fond of: the non-intellectual writer, the writer who stands apart from trafficking in criticism and analysis, the one transmuted into the spontaneous voice of the elementary people. This great Romantic myth is so obviously false that it only underscores precisely the contrary: the practiced artifice of Rulfo's artistic composition—something worth bearing in mind, for when the author apparently disappears ("it is not the author's voice that is speaking, but the voices of the characters," says one critic),[68] he has only intensified his presence. There are few writers of fiction in Latin America today whose writing is as sharply differentiated, characterized, and individualized as Rulfo's.

"It is a spoken language." "I wanted, not to speak like I write, but to write like they speak." "That is how I've heard people talk in my house since I was born, and that's how the people in these places talk," the author repeatedly declares.[69] But what we see is the result of his tenacious efforts to hone his style, as one critic proved by comparing different versions of the short stories. "The versions of his stories in *El llano en llamas* consistently slim down the text, eliminating words and popularizing the language, without destroying the stories' structures or making great changes."[70] On this, there is unanimous agreement among recent critics, reversing the initial critical reception of Rulfo's works, which were accused of overly economic writing. The features of this popular speech are, roughly, a simplified lexicon that cautiously admits dialectal and regional forms; a concise syntax, with apt use of set phrases; a tendency toward the laconic, even the elliptical, in the linguistic message; the minor key and a lack of emphasis (except when oratory is being parodied) that unite disparate discourse values into a single tessitura; muffled prosody, just as the explanatory contexts indicate; a stubborn eschewal of learned words; and the elimination of all intellectual terminology.

That this language should be perceived today as a transcription of popular speech only reaffirms the authoritative power of the linguistic construction of literature. Before long, it will be recognized simply as Rulfo's writing. Then readers will perceive that, despite his reliance on real sources, we are witnessing the deliberate construction of a literary language. To visualize this, we can turn to the many eyewitness accounts that Jean Meyer recorded over the course of the seven years while collecting oral histories from Jalisco farmers and their answers to his questionnaires on the Cristero War. These materials corroborate what we already knew by other means about American Spanish, especially as it is spoken by deeply autonomous social strata in regions that have been

Hispanized since colonial times. "This is the fierce and belligerent individualism of the *ranchero* who lives in isolation, who holds onto his inheritance, the Spanish language and traditions (if linguists would like to take a crack at it, they'd make some tasty discoveries)," said Jean Meyer on one of his first fieldwork excursions,[71] and at the end of his three-volume work on the Cristero Revolt, he added, "Their language is usually beautiful and their grammatical constructions correct, as is their use of tenses, with a marked tendency to use the subjunctive. . . . Everything passes through their eyes, ears, and mouth, and these men have prodigious vocabularies; it is said of them that they are quiet and that they entertain themselves with 'pronouncements, witty remarks, proverbs, clever sayings, and subtle and ingenious stratagems that cause wonder and admiration.'"[72]

Jean Meyer catalogues the long words they use and the abstract ideas they express spontaneously in their discourse, which reveals not so much a particularly intellectualist tendency as the collective usage of a language filled with abstract terms—a language derived from none other than the great baroque tradition that formed American Spanish, a tradition that the isolated, Hispanized regions still stubbornly conserve, just as they conserve artistic forms that can be called baroque and cultured in the strict sense of the words (the *espinela*, the *décima*). He then speaks of "the deeply rooted life of a popular culture founded on the Bible, Christian oral traditions, the books of chivalry, and courtly poetry."[73] This description is quite different from what critics have had to say about Rulfo's popular language; it is also quite persuasive.

It reveals the persistent creative effort it took to polish a literary language based on popular speech, from which words were selected, pruned, and rejected until Rulfo achieved expressive unity (which he continued to pursue in successive editions). It was not, then, "a language captured by the tape recorder," as Rulfo himself claimed,[74] but an interpretive point of view—a focal point for a worldview with a crystal-clear ideological quality and one that insists, in an entirely modernized mindset, on the unity of all the elements that make up the work: language, subjects, characters, settings, narrative structures, images, rhythms, exposition, and so on. It shows his persistent effort at creating an impoverished lexicon, selecting concrete particulars, and emphasizing a laconic and elliptical style that sharply contrasts with the learned phrases and intellectual turns that also are part of popular language, and the oratorical expository styles that are found in the models (frequently religious ones) that are readily accessible to an unlettered culture. His choices and rejections correspond to a specific and very new concept of verisimilitude and to a well-defined and equally new concept of mimesis, both of which are marked by a modernization grounded only in a nostalgic perspective, a return to the roots dreamed up through an anthropological concept of primitivism. These are the vectors that select the materials by looking for their affinity, their ability to join together in perfect harmony. This is quite clear in the absorption of the short stories by the voices that recount them, transmitting their homogeneous tonality to the whole collection. It is also clear in Rulfo's search for the poetic equilibrium ("monstrous" equilibrium, to use Arreola's word) that let him insert into a single story, "Nos han dado la tierra," both the very colloquial question "Hey, 'Teban, where'd you grab the chicken from?" and the surreal image "Somebody leans into the sky, cranes his eyes to where the sun hangs, and says. . . ."[75]

These modernizing operations, which include both mediating and transculturating functions, have their parallel in the narrower field of narrative forms. In this field, there was also an effort to recover systems peculiar to the rural environment, such as the scattered and derivative storytelling that forms the dramatic frame for the story "Acuérdate." The way this story branches out horizontally, sometimes until it completely loses the thread, is reminiscent of ingenuous medieval narrative forms. The same organization is used in the exposition of "Anacleto Morones" and in the dialogues of *Pedro Páramo*. In each of these cases, the normal transparency of a system for organizing (or disorganizing) the flow of a story has been replaced by its active presence within the tale itself as a way of signifying who is expressing it, just as was done with the lexicon and syntax, making them visible and literary in order to transform them into a tool of composition. This operation resembles the Surrealists' disconnection of elements, which, though drawn from the heterogeneous juxtapositions of the urban world, became a way of transmitting meaning and therefore served as testimony to a worldview.

In these brief notes on Juan Rulfo's astonishing literary output, we have tried to demonstrate two things: first, the active presence in a literature not only of the events and themes of a particular American cultural region but also of its specific cultural forms; and second, the original, inventive, innovative activity of a writer situated in the modernizing conflict. Such a writer creates a neoculture not merely by piling up contrasting elements but by constructing something new that assumes the problems and upheavals caused by the collision of cultures. Perhaps we should never forget that a writer is also, above all, a creator.

Part II

Introduction to Part II

In part I, we laid out the cultural and literary problems that Latin American literature went through under the impact of modernization during the twentieth century, focusing on how its regionalist writers transformed fiction. Though overshadowed by the dazzling and widely disseminated works of cosmopolitan writers, the regionalists fundamentally transformed the premises of their art and reclaimed narrative forms whose originality and ability to represent the genuine, widespread problems of Latin America have perhaps not been fully grasped before.

In Brazil, where the conflict between regionalism and modernity was actively discussed and even theorized in print, narrative writers from very different regions—and faced with specific cultural problems—offered a series of original artistic solutions. This is clear in the works of José Lins do Rego, Graciliano Ramos, and João Guimarães Rosa, among the most powerful Brazilian writers of the twentieth century; perhaps we should also include here Mário de Andrade for his novel *Macunaíma*. Alongside them there is a fairly extensive list of writers from all the regions on the map of Brazilian cultures who have faced similar problems in other instances of modernization up to the present. As a country that began by establishing its basis for nationhood without disturbing the lively autonomy of its regions, Brazil is a very fertile laboratory for examining these conflicts and its original solutions to them.

External pressure for modernization also affected the republics of Spanish America, however, often coming via versions of modernization that had developed in their capital cities. We outlined the case of one dynamic region, the Caribbean coast of Colombia, which gave rise to the

Barranquilla literary group and the works of Gabriel García Márquez. We also briefly covered central-western Mexico, a region centered on the state of Jalisco where an equally innovative literary movement arose, the clearest exemplar of which was Juan Rulfo.

In parts II and III of this book, we will explore a region where these conflicts grew extremely bitter not only because of the innovative impact that modernity had on the region after its introduction there around 1930 but also because of the static, rigid condition of the region's traditional cultural forms. This is highland southern Peru, with its center in the old capital of the Inca empire, Cuzco—a region that served as the battle flag of the *indigenista* generation of the 1920s and 1930s in the critical works of Víctor Raúl Haya de la Torre, José Carlos Mariátegui, and Víctor Andrés Belaúnde, to cite the authors of the most important intellectual and political reflections on a topic that led to a lively, modern questioning of what Peruvian nationality meant. In 1932, the Committee on the Constitution in Peru's Constitutional Congress ignited the controversy by dividing the country into political regions, thus reviving the nineteenth-century argument between centralist conservatives and federalist liberals. The committee was marked by the political prejudices of the various parties, and so it was deaf to the richly varied cultural expressions of Peruvian regionalism. Still, Jorge Basadre observed with his usual balance: "Regionalism, then, is valid insofar as it signifies understanding of, and interest in, the country's problems; that is, insofar as it helps to counter the foolish phrase, 'Lima is Peru, and the heart of the Union is Lima.' Regionalism is important in another way, then: for combating the exclusivist influence of the European model, the unexamined importation of prescriptions that arose from realities alien to our own."[1]

The perspective back then, and for a long time afterwards, was purely political.[2] In spite of Basadre's cautious warning, people on every side enthusiastically and ingenuously took up imported European prescriptions—even an intellectual as well versed in national reality as Mariátegui. The debate obscured the aspect of the clash that most interests us, its cultural impact (in the full anthropological sense of the term *cultural*), and the next generation was rather phlegmatic about recovering and asserting such a cultural view. Among the intellectuals who contributed most to that new, cultural direction, the leading role was undoubtedly played by José María Arguedas as a teacher, an ethnologist, and a writer.

He confronted the most complex and seemingly least tenable situation of any of the many culturally frozen hinterlands in Latin America.

He had, moreover, received simplistic doctrinal views from his predecessors that were unhelpful for finding effective solutions to the cultural
conflict. Besides, every previous solution that had been put forward had
been subverted by the unforeseen modifications that arose in the regions
of Cuzco and Apurímac, so we must first take a new look at the problem of the Andean cultural area (which, though it covers a vast region
crossing several South American countries along the Andes, has highland southern Peru at its core). We will then investigate the evolution of
Arguedas's thoughts on a subject to which he devoted his whole life, concluding with a recognition of his mestizo mediations between the country's two drastically divided cultural spheres. He found in that obscure
character, the mestizo, and in the saga of the mestizo, the archetype of a
transformative role that seemed to mirror what he himself undertook in
anthropology and literature.

The evolution of Arguedas's thinking, based on his patient study of
indigenous life in Peru, lined up with one of the great movements in
intellectual life. That Arguedas never particularly bothered to polish his
ideas or set them down in rigorous academic reports in no way detracts
from the originality of his research into a problem that has done more to
lead contemporary intellectuals astray than to enlighten them: the function of myth among Latin American societies. Armchair intellectuals
have written copiously on the subject, much more than Arguedas, who
studied it as an ethnologist and experienced it as an enlightened man.
Therefore, studying Arguedas's subtle investigations into the understanding of "mythic intelligence" can be thought of as an adult, responsible, and profound way of taking a second look at this very important
topic.

Part II of this book thus examines the steps that led Arguedas progressively from the problems of a hardscrabble region, to cultural solutions to
a seemingly endless conflict, and then to the higher forms in which the
spirit incorporates the forces that are in play and discovers a balancing
vision for them. Part III centers, in turn, on a study of a single book by
Arguedas, *Deep Rivers*. I see this novel as one of the great artistic creations
of Latin America, the equal of many more widely known examples of
the so-called new novel. The two chapters of part III are not intended
as an exhaustive study of the novel; that is something that a whole series
of recent books has already taken on, which is proof of growing critical
interest in *Deep Rivers*. Rather, these chapters delve more deeply into the
themes of part I: how artistic forms were developed out of cultural traditions, themselves forged by bounded communities in the rich regions

of the Latin American hinterlands, under the impact of a modernization that aimed at eliminating those very same cultures; and how writers rose up against that type of modernization, not in order to oppose it in vain but to put modernization to use in the service of rediscovering and reviving the cultural legacy they had inherited in childhood and whose survival they wished to guarantee.

In an era of rather childish cosmopolitanism, our aim is to demonstrate that one can indeed create new art on a high level based on the humble materials from one's own traditions and that such traditions can do more than provide picturesque themes; they can also be sources of well-designed techniques and shrewd artistic structures that fully translate the imaginaries of Latin American societies that have been crafting brilliant cultures for centuries. Instead of the Romantic themes that claimed to be faithful to their subjects, in the belief that this was the only way the nation could be represented, what we find in the transculturators' novels is a kind of loyalty to the spirit they attained by reclaiming structures peculiar to the Latin American imaginary and by revitalizing those structures under new historical circumstances instead of abandoning them. Those structures are the greatest inventions of the peoples of Latin America; they form the symbolic system through which Latin Americans express themselves and recognize themselves as members of a community—which is, in the end, the highest intellectual and artistic construction people are capable of producing.

CHAPTER THREE

The Andean Cultural Area

The innovations of modernity entered the hinterlands of Latin America from abroad after the First World War through the mediation of the region's capital cities, reviving and aggravating a number of cultural conflicts. The most prominent of these conflicts — and the one least likely to lead to a transculturation that could safeguard local values through their modernization — took place in the Andes.

The Andean cultural area, as we use the term, includes not only modern-day Peru (its historic core, the nerve point that most forcefully displays the whole area's problematics) but also a huge zone centered on the Andes mountain range and the many indigenous cultures that inhabit it. Since the Conquest, a dual society has developed here that has proved singularly resistant to the transformations of the modern world. The Andean area extends from highland Colombia to northern Argentina, including most of Bolivia, Peru, Ecuador, and the Andean part of Venezuela. The Inca Empire, at its height, spread across these ecologically comparable territories. This fact has led writers such as Víctor Raúl Haya de la Torre to revive the idea of Tawantinsuyu (the Quechua name for the empire), with its natural capital in Cuzco, because of the linguistic unity and overall cultural homogeneity that the empire imposed on the diverse cultures of the region before the arrival of the Spanish.

Despite imperial efforts at unification, diversity persisted under the iron rule of the Incas, especially in the last areas to be colonized on the borders of the empire, as witnessed in the survival of tribal or local languages (Ecuador), some of which are important living languages today, as well as the Aymara language (Bolivia), quite apart from the appearance of local artistic traditions. This diversity is even broader if we add the indigenous societies that never came under imperial rule, though they may have received influences from the Quechua culture of Cuzco, as in the case of the Chibchas and Taironas in Colombia, who developed their cultures autonomously, adapting them to their habitats, economic foundations, and forms of coexistence.

This diversity, which archaeologists and anthropologists have been puzzling out in recent years,[1] was transformed into superficial unity by an external factor: the Spanish Conquest and colonization as expressed with minor tonal variations throughout the entire area. Colonial rule wrapped variety in seeming unity ("Indians") and even heightened this unity by maintaining certain Inca imperial policies (adopting Quechua as a missionary language for evangelizing). Basically, however, it treated all Andean cultures as the same, relative to the new viewpoint of Spanish culture, and the enormous differences observable among the many indigenous Andean cultures simply dissolved. Meanwhile, Spanish culture itself functioned in a unitary way across the region; it drew forth from the colonizers an inner unity that was equally alien to the diverse roots of the Spanish conquerors. This Spanish unity was forged slowly by carrying out the task of colonization in order to establish Spanish rule, structure the region economically, and assemble the required administrative machinery. Evidence of this process of internal cultural unification over the course of several centuries after the Conquest can be found today in the similarities among linguistic behaviors throughout the Andean area, where a variety of Spanish is spoken with its own syntactic, semantic, and lexical norms, lending it a degree of unity relative to the Spanish spoken in other areas of Latin America. This is what Pedro Henríquez Ureña observed and reported in his language map of Spanish America;[2] his initial findings have since been corrected, but the revisions have not invalidated the existence of a clearly demarcated Andean linguistic area, which is none other than the unity that Spanish culture itself developed there.

Over the course of the centuries, a control regime was consolidated in which a foreign culture (European in origin) was imposed on top of the existing indigenous cultures—violently yet without destroying them (apart from the racial transformations that the original Andean populations underwent)—while also failing in its attempts to assimilate them, if any such idea had ever actually been seriously entertained. Throughout the area, the weakness of the middle stratum of mestizos—subject to the cultural dictates of the dominant group, whom they aped with little originality, and incapable for centuries to create their own coherent, systematic culture by developing a literature of their own—accentuated the dichotomy between the two opposing cultures, relegating the indigenous survivors to a traditional, folkloric conservatism, which on one hand gave them a bit of vital breathing room but on the other hand only allowed them to be more easily manipulated.[3]

After independence, the Andean republics inherited and perfected the situation established by colonial rule, setting it in a classist framework. One social class, heir to a local aristocracy based on its ownership of the land and control of menial labor, ensured the continued dominance of Hispanic culture by imposing itself on a class of rural workers, mainly Indians (but also mestizos, though the latter often served as the foremen and managers overseeing the indigenous workers, acting in the service of the landlords and only timidly advancing into work in the trades) among whom the old, autochthonous cultural traditions had been kept alive. As historical criticism has already shown, the Andean region did not go through the bourgeois revolution that was carried out elsewhere in the former Spanish Empire (Argentina, Uruguay, Chile), justifying the wars of independence. Upholding the economic structure created under colonial rule (one of the reasons why the *criollo* upper classes opposed the Bourbon reforms—so that their alliance with the bourgeois mercantile interests of the port cities was only temporary) served to maintain a social structure friendly to it. Both the economic structure and the social structure contributed to the survival of colonial culture after independence.[4]

Though this was generally true across the entire Andean area, there were nuances, depending on how developed the indigenous cultures were and how large and concentrated their populations were. Despite similarities, the province of Cundinamarca, built on the ancient kingdom of Bacatá, with a high degree of subjugation and acculturation,[5] reached a different solution than the Inca heartland, which put up more indigenous resistance than anywhere else in the Americas, so that Spanish colonial rule was imposed with great difficulty, leading to the curious alternation between two parallel capitals—Lima and Cuzco. Moreover, the political divisions that replaced Spanish colonial administrative districts, which were arbitrary enough already before being redrawn to suit the warring caudillos of the independence period, distributed this Andean unity among a number of republics. The cultural behavior of those republics then diverged throughout the nineteenth and twentieth centuries in accord with the orientations of their respective capital cities.

Thus, the Andean zone that became a part of Argentina was harshly incorporated into that republic by the victories of nineteenth-century liberalism and the centralist rule of Buenos Aires, and it was subjugated (always partially, always reluctantly) to the capital's modernizing dictates. Venezuela incorporated its western Andean region in the same way, though it did so much later during the twentieth century. However, most of the Andean area remained under the rule of conservative administrations in La Paz, Lima, Quito, and Bogotá, and it was structured according to a principle of socioeconomic continuity that tied the region back to the colonial regime, in effect prolonging colonial rule in flagrant disregard for the general mood of the times. The region did not seek another way out, as Paraguay did under nineteenth-century dictators José Gaspar Rodríguez de Francia and Carlos Antonio López, when it aspired to self-sufficient national development under paternalistic rule that would keep the country independent of Western expansion into Latin America. The Andean region simply went on using its established model to grow rich.

The counterpart to this historical behavior was the fact that both cultures, indigenous as well as Spanish/European, became equally static—frozen in place—facing one another across the divide of class ideologies that condemned them to parallel stagnation and endless repetition of ancient models. The subjugated culture was not the only one that stagnated; so did the dominant culture. However, national integration would have taken a tremendous effort at transculturation, which was rejected by each of the three groups that made up the area (as witnessed by the failure of the mestizos, who were called on to take up this task but who did not do so for centuries). Likewise, the economic foundations of the system were never transformed, and they continued to rely on backward forms of agricultural exploitation and the extraction of raw materials in accordance with the rise and fall of European economic demand. As a result, creativity was immobilized in the region, and progress was sacrificed to preexisting formulas, which, inevitably, grew outdated.

It is an example of the Hegelian master-slave dialectic that I think has no equal anywhere else in the Americas. The master cannot replace the slave because the former needs the latter (the existence of the master in itself implies the existence of the slave); instead, he elicits the slave's submission by means of which he constrains the slave's creative abilities, transforming him into an automaton who receives orders. As a result, the master also transforms himself into an equivalent component of the system, symmetrical to his slave. He makes himself slave of that regime of submission, and by the same token his own creative abilities are frozen—garrisoned—in the repetition of attitudes and values. He, too, becomes an automaton, except that he's the one who gives the orders.

The persistence of the semifeudal economy that exploited the subjugated indigenous people and mestizos of Colombia, Ecuador, Peru, and Bolivia affected the social organizations and politics of these countries, paralyzing them. A national consciousness based on a vision of the future did not emerge in any of these countries—unlike the European world, where a transformative bourgeoisie mobilized the lower social strata and created the seeds of nationalism. Throughout the nineteenth century, the timid liberalism of the Andes was defeated or diluted over and over again by deal making and concessions. There was not even a liberal movement to support a revolt from Spain until the oligarchs decided they needed it, and when they did, the result was impoverishment across the board. Therefore, we do not take José Martí's familiar phrase, "our America, which must be saved together with her Indians,"[6] as exhausted rhetoric but rather as an intuition that points to this obscure communality of fates. This mutual dependence was never recognized in the Andean area, and it was not transformed into integration when the world's new economic structuring required it. The region has paid dearly for it.

Standing up to this rigid system could only be done under its own conditions. An endless series of local rebellions—disconnected, provincial, anachronistic—served as evidence of dissatisfaction with the situation, but they were simultaneously tainted by the system's own uncreative rigidity. In the field of literature, the system likewise could only be opposed through the methods of the pamphlet, the diatribe, the indictment, and the denunciation, with naive confidence in the power of the unconsciously sacralized word. We see this in Montalvo's boast: "My pen has killed him."[7]

Nowhere in the Andes was this unsubmissive attitude as strong or consistent as it became in Peruvian society, the site where the conflicts described were most intense and the contradictions in the system most jarring. Lima was therefore the city where the idea of critically reexamining the system arose, once it became patently clear (with the loss of Peruvian territory to Chile during the War of the Pacific, 1879–81) that the system was incapable of confronting the conditions of the modern world; the starting point for this reexamination would be the fragmentation of Western culture by the emergence of new social groups. It was in Lima where criticism (which is simply a means of regulating the deficiencies of any system) was elevated into an autonomous, independent, and sovereign value, thus reproducing the characteristics that gave birth to European criticism during the eighteenth century under the stifling rule developed by the aristocracy as they fought the bourgeois insurgency, when criticism became a weapon used to destroy a structure that could not adapt to the new requirements of society. Pessimism about the present (but an extreme, crushing pessimism) and optimism about the ideal (but an optimism overflowing with utopian hopes) were the basic tools of this critical reexamination. This has already been noted in the ideas of Mariátegui, who was perhaps unaware of the degree to which both he and his precursor, Manuel González Prada, honed their criticism under the cultural conditions determined by the master-slave dialectic, and those conditions were what gave rise to the emphases, the probing questions, the categorical nature of their criticism, and the absolute independence they granted to the idea of criticism, which later generations took as a defining characteristic of that intellectual activity. Lately, we have seen it reappear in the intellectual discourse of Mario Vargas Llosa.

No one was wrong to criticize the "pus bursting forth" from Peru's social body (in Manuel González Prado's apocalyptic metaphor),[8] though their statements were sometimes cloaked in the distortions that the system introduced even into the best criticism, which one intemperate spirit who knew this history well, Jorge Basadre, has termed "abstract progressivism."[9] The indictment that González Prada began to formulate during the late nineteenth century, that his disciples Clorinda Matto de Turner and Federico More further developed and that we see in the works of Haya de la Torre, José Carlos Mariátegui, César Vallejo, Luis E. Valcárcel, José Sabogal, Luis A. Sánchez, and the entire *indigenista* movement for reclaiming society, was aimed at the stagnation of the Andes. Such writers as Baldomero Sanín Cano in Colombia and Alcides Arguedas in Bolivia contributed to it from nearly opposite positions, and the generation of the 1920s and 1930s — nativists, criollistas, and indigenistas, according to the demands of the various parts of the region — devoted themselves to it.

Their point of departure: dissatisfaction with backwardness, anachronisms (a judgment unconsciously influenced by the European model they used), and static cultures that made it impossible to unify the country; they idealized indigenous culture beyond all bounds, while they condemned without mercy the culture with which the intellectuals were actually familiar. Their negativity could be defined in several different ways. For Luis Alberto Sánchez, writing about the field of literature: "In Peru there has always been a tendency to reject, implicitly or openly, anything new because it is new, whether in literature or in politics, in painting or in sociology; and, in consequence, to be frenetically backwards."[10]

Jorge Basadre expressed the same idea with regard to the field of history, phrasing it with his characteristic discretion: "The history of Peru in the nineteenth century is a history of lost opportunities and squandered possibilities."[11]

Haya de la Torre and Mariátegui insisted on explicitly grounding all of these negative statements in economic and social conditions, finding the explanation for the country's paralysis in the land tenure system and the social structure that was based on it. Both were mainly interested in a politics of protest and practice, and it was in the service of their politics that they analyzed Peruvian culture through its texts. This backwardness of Andean culture also affected its literature during the nineteenth century—even earlier, if we look back at the weakness of its eighteenth-century transformations when compared with other regions of Latin America where the historical acceleration that began back then had proved a precursor to independence. The poverty of Andean contributions to nineteenth-century literature resulted from the fact that the entire Andean area was stuck in exhausted models of a culture of domination that refused to forge a modernized national unity—models handed down from the heirs of the Spanish Empire, who held on to power much longer here than elsewhere in Latin America.

The issue is not how long it took Andean writers to turn to Romanticism, nor how insipidly they did so (given the general poverty of Romanticism all across Latin America), but rather their nostalgic adhesion to a culture in decline—the culture of Spain—whose literary traditionalists[12] remained the primary inspiration of the best talents in the Andean area, justifying the judgment of "colonialist literature" that their twentieth-century critics passed on their works. Nineteenth-century Andean writers pursued such projects as the push for linguistic purity in Bogotá; the *costumbrista* novel *María* (1867) by Jorge Isaacs of Cali; Ecuadorian writer Juan Montalvo's remarkable venture of writing the *Capítulos que se le olvidaron a Cervantes* [Chapters That Cervantes Forgot, 1895]; the timid compromises of Ricardo Palma's *Tradiciones peruanas* (1872–83); and the costumbrista novels that Colombian Tomás Carrasquilla (1858–1940) wrote in imitation of Spanish writer José María de Pereda (1833–1906).

Projects such as these were not pursued in other cultural areas of Latin America, where the new ideas of modernity (Romanticism, political liberalism, individualism, free trade, export economies, and, soon enough, realism, positivism, bourgeois dominance, and technocratic rule) took root early. In Brazil and the Río de la Plata area, these trends led to the works of such writers as Domingo Faustino Sarmiento and Machado de Assís, at which point we find ourselves immersed in a narrative language that belongs to contemporary civilization. This does not mean that theirs were the only possible models for artistic creation, nor does it mean that all models necessarily had to correspond to the European cultural norms of the moment; simply, the Andean area produced no original, local models that indicated any degree of inventiveness that might surpass the restricted degree of social mobility in the Andes.

No matter what value we might place on the works of Ricardo Palma— whom Mariátegui himself began to rehabilitate, treating him as an interpreter of the people of Lima—there can be no doubt that his "Peruvian Traditions" of 1872 reflected a derivative aesthetic solution that continued to draw its inspiration from Spanish Romanticism, if not from the masters of Spanish Golden Age literature during the sixteenth and seventeenth centuries. However, 1872 was already a decade past the publication of *Martín Rivas* by Chilean novelist Alberto Blest Gana, which, in the field of literature alone, exemplifies the changes that had been taking place in Chile, just as surely as Palma's works exemplified the changes that were *not* taking place in Peru, prefiguring the outcome of the ill-fated War of the Pacific. Though it is difficult to share Mariátegui's judgment that González Prada founded so-called Peruvianness in literature, it is nevertheless clear that (for Peruvian literature) modernity, expressed in the highly colored styles forced upon it by the rigidity of Peruvian culture, began with him. This made him the leader of all twentieth-century Peruvian writers, yet it relegated him to his own modernizing offensive. It is thus correct to see in his poetry the initial signs of a kind of modernism, though these obviously differ from the signs of Rubén Darío's modernism, which are usually treated as distinguishing the modernist literary movement (they do not line up with the famously modernist features of José Martí's poetry), allowing us to place subsequent Peruvian poetry accurately. Other than the imitative verbosity of modernism in Peru, typified by Chocano, Peruvian poetry found its expression very late—when it was already on the brink of incorporating futurism— in the refined and rigorous creations of José María Eguren (*Simbólicas*, 1911), which belong to the school of González Prada.

Throughout the Andean area, modernism was feeble, late in arriving, and a distinctly minority movement in poetry. The solution found by Bolivian poet Ricardo Jaimes Freyre (1868–1933) was the same adopted by Rubén Darío: moving to another culture area, one with a dynamic center—in Jaimes Freyre's case, Buenos Aires. The wisdom of this solution was inversely confirmed by Colombian poet José Asunción Silva. The bullet with which this elusive modernist ended his life in 1895, before he had even pulled his small output together into a book, also ended his attempt to reinvent the poetic language of Colombia, abandoning it to the pageantry of Guillermo Valencia (1873–1944) for at least another thirty years. González Prada's failure as a politician, the individualistic extremism that he practiced to the end of his life, underlines both his stubborn loyalty to his ideas and the intellectual bankruptcy of his setting—the continuing absence of anything beyond rebellious individuals in Peru, which is to say, the absence of a coherent social group.

González Prada's genius lay in his ability to perceive the ties that bound the dominant and the subjugated, despite the rigid compartmentalization that both sides thought separated them. He saw clearly that the disdain white Peruvians felt toward the Indians and the subjugation under which they held them were mirrored by the Europeans' disdain for and subjugation of white Peruvians.[13] This view opened up the possibility of understanding how the dominant culture was a dead end, given the two factors that constrained it: its dependence on the foreign world and its isolation from its own hinterland.

Incapable of integrating Peruvian nationality, which would have meant surrendering to a vast transculturation, the members of the dominant culture did not have a nation to back them up, nor could they conceive of the need to forge one as a way of ensuring their own survival in power. Forced by the established system of submissiveness to be a mere replica of the servant in the dominant sphere, they lacked the dynamic elements they would have needed to face up to the process of modernization (and of subjugation as well, for the two went hand in hand) emerging from Europe. The whites in the Andean area became the Indians of the Europeans; they rejected the transformations required by capitalist development and squeezed themselves into the formulaic roles they had acquired under colonial rule, turning the Spanish culture that had given them life into a mere folkloric remnant. As a result, they were exploited in exactly the same way they exploited their own indigenous people, with no chance of making progress, becoming up-to-date, or gaining the strength they would need to achieve autonomy.

Despite the corrections to González Prada's positions that Mariátegui made, from another perspective and in a different time, we must agree that González Prada was astonishingly clear-sighted in his ability to detect the precise defects of the culture of his era and recommend the only workable solutions for the society in which he lived. His attack on Castelar, on the remnants of an ideologically nostalgic literature pining for colonial times—in contrast to which he declared that examining the historical present was the central mission of literature—went on the new generation's checklist. His full-on opposition to archaizing language and ornamental wordplay, to which he contrasted language as precise and refined as distilled alcohol, along the aristocratic lines of Voltaire's encyclopedism, led not only to Eguren's experiments in poetry but also to Mariátegui's rigorous, biting style. His antagonism toward Palma is key in this context; so long as literature continued endlessly compiling short tales, regardless of theme, style, or language (though all these necessarily had to be ideologically nostalgic, like the narrative system itself), there would be no way to attain the organic structures that the European bourgeoisie had succeeded in imposing on the novel at the time of their triumph in the nineteenth century, establishing vast harmonious mechanisms that betrayed the rationalizing capacity of the liberal enterprise they had undertaken. In the parallel field of science, only a scientism devoted to the application of the most extreme system of rationalism could develop the mental forms suitable and favorable to building a modern society. His guiding desire was modernization; his desperate fear was backwardness in comparison with the regions farther south (Chile, Río de la Plata), where he saw the new model bearing fruit.

The actions of the dominant culture in the Río de la Plata area were the exact opposite of those that characterized its counterpart in the Andes. Mariátegui, never deluded about the modernizing mission that would fall to those who shared his socialist revolutionary thought, saw this quite clearly. The largest city in the Southern Cone area, Buenos Aires, had joined the foreign Franco-British pressure groups as a dependent, taking up their universal project of socioeconomic remodeling and partially adapting it to local conditions. To carry this out, the city coercively transferred their impositions onto the societies in its hinterland, subjugating them by force. At the same time, it imbued them with a renewed set of values that were essential to their new functions and to the roles that had been assigned to them; the city was therefore key to their ability to progress and even break their own subjugation.

Indigenismo for Mestizos

The rigid dichotomy at the heart of Andean culture led to an indictment of colonialism, and by the same token it motivated the idealization of the indigenous people, giving rise to a long-lived and fruitful school of thought, *indigenismo*, which enjoyed special esteem in Peru, Bolivia, and Ecuador (with reverberations in Mexico) from roughly 1920 to 1950. The rigidity of Peru and Ecuador led to a geocultural interpretation of both Andean cultures that divided them into coastal and highland regions (in addition to their rainforests), though it didn't go so far as to allow for progress in each region. Their cultural rigidity also led to innumerable features that, with apologies to anthropologists, we might call archaic or, to put it a different way, close to their roots or embedded in profoundly Latin American behaviors.

This rigidity (against which the indigenista generation rebelled) had helped preserve many features of indigenous culture that were now seen to be functionally useful—for otherwise, they would have disappeared—and as serving to maintain the subjugated society's identity and behavior. In a way, they were evidence for the past that had been retained by the lower strata, helping them to cohere socially and elaborate their own worldview, indispensable to the continued existence of a human group. These cultural traits also stored unexpected potential if they could be reinvigorated creatively. That was the mission taken up by writers of the indigenista generation. In their revival of intellectual life, they were assisted by the great many newspapers that served as their mouthpieces, especially in the provinces, as well as by their endless verbose polemics; their noble-minded, lyrical protests; and some rather elementary exercises in art and literature. They achieved their fullest theoretical expression through pieces published in the journal *Amauta* under the editorship of José Carlos Mariátegui.

This was the fourth time in the history of conquered America that the figure of the Indian was used as Exhibit A in an indictment. The first was in the missionary literature of the Conquest. The second was the critical literature of the mercantile bourgeoisie in the years just before and after independence, which used the neoclassic style as its instrument. The third was during the Romantic period, when the figure of the Indian was used in expressions of lingering lamentation over his destruction, as a translation for white society of their own native-born status. Now, in the twentieth century, the Indian appeared for the fourth time, in the form of a denunciation presented by a new social group that had arisen from the white and mestizo lower middle class. Of course, in none of these cases was the Indian himself speaking; people from Spanish, criollo, and mestizo society, respectively, spoke in his name. In each case, what motivated the discourse, apart from individual conviction of the rightness of the Indian's side, were the implicit claims on behalf of the social groups that actually formulated it. These were minority groups within their societies, but they were groups with great social mobility and well-defined projects for social progress, and they padded out their own demands with those of a much larger social group that had no voice and no means of expressing its own complaints. This is not to diminish the indigenista movement, which led to a new consciousness of how to treat more justly the descendants of indigenous cultures and to the archaeological recovery of a rich past; rather, it is to situate indigenismo sociologically and thereby understand its specific characteristics in the arts and literature—the fields where it fought its greatest battles.

The first person to acknowledge this was José Carlos Mariátegui. In his feverish tour of Peruvian literature, he told us, "A critic could commit no greater injustice than to condemn indigenist literature for its lack of autochthonous integrity and expression. Indigenist literature cannot give us a strictly authentic version of the Indian, for it must idealize and stylize him. Nor can it give us his soul. It is still a mestizo literature and as such is called indigenist rather than indigenous. If an indigenous literature finally appears, it will be when the Indians themselves are able to produce it."[14] Like all movements inspired by a passion for social justice and grounded in legitimate demands, indigenismo came to encompass a wide variety of personalities, movements in the arts, philosophy, politics, cultural situations, and levels of education. Practically every position, other than strict old-fashioned conservatism, fit under its umbrella, which at first included everything from the idealized nostalgic post-Romanticist lyricism of Luis E. Valcárcel[15] to positions that reveal the recent incorporation into Latin America of the diverse socialisms of Haya de la Torre, Mariátegui, and Hildebrando Castro Pozo,[16] who were the ones who truly built up indigenismo ideologically.

After analyzing (sociologically, not aesthetically) the works of the first generation of indigenistas—the art of José Sabogal and Guayasamín; the fiction of Enrique López Albújar, Jorge Icaza, and Jesús Lara—we are forced to conclude that their tone is more mestizo than Indian; indeed, that mestizo tone defined the movement's greatest triumph, Ciro Alegría's novel *El mundo es ancho y ajeno*.[17] We discover the worldview that inspired these works and gave them meaning, a worldview elaborated by a new social stratum springing up in provincial towns and cities thanks to a new educational system that allowed it to rise from the incipient lower middle class, called forth after the First World War by a fragile modernization process that demanded a broader, better qualified work force. At the same time, this class had found its rise checked by the remnants of the old social structure, which was dead set against the process of modernization. Confronting this obstacle, the tools this class used for critical action and spreading its message of social and political protest were literature and art (this in itself shows the level on which it was operating). In so doing, it turned to indigenismo, but what it was really expressing was a mestizo movement—call it *mesticismo*. It was a mesticismo, however, that dared not reveal its true name. This fact underlines the ambiguity with which it was used in this emerging situation as well as the sparse intellectual resources that the new social stratum had at its disposal to aid it in its social rise.

We therefore recognize this indigenismo as a specialized branch of the regionalist movement in art and literature that began its triumphant rise much earlier in other regions of Latin America (around 1910) and that, by a decade later, had already produced the works of Manuel Rojas, José Santos González Vera, Baldomero Fernández Moreno, Alfonsina Storni, Ramón López Velarde, José Eustasio Rivera, Rómulo Gallegos, Juana de Ibarbourou, José Pedro Bellan, and Monteiro Lobato—in other words, the literature of the emerging middle classes that were promoting the progressive democratization, through accelerated reform, of countries all across the continent.[18] These middle classes were behind the Argentine university reform of 1918, but they were also capable of unleashing the Madero movement at the outset of the 1910 Mexican Revolution.

What we are witnessing is a new social group created by the imperatives of modern economic development. This group's educational differential varied according to region and regional economic progress, and the group made specific claims on the society to which it belonged.[19] Like any group that has gained mobility (as Marx pointed out), this social group extended the demands it formulated to all other oppressed social groups and set itself up as the interpreter of the demands of those other groups, which it saw as its own, thus swelling its ranks by the thousands. No doubt the members of this group truly felt solidarity with the exploited masses. However, there is also no doubt that, for them, the masses served as cover, given that the masses faced more flagrant injustices than they did; in addition, the masses enjoyed the undeniable prestige of having forged an original culture in the past, something that could not be said about the emerging lower middle class. In their silence, the masses were, if anything, even more eloquent, and they were in any case more conveniently interpretable by anyone who had the proper tools: the written word and the fine arts.

Perhaps this was the trick that rendered the artistic efforts of the indigenista movement infertile like other subterranean errors in the field of ideas. In the end, it was a literature written by and for the rising lower middle (or mestizo) classes, who, because they were rising, were eager for the culturization that they absolutely needed in order to fulfill their project. This closed circuit nevertheless passed through the indigenous theme, which it used only as a point of reference, never as an element that might be put to the test in reality, given that the audience for indigenismo was never at any time composed of Indians. The same was true of Bartolomé de Las Casas's reports on the destruction of the Indies (1516–52), Manuel José de Lavardén's tragedy in verse *Siripo* (1786), and Juan Zorrilla de San Martín's epic poem *Tabaré* (1888). All of these, as much as Jorge Icaza's indigenista novel *Huasipungo* (1934), were material for consumers from the same overall culture, the members of which were drawn from different strata (Spanish, criollo, mestizo) during successive eras. All dealt with a somewhat exotic theme, with aims that cannot be found in their discourse of explicit denunciations (moral, political, metaphysical, and social, respectively, in the cases mentioned above) but rather in their literary and artistic sources, their aesthetic structures, and their cultural worldviews — those worldviews being the implicit facts that led to the creation of, and therefore set the tone for, the corresponding texts.

We no longer need to treat the movement as cautiously as Mariátegui did when it was just starting off and when great things could still be expected of it. It was an incipient movement when he wrote in the early 1920s; today, forty years have gone by, its historical cycle is closed, and it is no longer time for prophecies but for a balance sheet. The balance looks bad. If that is the case, the fault lies rightly with the mistake that entered into play when the movement was first dedicated to characters and topics drawn from the functioning of a subjugated and repressed culture, which the movement itself had no real way of evaluating. What these writers were generally ignorant of was the indigenous culture of the present, the living and genuine culture that existed under the tattered clothes and oppressive injustice. This was for the simplest of reasons: because they thought indigenous culture nonexistent or inferior (hence their haste to turn back the clock and mythify the past, salvaging only things from the time of the Inca, that is, the legends, in the culture of the present). In this, they were only demonstrating which cultural sources they relied on: none other than those of the dominant culture, whose value system they turned upside-down. The indigenista movement saw and explained the Indians using resources drawn from the emerging mestizo culture, which frankly was none other than the bastard child of its father, the eternal white conqueror, and was at that moment devoted to demanding the recognition and legitimacy that its progenitor had denied it. It took from the dominant culture all of the elements it considered useful, simplifying and clarifying them through its close contact with the actual functioning of the society in which it existed—that is, through its tough determination to survive in a hostile environment. This allowed it to deflate the pompous rhetoric that people such as the two Francisco García Calderóns and the two José de la Riva-Agüeros, not to mention their ancestors, continued to wrap themselves in; it also allowed it to be more indulgent toward Ricardo Palma.[20] As it struggled toward legitimization, the indigenista movement discovered one interpretation of reality that it made its own, because of its clarity and realism, while also simplifying it. That interpretation was Marxism, which in that era came in a mechanical and simplistic form. A man as intellectually gifted as Mariátegui could equate communism with a religion, which would seem to make him an intellectual descendant of Karl Kautsky and his critique, but he was simply taking up the only view of scientific socialism that could be formed in an undereducated environment that was just beginning to develop and that still contained great reserves of blind faith, waiting to pour them into some new cult of the saints.

The mistaken view of this mesticismo, with its indigenismo disguise, helps us understand why a novel such as José de la Cuadra's *Los Sanguri-mas* (Ecuador, 1934) today seems to offer so much more truth and effective artistry, now that the period of tumultuous polemics has passed, than do the indigenista novels of Jorge Icaza, though in their time Icaza's novels reached an audience that now strikes us as inconceivably huge. De la Cuadra's short novel takes the worldview that governs its literary devices, which coincides with the accepted (and therefore delightful) mestizo view of the world and adapts it to the themes, characters, setting, and functions of his work, establishing an autonomous and harmonious whole. In Jorge Icaza's works, on the other hand, the collision between the two worlds—which would become glaringly obvious after José María

Arguedas published the stories and novels in which he internalized some indigenous cultural values—created an internal contradiction that frustrated his creations aesthetically.

In retrospect, it is clear how impoverished mestizo culture was in the Andean area when it appeared, rather late on the scene, as an equivalent of the criollo or regionalist cultures of other areas. It is equally clear how quickly this mestizo culture developed and transformed itself, reaching adulthood within a few decades—an achievement that can be dated with some precision as the time when it abandoned the indigenista theme, for, once its control over its resources showed that it had attained an evolved level of social development, it let go of its exclusive concern with indigenismo and began to deal with a more diverse reality in which urban life played a major part. Many of its early solutions had their counterparts in other areas of Latin America, such as Central America and even Mexico, which to different degrees and through different conflicts were undergoing a similar evolution. It was, on the other hand, quite different from the areas that had experienced significant progress in the internal development of their middle classes by 1920 or where members of higher social strata had joined the indigenista movement and made important contributions. In such areas, the huge middle sector of society climbed higher through a succession of intellectual contributions until it could test its ability to handle comfortably the tools it had inherited from the upper classes. On the other hand, the Andes would pay a price for this long period of stagnation: the lack of preparation of the emerging mestizo group that had lived under conditions of servile dependency and was just now starting off on its own historical trajectory or was perhaps simply forced by modernization into its own trajectory.

Regardless of its initial poverty, this culture was a product of increasingly blatant expectations and of a social eruption that occurred in spurts throughout the 1920s, 1930s, and 1940s, until it was strong enough to absorb other middle social groups into its universe of values. This is demonstrated by the success of the literature produced by the first indigenistas and also by its close connection with the literature of the regionalists in other parts of Latin America. During the 1950s, a series of regional book fairs flooded Peru with published books. One of the writers behind this system of accessible mass editions, Manuel Scorza, was the one who brought back the socially conscious line of indigenismo and carried it through to its final conclusion in a series of novels beginning with *Redoble por Rancas* (1970). In November 1957, the publishers Mejía Baca and Villanueva of Lima organized a book fair for which they reissued novels by Jorge Icaza (*Huasipungo*, 1934), Enrique López Albújar (*Matalaché*, 1928), and Ciro Alegría (*El mundo es ancho y ajeno*, 1941) in print runs of half a million copies each, along with the regionalist classics *Cuentos de amor de locura y de muerte* by Horacio Quiroga (1917), *Doña Bárbara* by Rómulo Gallegos (1929), and *Los de abajo* by Mariano Azuela (1916). One newspaper, in a review of the event, lamented that they had not also included *Yanacuna* by Jesús Lara. Indeed, that was the only one they left out.

With its scope and ambiguity, indigenismo had produced quite a wide variety of works. Even Ventura García Calderón wrote (folkloric) indigenista tales back then, and there was no lack of rash idealizers of the pre-Columbian past who, in singing their uplifting anthems, lost sight of the present-day Indian and came to believe in the possibility of reestablishing a time and culture that had been destroyed. Likewise, there were those who proceeded to reinterpret that past in light of more recent ideas until they succeeded in imposing a new myth, summed up in the title of a famous book: *El imperio socialista de los incas* [The Socialist Empire of the Incas].[21] That myth had already become a commonplace of socialist political thinkers who saw the survival of the *ayllu* as the key to connecting archaic economic structures with more modern ones, leaping across the millennia in the blink of an eye.

These contradictions explain why the indigenistas were constantly embroiled in internal controversies; they were also the sources of Mariátegui's tough thinking when, in contrast to so many wide-eyed idealizers of the Incan past, he insisted on a social and economic analysis of the Indian problem, just as he insisted on the central function of the intellectual avant-gardes from the capital or port cities. Both themes, in fact, were one and the same.

Mariátegui rejected the strict dichotomy set up by González Prada and further developed by Federico More—between coastal Peru, seen as entirely reprehensible, and highland Peru, the guardian of all the country's values; such a division ignored "the protests of a vanguard that represents a new national spirit in Lima as in Cuzco, Trujillo, and Jauja."[22] In the same way, he refused to accept any solution to the indigenous problem that was based on ethical or cultural considerations rather than on fundamental explanations, which were economic and social in nature. This came to define the direction of his thought as he expanded on González Prada's distinction between the problem of race and social problems, as applied to the Indian.

As early as 1927, in his prologue to Luis E. Valcárcel's *Tempestad en los*

Andes, Mariátegui wrote, "As long as the vindication of the Indian is kept on a philosophical and cultural plane, it lacks a concrete historical base. To acquire such a base—that is, to acquire physical reality—it must be converted into an economic and political vindication."[23] He expanded upon this conviction in his *Seven Essays* and portrayed it in even more dramatic terms: "Any treatment of the problem of the Indian—written or verbal—that fails or refuses to recognize it as a socioeconomic problem is but a sterile, theoretical exercise destined to be completely discredited. Good faith is no justification. Almost all such treatments have served merely to mask or distort the reality of the problem. The socialist critic exposes and defines the problem because he looks for its causes in the country's economy and not in its administrative, legal, or ecclesiastic machinery, its racial dualism or pluralism, or its cultural or moral conditions."[24]

As is well known, Mariátegui alternated among a variety of interpretive systems, depending on the case at hand. For the Indian case, he rejected all racial explanations, yet he turned to exactly such an argument to analyze the case of blacks in coastal Peru, stooping to consider even psychoracial factors. This ambivalence resulted from his polemical way of thinking, which functioned in response to specific propositions that he put together as he went along in a rushed and slapdash manner.

It was for the same reasons that, in his zeal to combat the sterile explanations (some lyrical, others fraudulent) of the Indian problem that tried to hush up the central fact of its economic foundation, he so emphasized the economic element that he lost sight of any other aspect that is a normal part of human group identity. This was another example of the operational simplification which we have pointed out as a characteristic of the first phase of mestizo culture, resulting from the immediate needs of the new social sector's education and actions. It was and still is obvious that the Indian problem necessarily passed through its economic foundations (landownership and agricultural systems), but it also was and is obvious that those foundations did not answer all the questions raised by the integration of an ancient cultural structure into modern society, as became clear when the capitalist economic system began to unfreeze the stagnant indigenous groups. Nevertheless, Mariátegui persisted in his opposition to so-called culturalist interpretations: "All that survives of Tawantinsuyu is the Indian. The civilization has perished, but not the race. After four centuries, the biological material of Tawantinsuyu has proved to be indestructible and, to a degree, immutable."[25]

Though the culture of Tawantinsuyu, as such, had obviously disappeared, and though it was ridiculous to think that it might someday be resurrected, there still existed the cultural structure that replaced it, linking the living community back to its roots. That cultural structure was what allowed Indians to survive as Indians, not the biological reasons adduced by Mariátegui, which might even work against his arguments, given the difference in historical growth rates of the white, mestizo, and Indian populations. The bond that allowed this oppressed society to continue living and that made it a singularly legitimate cause for protesting the entire structure of social, economic, political, and cultural domination (cultural, in the proper sense of the term) was none other than its conservation of cultural norms that could be traced back to ancient Tawantinsuyu, beginning with the Quechua language, however many significant transformations these norms might have undergone. In any case, these communities enjoyed a culture whose functionality was evident and indispensable.

Though in other texts Mariátegui was quite sensitive to these values — and, despite his own declarations, was even open to idealizing them beyond any scientific, objective measurement — he was generally faithful to an exclusively socioeconomic interpretation that ignored all other elements of social life and even shut its eyes to the key importance of culture. In this way, his arguments became clear, simple, and categorical, but they also became a form of mesticismo probably because what we see here, in his way of choosing certain elements and preferring others, is the outlook of a different culture — the mestizo culture — and its filters for ordering reality. Two compatible factors were prominent in that outlook: the realist and the economistic, which we detect not only in all of Mariátegui's texts but also in indigenista fiction and in the rationalized reworkings of indigenous art. Realism, an offshoot of the European naturalist novel, is the petitio principii of indigenista art. Whenever indigenismo seemed to forsake realism in favor of reconstructing popular legends imbued with elements of the fantastic, it still continued to use the stylistic devices of realist fiction, and we discover that its creativity was grounded in its control of the rationalized coordinates in much the same way that eighteenth-century Spanish Enlightenment writers (Tomás de Iriarte, Félix María Samaniego) wrote fables using conventional connections, articulations, and linguistic behaviors. This realism, moreover, consistently views economic factors as driving the narrative action, and it therefore orders its dramatic crises in an immediate and simplistic way, showing us the general poverty of its view of man. The partial progress seen in Ciro Alegría's work only proves, by contrast, the limitations that an elementary and mechanistic worldview of reality placed on earlier works, such as Icaza's.

Even when Mariátegui rebelled against nineteenth-century scientism and the shortcomings of rationalism, palpably picking up on the debates that were just then roiling European thought and that Georg Lukács would later critically assess;[26] even when he drew a contrast between rationalism and the functionality of myth, repeating here too a commonplace of the European avant-garde's irrationalist rebellion by declaring that, for man, "only Myth possesses the precious virtue of filling his deepest self,"[27] he was elaborating a concept of myth that was almost identical to the nineteenth-century rationalist philosophers' concept of the ideal. This concept can also be traced in avant-garde literature, where it functioned as a learned substitute within the structure of modern society for genuine mythical thinking and from which the modernized human psyche was completely alienated. As such, it was an attempt to recover values that had disappeared with the development of industrial society and could only be attained now through reorganizations that were unsatisfying yet good enough to make up for the loss, as seen in the mass movements of the interwar years.

It is characteristic of all emerging social groups, regardless of their size, wealth, or poverty that they should attempt to impose their own filters for interpreting reality on all other social groups. They interpret the other groups through those filters and then try to force the filters on them so that they, too, will appreciate their values; what they basically propose is the general homogenization of the social body based on their own scale of values. Mestizo culture in effect demanded the universal mestizo transformation of Andean society, even of the remaining indigenous peoples whom they exalted but for whom they proposed a profound acculturation under mestizo guidance. That was the educational function that fell to the avant-garde. A political thinker such as Mariátegui could not fail to notice the relevant role that the avant-garde should play in initiating and framing such a movement, in which it would capitalize on general unrest in order to put a stagnant nation on the move. The place of mestizo intellectuals in the avant-garde was key: they already had some degree of education, quite a bit more than millions of indigenous people had; they had a coherent and simple vision of their class interests, which as they saw it coincided with the nation's interests; and after many failed attempts, they had managed to create a cultural worldview of their own that drew together contributions from many varied sources into one coherent whole. They therefore constituted a powerful instrument for leading the Indians toward economic and social progress, as well as toward integration into mestizo culture.

Those who, at the time, thought through these problems from the socialist viewpoint did not fail to speculate about this question of leadership and what it meant with regard to incorporation into the modernizing process on a non-capitalist basis. Hildebrando Castro Pozo expressed this view succinctly:

> At present, the Indian does not know, and will not know for many decades, how to solve the problem of his land tenure, much less that of his acculturation. For the moment, today, he needs leaders; and these can be none others than those who love him most and understand him best, those who have no pressing interest in defending their class or prerogatives, and those who under certain circumstances not only have joined their futures to his, but who do not live off of his ruthless exploitation. And this ideal rational leader, the one who began the crusade for the Indian's rights, cannot and must not be any other than the mestizo.[28]

Realism and economic reductionism, born from the mestizo's struggle to advance in the face of dogged opposition from the oligarchy's interests, both proved good ways of explaining social reality in their time, but only to the degree that social reality yielded to the imperatives of modernization, for those imperatives are what open up new prospects for the lowest groups on the social pyramid. This mestizo culture began to exist dynamically when it clashed with the holders of power — a moment that the mestizos arrived at due to the effects of modernization, the key progressive factors in their power struggle against the antiquated ruling classes. That was how mestizo culture, born in the shadow of the Western cultural forms that belong to the dominant classes, became a child of modernization. Modernization allowed mestizo culture to take off, and modernization helped it to stand up to the traditional powers. Modernization was not only a dependent process bent on technological contributions for unfreezing and subverting the existing economic structure but also an ideological repertoire for interpreting and adapting that structure to the specific demands of the new social group.

The same Western source that had given the region liberalism now sent socialism, which would operate on two fronts. First, it validated modernization as indispensable for assuring the nation's progress and righting the imbalance between the nation and the global power centers, which meant acculturating the indigenous population in order to incorporate them rapidly into the broad and productive workforce that an operation of this type urgently demanded. Second, it aided the mestizos in their struggle against the oligarchy, which they considered unfit for the historical task at hand. They sought to rebuild the nation on new social bases, and they felt that mestizo culture was in a position to lead this enterprise. One therefore sees that the incipient mestizo culture had discovered in modernization and socialism the two additional factors that, by legitimating the basic factors of realism and economic reductionism, would complete the interpretive panorama of the mestizos' situation and of the role that they were to play in the immediate future. These four factors are simply the expression of a single principle on different planes of reality, underlining the operative simplification behind this thinking.

What this framework overlooked was the positive value of indigenous culture. Indigenous man was valued, true, as an individual who could be compared or equated with the mestizo and linked, albeit paternalistically, to the enterprise of social transformation. However, indigenous culture, which seemed fatally outdated to modernizing thought and a genuine stumbling block on the road to progress, was not equally honored. The intellectual legitimacy of indigenous culture was denied, and from that moment on the problem of safeguarding its intrinsic features for the upcoming and widely heralded process of transculturation was also ignored.

It should be pointed out that those who did value indigenous culture were, above all, the idealists, dreamers, utopians, poets, and unrepentant idealizers of the past. They had no real basis for supporting their views, and this fact warranted their harsh condemnation by modernizing socialists; they valued the cultural otherness that indigenismo represented, and as their ideas did not rely on realism or economic reductionism, they were able to fulfill their idealizing function freely, even heedlessly. Their ranks might have included reactionaries, nostalgic idealizers of the past, and people motivated by ideologies unfit for the present circumstances, but the role played by the full corpus of their propagandistic writing was far from negligible. Thanks to them, a later generation—intellectually better equipped and better informed about reality because its transformation had already begun—took indigenous culture, the element that the modernizers had looked down on, into account. They worked hard to understand it and to genuinely know it (and therefore to respect it), searching for ways to preserve its traits when the time for transculturation came. This generation was quite aware that the area's destiny lay in the hands of the mestizos; that modernization was an unavoidable condition whose effects could be catastrophic, given the backwardness and compartmentalization of the Andean countries; and, finally, that the area was undergoing radical changes in land tenure and in the rational exploitation of the land. At the same time, this generation continued to believe that every nation has—let us use the word without fear—a soul, a center that establishes its identity and destiny as a community, and this soul is expressed through the construction of a culture. If a transformation in economic and social conditions must necessarily bring about fundamental changes in that culture, those changes cannot destroy the center of identity or the key values on which the culture is built.

This change in attitude can be appreciated by comparing two readings of a literary text, performed by important representatives of the first and the second generation from this period. Reading *Cuentos andinos* [Andean Tales, 1920] by Enrique López Albújar, Mariátegui discovered a Peruvian from the coast who had a rare ability to understand "the Quechua soul," and he tells us that "in its harsh sketches," this book "grasps the elementary emotions of life in the sierra and charts the soul of the Indian."[29] Only a few years after this reading, the young José María Arguedas, Mariátegui's junior by eighteen years, performed a different one: "Then, when I reached the University, I read the books that attempted to describe the indigenous people—books by López Albújar and Ventura García Calderón. I felt so indignant, so surprised, so disappointed, that I considered it essential for me to make an effort to describe the man of the Andes just as he was and just as I had known him through living in very direct contact. . . . Both describe the Indian as a stone-faced, mysterious, inscrutable, fierce creature, an eater of lice."[30]

López Albújar, born in 1872, was a typical regionalist writer still in the grip of nineteenth-century naturalism: a Mariano Azuela (1873–1952) who hadn't lived through an agrarian revolution or an Horacio Quiroga (1878–1937) who had never set eyes on the jungle. He could deftly structure a horror story such as "Ushanam Jampi" or retell a legend such as "Las tres Jircas" in a very economic style, in each case applying his mechanistic view of reality as best fit his narrative method. One finds nothing in these texts that might reveal "the soul of the Indian," although one does find behaviors that come within the purview of the penal code, which (as a federal judge) he had reason to know well. In literary terms, this meant cutting out much of reality, circumscribing and clarifying actions while at the same time pruning their meaning, transplanting them from the cultural plane where they were produced and legitimated to another plane where they lost any context or nuance. This literary operation, which can be found in many other indigenista texts, repeats what we have observed in so many descriptions of Indian life from colonial-era church and governmental literature: actions that were culturally acceptable to society under the Inca Empire became examples of monstrous savagery when transferred to different cultural parameters. What we see, then, is how one culture functions when it sets about interpreting the external, objectified products of another culture. Hence, we discover that the indigenismo of López Albújar, like that of his occasional apologist, José Carlos Mariátegui, is actually a mesticismo with well-defined limits.

This does not mean, however, that José María Arguedas's culture was not mestizo as well. It could not have been otherwise, even if, in Arguedas, one might perceive a certain indifference toward the mestizo social sector, which he nevertheless continued to consider the country's future. It was just that, in passing from one generation to the next, the vision had deepened. It had become imbued with values that the ideological leaders of the mestizo movement had implicitly scorned, thus hinting at an initial division within the movement that we might also be able to discern in other aspects of national life.

The generational transition had meant taking a second look and led to the discovery of previously overlooked areas of indigenous sensibility, thought, and imagination. With these discoveries, the first indigenismo came to an end, and a new art and literature came about that cannot be described as indigenista, insofar as that term retained its initial meaning, nor can they be called simply indigenous, as Mariátegui had hesitantly speculated, because they were not directly created by Indians either. The participants in this enterprise were mestizos and whites, without distinction; the level of intellectual work became hierarchical and specialized; sociologists, anthropologists, and folklorists arose and took part in an adult exploration of relevant knowledge; and, in particular, artistic creation recovered its autonomy and was no longer used exclusively in the service of a social project.

The 1950s marked the triumph of the indigenista movement, meaning that it had attained its principal purpose: eroding the values of the dominant culture, hastening their fall into a crisis of disrepute, and forcing the nation to accept new proposals. Nevertheless, at the very moment when it had won a greater social space than ever imagined by the avant-gardes and intellectual coteries among whom it had been developed, its proposals were seen as old-fashioned compared with the contributions of the new generation. This was the moment that gave us the fiction of José María Arguedas, the poetry of Javier Sologuren and Emilio Adolfo Westphalen, the paintings of Fernando de Szyszlo, the criticism of Sebastián Salazar Bondy and Alberto Escobar, the sociology of José Matos Mar and Carlos Delgado, and the works of many others. Specifically in the field of letters, the anthology *La narración en el Perú*, edited by Alberto Escobar,[31] can stand as an indicator, for it was based on a new conception of literature that included not only narrative forms traditionally classified as literary but also folktales, fragments of historical documents, materials from indigenous societies, and materials with clearly foreign sources with an eye to integrating all of these texts into a single literature. It was this same proposition that sought to integrate "all the bloods" of the nation, which is not the same thing as having one supplant another.

Regionalism and Culture

Arguedas, like Guimarães Rosa in Brazil, belonged to the first generation to arise after the conflict between *vanguardismo* and regionalism had broken out (in the same sense that Juan Rulfo and Gabriel García Márquez belonged to the second generation in this line of polemics, in that their first books were published in the mid-1950s, twenty years after those of their predecessors). Arguedas was thus a direct heir to the concepts that arose from that debate. It was up to him to test the changes worked by time (or modernization), their effects perhaps anticipated but not witnessed by the theorists who first commented on the controversy.

Arguedas traced regionalism—to which he dedicated his life, his experience, and his art—in a straight line back to Mariátegui's redefinition of the concept and particularly to the model of it that Mariátegui used when he introduced his own modifications. The classic tripartite division of Andean geography and culture into coastal, highland, and jungle regions, as well as the value newly placed on highland culture in contrast to coastal culture (the latter typified by urban Lima), reflected a theoretical generalization that was based on a specific regional model: the model of southern Peru, where the Andes squeeze in upon the coast and seem to smother it with mountains.

Mariátegui had written of "the sincere and profound sentiment of regionalism in the south, specifically in the departments of Cuzco, Arequipa, Puno, and Apurímac. These departments constitute our most clear-cut and integrated region. Trade and other relations between them keep alive an old unity inherited from the Inca civilization. In the south, the 'region' rests solidly on its historical foundations with the Andes as its bastions."[32] This was the region where Arguedas spent his childhood and adolescence, and it became the setting for his works. He drew his characters and the conflicts in his fiction from it. In 1928, when Mariátegui wrote the above description at the age of thirty-three, José María Arguedas was an adolescent of seventeen who lived in those places, where he had spent most of his life, preparing to move to Lima.

The regional complex is characterized by three traits, though most indigenistas of the 1920s only dealt with two of them, using them to transform the complex into a prototype. These traits allowed them to construct a clear, homogeneous structure, which for many years continued to function in Peruvian intellectual life as a sort of model that all writers were measured against and by which their works were classified. When Arguedas himself tried to explain what distinguished his art from Ciro Alegría's, he attributed the differences between them to the fact that Alegría had been born in the northern highlands and described the characters of that region, whereas he himself belonged to the southern highlands.[33]

The first trait characterizing southern Peru is a historical and cultural one. This was the region where the foundations of Quechua civilization were laid, the site of what Wissler described as a typical "cultural center,"[34] which explains why certain values were highly concentrated here, as highly concentrated as they could be in a community. In 1949, Arguedas declared that the departments of Cuzco, Apurímac, and Ayacucho "constituted in ancient times the center of diffusion for Quechua culture; in the present, all their inhabitants speak Quechua and in no other region are the survivals of ancient Peruvian culture so densely concentrated or so profound."[35]

The second trait, closely linked to the first, is the regional habitat and its relationship to the isolated conditions that served for centuries as a kind of natural fortification here. Mariátegui spoke of bastions, which was a fine semantic way of getting across his thoughts on this. Arguedas explained the situation with scientific objectivity: "A horse-drawn coach never crossed the mountains from Lima to Cuzco, nor from Lima to Trujillo or Arequipa. Draft animal locomotion was not practicable on the coast, nor in highland Peru: the loose sand of the desert and the chasms of the mountain ranges precluded it. The villages of Peru were always isolated by its invincible topography. . . . The geographic isolation of the villages is what determined the great power and influence that native culture had, and continues to have, in Peru."[36]

This geographical isolation was viewed mainly from a positive angle, less so from the angle that highlighted its notorious drawbacks. It was obviously also responsible for the lingering presence of outdated and exploitative socioeconomic regimes that grew during the colonial period, when a minimal transportation system had in fact existed to serve the needs of the empire, but those regimes had fallen into crisis at independence, after which isolation only increased in the region, bringing about a kind of refeudalization there. The penchant for positive interpretations emerged from the intellectual search for what was authentically American, popular all over the continent since the 1920s. This trend gave us an explosion of essays (from Samuel Ramos in Mexico to Ezequiel Martínez Estrada in Argentina) and the theorizing of movements such as nativism, indigenismo, and négritude, by writers from the emerging middle classes. What all these movements had in common was their search for a hidden inner history of Latin America that had been preserved alive in the lower strata of society.

In the same article, Arguedas presented a culturalist view—not a conservative or reactionary one but rather one that was attentive to historical trends that might prefigure the future. Aware that a process of transculturation was coming (there was no other way forward, other than gated reservations that would transform the ancient cultures into ghettos) and might prove fatal to the cause of achieving national unity, he saw this isolation as an unexpected asset that reduced the distance between the two cultures, tempered the intensity of the predictable clashes, and introduced a mediating regulating mechanism that facilitated a degree of adjustment between the historical times of each culture.

This was something Arguedas had already noted in 1947. "The isolating power of the mountains was an ally of native culture, for it slowed down the rhythm of Western penetration, aiding the retranslation of cultural characters imposed with the greatest violence by the European invasion: such as, for example, the case of religion and the endless series of cultural complexes that are based on and revolve around religion and its external practices."[37] The region's habitat, however, did not function only as a protective wall. It also had a clear influence on the construction of regional culture, insofar as the latter was a human response to geographic and climatic conditions, modifying them or wisely utilizing the possibilities they offered. Throughout the region, this modeling of nature had been carried out since the days of the Inca Empire, with terraced agriculture, irrigation farming, the development of specific times for sowing crops, and the constant struggle to improve the utilization of water.

This was a region where a close relationship had developed between society and its habitat over a period of many centuries. The society profoundly humanized the habitat, creating what some anthropologists call an environment, in which its various contributions were combined and counterbalanced.[38] Southern Peru was hardly the only place where the literary products of indigenous culture (songs, tales, legends, proverbs), as well as its religion and moral beliefs, had integrated nature into the worldview so coherently and systematically that they could resist being worn down by the penetration, however delayed, of Western culture. As we observe in other rural societies, the cultural structure that was developed in this region intimately absorbed the features of the habitat, adapting man to his environs. There is no better medium for seeing this than folklore. Commenting on a collection of tales from the oral tradition, Arguedas observed that "they describe the people's attitudes, the landscape, the smallest details of the setting in which the characters move, in such astonishing exactitude and depth that the physical world and the living world of animals, men, and plants appear so intimately and vitally connected that, in the world of these tales, everything moves in a community that we might call musical."[39] It is a fitting description of the problem. This is about the origins of a musical community, a phrase that inevitably calls up associations with the comparison that Claude Lévi-Strauss drew years later between mythical tales and musical structures. Physical reality and cultural inventions play and interweave according to harmonic rules that are also modes of thought, and they construct a harmonic world—the basic cultural operation is to harmonize all of these elements, employing the most varied formal structures, especially when facts from the age-old habitat must be included among them.

This was not a sort of animism, which even in indigenous beliefs alternates with other views (as seen in the metamorphoses of *huacas* and in the fixed hierarchies between creator gods and *wamanis*), so much as it was a precise evaluation of the role that the physical elements play in community life. It is an appreciation of the might of the river and the mountain, of their function in a well-known natural order, and of the roles of plants and animals as participants in a labor that they accomplish alongside men. None of these elements are seen as separate from humankind; rather, they are interrelated with it, somehow joining in with it to build culture. Therefore, though there was no animism in Arguedas, neither was there alienation.

One of the features of Indian culture that famously persisted in Arguedas, in the form of the child's worldview he sometimes employed, was the sense of the unity of human life and habitat, of culture and nature; that is, the holistic and harmonic — musical — comprehension of the environment. As the child admits in *Deep Rivers*, "I, who felt as if even the things owned by others were mine! The first time I saw a line of weeping willows shimmering on the bank of a stream I could not believe that those trees might belong to someone else! The rivers were always mine; the bushes that grew on the mountain slopes, the village houses with their red roofs streaked with lime; the blue fields of alfalfa, the golden valley filled with maize."[40] Remnant of a worldview whose Indian origins we may recognize but which we can find today in numerous rural societies all across Latin America, in their habits and customs as well as in their spontaneous literary productions. These are features that belong to the regional cultures of rural life rather than to any specific Indian culture, but Indian cultures have colored them with their particular ways of appreciating the world, and they use them to translate their forms of thinking.

The third trait of the regional complex is the most paradoxical. Southern Peru was marked not only by a well-protected traditional indigenous culture, adapted to a specific habitat with which it had interwoven its worldview, but also by its own particular social situation. The regionalist model of southern Peru attained the particular expression that it did because it derived from a regime of intense despotism and servitude, so intense that it had almost no equal in the Andes. Through his ethnological research, Arguedas was able to detail how this trait functioned and the constitutive role it played in forming a culture. His scientific research was carried out thirty years after de la Haya's and Mariátegui's manifestos and was enriched by his experience of living in the heart of the region's indigenous communities as an adolescent. He published this work in two long studies of the Mantaro Valley and the city of Huancayo, both in the central highlands of southern Peru,[41] and in a curious sort of "Puquio Revisited" in which he proceeded to examine the transformations that had occurred in the region where he had spent his early childhood years.[42]

In his first analysis of a regional Indo-mestizo society (Huancayo), Arguedas discovered that a process of incorporating features of Western culture had taken place without harming the conservation and the further development of traditional values; noticeable economic improvement, the use of modern technology, and considerable social freedom had not torn asunder the original fabric of the indigenous society or its basic cultural norms. This, he argued, demonstrated that the society had become "a center of cultural diffusion, compensating for the cosmopolitan modernizing influence of Lima,"[43] which in turn made it recognizably more effective as a regional model than societies that defensively hunker down behind geographical bulwarks to hold onto the past. Seeking the reasons for this exceptional situation, he found them in the behaviors that the conquerors of the region were obliged to adopt, as well as in the motives that led to an equilibrium between cultures during the colonial period, when the local Indian culture was not forced into a system of subjugation; the opposite conditions explained the contrasting situation in the departments of southern Peru.

From his analysis, one sees that the prevailing social system is the third trait that defines a regional culture and that the model presented by the indigenistas of the 1920s was a case of a subjugated, beaten-down society that clung to its traditional culture in order to survive within the narrow limits that were permitted to it. Arguedas, who had lived within this model and had learned from the cultural elements passed down from the remote past that it conserved and reworked in light of contemporary circumstances, painstakingly described how this social factor worked:

> The picture of the communities in the south is very different. They have long been locked in an unequal everyday struggle against the voraciousness of the neighboring landowners. And there were only two forces in these regions, in nearly perfect opposition: the indigenous community, consisting of illiterate people who held fiercely onto their ancient customs; and the landowner, a lord over Indian tenants who worked for him for practically nothing, who had no greater ambition than to reduce all the Indians of every surrounding community, near or far, to tenancy under him. The mestizo and the small landowner were insignificant forces, necessarily allied with or in service to the great landowners, for they had no other way to eke out a subsistence living.[44]

The positive cultural value that indigenismo saw in these communities, given that they had preserved their originality as indigenous cultures, had its other, tragic side: they had preserved it as the result of centuries of harsh exploitation. On the other hand, indigenismo also fought to end that exploitation but without questioning the consequences that change would bring. Indigenismo demanded equality of economic, political, and social rights; integration into the development of the country; the acceptance of modernizing norms; and, for the socializing sector, the use of cooperativist or socialist forms of production. Such forms of production would likely have had fewer corrosive effects on indigenous cultures than the capitalist development systems that were actually employed, whose effects Arguedas was able to study in the 1950s. This was the problem he faced that the indigenistas of the previous generation had not foreseen: the effects that an abrupt socioeconomic thaw would have on traditional cultures.

This matter comes up time after time in Arguedas's theoretical works. Those works are little known, since they were never published in a collected volume, so going over his conclusions is worthwhile. It will also help undo stereotypes about Arguedas (that he was intuitive, a primitive genius, possessed by his passion for all things indigenous, a sort of Indian who spoke perfect Spanish) by demonstrating his lucidity, his vast knowledge of the problems of his time, and the coherent, conscious nature of his transculturation project. It was not a matter of sheer nostalgia for the past nor some obscure way of repaying a debt of gratitude; rather, it was a well-grounded intellectual statement about what the mission of a Peruvian writer should be during his era and what he should do in order to contribute to the solution of his country's central problems. His book *Todas las sangres* was in equal parts a novel and a program for governance. All of his other works answered to his summons for social service in the region where he gained his knowledge and abilities.

Mariátegui was unable to see what Arguedas saw: the effects of modernization in those years. Much like Claude Lévi-Strauss, who in 1935 was one of the last anthropologists to observe the isolation of the hinterland regions of Brazil before it was subverted by the plans of the highway builders,[45] Arguedas knew the Andes both when they were defensively closed in upon themselves and when they were being transformed. "Beginning only twenty years ago, the ancient cultural areas that were respected throughout the colonial period have been torn apart and rearranged by the highways. . . . Finally, a new demographic occurrence has been observed that will have a decisive influence on the future cultural configuration of Peru: the constant and growing migration of the highland population towards the coast, especially to Lima and other cities. . . . In the great capital city, which has tripled in population over the past twenty years, highland migrants have become cells spreading Andean culture."[46] This text was written in 1952. In another, written in honor of José Sabogal upon his death in 1956, Arguedas returns to this point: "In recent decades, the influence of modern culture on the Andean regions of Peru has penetrated much more deeply as a consequence of the opening up of routes for mechanical travel. These routes have reduced travel time from the capital to the provinces, from the coast to the highlands and the rainforest, in revolutionary proportions. In thirty years Peru has leapt from a feudal communication network to one of highways and airplanes."[47]

Modernization had taken the ancient bastions of the Andes by storm and had settled in. Mountains no longer held off the assault of Western culture and no longer served to reduce the time that separated Western from indigenous culture to the effects of a progressive appropriation of new elements. Under these conditions, it was the purest, most traditional cultures that proved most defenseless and surrendered to an acculturation process that robbed them of identities they had jealously defended for centuries. It was not only in the crowded neighborhoods of Lima, where the myriad of rural highlanders to whom Arguedas dedicated his last, posthumous book had migrated, that both positive and negative influences were felt, but also in their home communities: material improvements alongside gaping inequalities, but above all the loss of their roots, the destruction of a cultural balance that was never replaced by anything similar, and the obliteration of a communitarian worldview that was replaced by the so-called skeptical individualism of contemporary bourgeois society.

When Arguedas returned after an absence of twenty years to Puquio, where he had spent his early childhood, he discovered as an anthropological researcher that it was no longer the "capital of an old-fashioned, predominantly colonial-style farming and livestock area" but instead had been "transformed . . . into a trading center with an active economy," and he analyzed those changes.[48] He observed higher economic levels, development of the mestizo sector of society, a diminishment of the landowners' despotic authority, adaptation to modern production techniques, and so on. He also observed the unraveling of root values and, hence, deculturation—in short, a vacuum, where there was not even a possibility of rearticulating society within the modern culture of domination:

> As for the Indians, we observed that this process is tending to emancipate them from the despotism that the aristocratic and mestizo classes have exerted over them, traditionally and also up to the present day. However, at the same time, the process is removing

the Indians from the foundations on which their traditional Indian culture rests, even though it is not clear what elements are to replace those foundations. The Indians are apparently following an open road to skeptical individualism, loosening the ties to the gods who have regulated their social conduct and harmoniously inspired their arts, in which we contemplate and feel a beauty as perfect as it is vigorous.[49]

This is a process we can follow, using cultural worldviews as our guide, thanks to a myth developed by a number of different indigenous communities in Peru. This myth has been collected by many researchers, including Arguedas himself in the Puquio region, as sociologists and anthropologists have found it extremely interesting.

It is the myth of Inkarrí (from the Quechua-Spanish phrase *Inca Rey*, the Inca King). Judging from its internal characteristics, the myth was a colonial creation. It tied together elements of pre-Hispanic myth, some of which were recorded in the texts of Inca Garcilaso de la Vega (1539–1616), and later elements, demonstrating the persistence of the self-affirmation of indigenous culture and the hopes it held out for its restoration across the old territory of the Inca Empire. The original component of the myth tells of the burial of the culture hero's head after his death. Buried either under the city of Lima or Cuzco, the immortal head is orchestrating the regrowth of the entire body; once Inkarrí is whole again, he will rise to rule over men, exercising his civilizing power.[50] It is clear, as Bourricaud noted, that what we see here is a cultural protest on the part of a people who have been subjugated but not defeated, for the myth itself continues to encourage their hopes for their restoration to power, which will happen here on earth—not in our heavenly promised land—when their traditional culture is restored.

As Arguedas observed in his notes, in the city of Puquio, after twenty years of transformation, this highly significant myth is only known by the grandparent generation, the older members of society. The intermediate generation—men between the ages of thirty and forty—have some vague and confused notions of the myth, but they are incapable of developing it organically or of perceiving its rebellious scope, frequently combining it with Catholic religious stories, as their elders do.

The youth generation is completely unaware of it. In the process of acculturation that has taken place over the past several decades, their loss of cultural values of their own has also led to a loss of communitarian protests, which were swallowed up by other protests pertaining to the class structure of modernized society.

In this point, we can measure the importance of transculturation and understand Arguedas's sudden insurgency against what he saw as an acculturation. A society's progress, its rising living standards, and its adaptation to the exigencies of a technological civilization (positive changes, for most people) should not have to result in its loss of identity, the destruction of the cultural bases on which a society had been founded for centuries, its distinctive note, or its contributions to global human society.

Here is where we can fully understand what Arguedas meant to accomplish with his writing. Like the mountains of the Andes, he sought to protect a tradition, the one that for him had formed his fullest childhood world, and to reinsert it among the dominant modern cultures. He set himself a titanic task, and to that we owe an exceptional body of work.

CHAPTER FOUR

The Saga of the Mestizo

José María Arguedas, Peruvian novelist, has overshadowed José María Arguedas, Peruvian ethnologist, almost to the point of making him disappear. Indeed, it will surprise many fans of his fiction to see his name on the cover of a collection of essays in cultural anthropology about the formation of a truly mestizo and original culture for all Peru.[1]

This is not because there was a huge gulf between his two activities, as is typical for Latin American intellectuals: on one side, a literary vocation, free, unremunerative, and sporadic; on the other, a profession that fulfills the social demand for paid work—what Mallarmé referred to when he complained, "What jobs our society inflicts on its Poets!"[2] Rather, both activities developed as if on parallel paths, mutually complementary and interconnected, arising from a single creative impulse that adapted to the two disparate forms without losing their common root. Arguedas did not compartmentalize his fields of expertise; instead, he built a holistically meaningful corpus of intellectual work. Its meaning emerged from many channels, at least three of which we can distinguish: we may speak of José María Arguedas as writer, as folklorist, and as ethnologist. Facts from any one of these three identities alone, even that of fiction writer, would not suffice to understand the author's full intellectual adventure.

He dedicated his entire adult existence—from the 1930s, when as a youth of twenty he studied at the Universidad de San Marcos, to his death in 1969, when he had already served as professor and chair of Ethnology at the same university and had joined the faculty of the Universidad Agraria La Molina as head of its Department of Sociology—to literature, folklore, and anthropological research, all at one and the same time. For him, these three disciplines were interconnected, and through them he expressed a single will and a single intellectual project whose roots were necessarily political and social.

The unity of José María Arguedas's life derived from his early selection of one area of reality to study and one philosophy for interpreting it. The area of reality that he chose can be defined as follows: the situation of indigenous culture, heir to the culture of the Incas, in the heart of contemporary Peruvian society, and the indispensable means by which it should contribute to the formation of a vigorous, free, and modern national culture, alongside all of Peru's other cultural roots. This choice necessarily led the young intellectual to join the *indigenista* movement, which his elders had already founded, though it would later be up to him to rework it in accordance with the changes that were taking place in the country's social and cultural structure. As for his philosophy, it was a legacy of Mariátegui's thought. Arguedas took up its rebellious spirit, a spirit of protest and social activism, which should not be confused with his forerunner's Marxist philosophy, but he nevertheless confidently adopted much of Mariátegui's socioeconomic analysis of Peruvian reality, together with his ideological presuppositions. Above all, Arguedas adopted Mariátegui's bristling nationalist spirit and sense of urgency about the transformations that the historical moment demanded and made them his own.

In his October 1968 acceptance speech for the Inca Garcilaso de la Vega Prize in literature, Arguedas looked back from the perspective of a man who had completed his life's work and had already resolved on his own death, and he synthesized the early adolescent impulses that had given his life meaning. "His sole ambition was to pour out into the current of wisdom and art of the Peruvian *criollo* that other stream of art and wisdom of a people who were considered to be degenerate and debilitated, or 'strange' and 'impenetrable,' but instead were really doing nothing less than becoming a great people, oppressed by being scorned socially, dominated politically, and exploited economically on their own soil, where they accomplished great feats for which history considered them a great people."[3] The intellectual career of José María Arguedas can be traced from this early activism, from the time he was vividly steeped in the intellectual climate of the antifascist decade, "full of great rebelliousness and great impatience" and "eager to fight, to do something," through the "socialist theory" that "channeled not only my whole future but also whatever energy there was in me."[4] Today we can define his career, in retrospect, as a cultural service that contributed to the formation of Peruvian nationality.

For more than three decades—from the publication of his first important works in 1935 (his collection of short stories, *Agua*, and his articles on the situation of the indigenous people) to his death in 1969—his creative writing, field research, study of anthropology, folkloric descriptions, and work as a professor and as an administrator of cultural institutions all contributed equally to achieving the same goals. He seemed to embody the old Romantic principle of the so-called citizen poet, without needing to resort to the more recent and widely bruited slogans about the politically committed poet. Unlike his contemporaries who made more noise but may prove less enduring, he refined this principle in himself by becoming immersed in real, concrete life and by vividly sharing in the life of a community; such experiences confirmed the justice of his political demands, but on the other hand, they corrected, emended, and reoriented those demands realistically. This authenticity saved him from the rhetoric that besets so much protest literature in Latin America. The dialectic of the concrete functioned here not only due to Arguedas's respect, as an intellectual, for the lessons of reality, as well as the humbleness with which he accepted its suggestions, but also due to his integrity as a researcher, which led him to recheck his first, rather schematic and Romantic assessments and adjust them progressively as his knowledge became broader, better grounded, and more reflective of Peruvian reality throughout the course of his studies and concrete experiences.

His early views were dominated by political activism and the urgency with which the matter was viewed then. The imminent arrival of socialism was an article of faith during the 1930s. This militant passion fanned the embers of the rushed and fervent writing in his early short stories,[5] but it did not advance his understanding of Peruvian reality, nor would it have lent his adult writings the exceptional qualities they possess: their generous and lucid breadth of vision, their artistic and intellectual effort to encompass the country's society as a totality, and their ability to take on its greatest and most complex problems without simplification or compromise.

Twenty years after his cultural initiation during the 1930s, in the shadow of the Amauta generation, Arguedas critically analyzed his first two works of fiction, *Agua* (1935) and *Yawar Fiesta* (1941). In his analysis, the fact that each book was different in tone was the result not of his own intellectual development but of his fidelity to the necessarily different realities that served as sources for the two works—that is, to the principle that a writer must follow the historical truth. Thus, his first book, *Agua*, arose out of "a pure hatred, the kind that springs from universal loves up there in the regions of the world where two factions confront each other with implacable cruelty—one group that bleeds and another that squeezes out the last drop of blood."[6] Simplifying the conflict in the *Agua* stories by contrasting the feudal landlords' brutality with the indigenous people's just demands was thus a consequence of the equally simple and dichotomous reality that reigned in the villages of the southern highlands. In the same essay, Arguedas hastened to demonstrate that his second book, the novel *Yawar Fiesta*, abandoned his earlier book's schematic and elementary concept of Peruvian society because it had to reflect the life of the big towns, as a result of which he had been obliged to present no fewer than five types of characters, deemed representative of the five social strata or classes that he distinguished in provincial capitals: Indians; traditional landowners; newer landowners with political connections; bivalent mestizos; and students, who similarly wavered between their towns and the social order of Lima that was to swallow them. (The same social schema guided Arguedas's later novels but was especially apparent in *Todas las sangres*, from its opening distribution of roles between the landowners Don Bruno and Don Fermín to its culminating assignment of a role to the culturally mestizo Indian, Demetrio Rendón Willka.)

In this analysis of his novel, which differs little from French sociologist François Bourricaud's unfinished analysis of *Yawar Fiesta*,[7] one clearly sees the sociological view of art that was always Arguedas's hidden inspiration. We can chalk this up to the powerful influence that the Amauta generation, with its interpretive norms for literature and art, held over him. Indeed, it was that generation, and Mariátegui in particular, who set the criteria of realism, typicality, reflecting the social structure, and ideological tendentiousness, all of which came from a fairly rigid application of Engels's precepts. This mechanical view, which had been a vital support for social art during the progressive decade that César Vallejo kicked off in the Andean area with his novel *El tungsteno* (1931), points to the narrowness of the indigenista concept held by the Amauta generation. Arguedas would later counter the narrowness of these criteria not by critically confronting them but by successive correcting and, even more, progressively expanding upon them. In the change between his two first books that he observed in retrospect (writing from the perspective of 1950), the evolution of his thinking was already clear, and although the change referred specifically to the arts, it actually derived from his sociological analysis of Peru, which always guided his thought.

The way he defined himself with regard to *indigenismo*—a movement in which he was both insider and outsider—had roots in the tremendous changes that took place in indigenous communities in Peru when modernized capitalism brought about their sudden, violent unfreezing. This explains his characteristic wavering between drawing close to the movement and distancing himself from it.[8] On one hand, he always maintained a close bond with the principles of Amauta, expressing his gratitude to Mariátegui even in the last pages he wrote, and indeed he never stopped constructing novels that, aside from all other possible readings, always allowed for a clear and socially conscious reading in which particular characters served to put the behavior of broad strata of Peruvian society on display.[9] On the other hand, he did nothing but modify, emend, and perfect the vast set of indigenista principles.

The term *indigenismo* was coined by the postmodernist generation in Latin America, who gave it the meaning that became accepted across the continent. As in the parallel and contemporary cases of *négritude* in the Caribbean and the literature of the revolution in Mexico, it specifically addressed the cultural problematics of its own region, but it was a local formulation of the generalized trends of regionalism, *criollismo*, and nativism that were ascendant in Latin America after the modernism of the nineteenth century, which developed during the 1910s and 1920s. It proposed a new assessment of reality and of the workings of the continent's modernizing societies, as viewed by the rising lower middle classes who were embarking upon their struggle against the consolidated structures of power. Their frank, coarse realism; their aspiration for a supposedly objective, even documentary, take on their milieu; their powerful, clarifying rationalism; their simple, emphatic, black-and-white mental schemas, which put forth simple yet effective interpretations of the world; their strength, which lent their literature a harsh, gruff tone; their spontaneous emotionalism, elevated to the status of a positive moral and artistic value; their combativeness, which twisted the denotation of any text into a reference to the generalized discourse on society; their trust in the proliferating ideologies that only disguised the concrete actions of this rising social class; their morality, which translated into permanent political activism: all these traits can be found in the novels, works of art, social and economic studies, and political slogans of the era, and all can be found together in the language utilized by these texts, whether

Mariátegui's *Seven Interpretive Essays*, López Albújar's *Matalaché*, or José Sabogal's paintings.

Such was the indigenismo that Arguedas was to revise without turning his back on the movement. All of this is explained in his essay "Razón de ser del indigenismo en el Perú" (Raison d'être of indigenismo in Peru), a posthumously published work whose date of composition is unknown. In it, he begins by dispensing with the nineteenth-century contributions of Manuel González Prada (from whom he had always maintained his distance) and turning specifically to the twentieth century, within which he distinguishes three periods of indigenismo. First came the early twentieth-century period, in which the movement was timidly supported by the works of Julio C. Tello in opposition to the so-called Hispanist thinking of José de la Riva Agüero and Víctor A. Belaúnde, though all glorified the ancient Inca culture that was just then being revealed by archaeologists and bibliographers (Paracas, Machu Picchu, Guaman Poma de Ayala, and so on); there was no parallel reevaluation of post-Conquest Indian culture, however.

The key second period was led by José Carlos Mariátegui. During this period, the social and economic rights of the Indians were vehemently asserted; writers and artists were urged to take up contemporary Peru as their theme; and an abundant body of work on the wretched, abused, despoiled Indian was created. "With the passage of time, this work now seems superficial, of little artistic worth, and almost none of it survives, but it fulfilled an important social function," Arguedas added.[10] Nevertheless, his main objections were not to the artistic poverty of this indigenismo, which might even have been set down to the learning period it was going through (just as Mariátegui adduced), but to two other aspects. First, the undivided and exclusive emphasis placed on the Indians and those who dominated them, superimposed on the coastal–highlands dichotomy and leading to the widespread dualist thesis of Peruvian criticism,[11] did not do justice to the true complexity of Peru's social structure, did not recognize the important contributions of the new sectors of society (the mestizos), and did not take into account the subtle differences *within* the classes that were arrayed against one another (very distinct kinds of indigenous communities, very distinct kinds of landowners, and so forth). Second, the indigenistas had no serious understanding of Indian culture ("Mariátegui had no information about indigenous or Indian culture at his disposal"),[12] so they were incapable of appraising it or humbly recognizing the many products it had created (clothing, instruments, dances, objects of worship, utensils, foods, and so on) or the originality of its beliefs and customs.

The third period of indigenismo, coming after Mariátegui and Valcárcel, and with Ciro Alegría and José María Arguedas as its most prominent narrative writers, was distinguished by the effort to rectify the shortcomings mentioned above. While preserving the social, economic, and political demands made by the indigenismo of the *Seven Interpretive Essays*, it would endeavor to perfect them through a better understanding of the reality and a wider focus on Peruvian society based on more solid documentary evidence. The dominant note in this third indigenismo would therefore be culturalist, and it would no longer be exclusively about the Indian. With that, the movement's own name would become questionable,[13] at which point this new opening could be seen as the true foundation of the national period, the Peruvian period, the period of the country's culture, the period leading up to the profound political and social changes that would soon have to take place. Referring solely to the theme of literature, Arguedas defined this indigenismo as follows: "Building on these earlier experiences, Peruvian narrative aims to encompass the country's whole human world—as complex, with all its internal conflicts and tensions, as its social structure—and the world of its ties, largely determinative of those conflicts, with the powerful external forces of the imperialisms that try to mold the behavior of its inhabitants through their control of its economy and of all the means of cultural diffusion and political authority."[14] There was a palpable effort here to make the concept of *indigenismo* overlap with the concept of *Peruvianness*. This modification—which distinguished not only Arguedas's fiction from López Albújar's but also his ethnological essays from the political essays of his mentor Mariátegui—came from gradually delving into the substantial changes that had been taking place in highland Peruvian society in the decades after 1930.

This led to a curious paradox. The archetypal indigenismo, that of Amauta, was, as we have seen, the ideological form that mestizo consciousness adopted when it supported the movement as a tool in its struggle for social ascent; indigenismo was put forward as the interpreter of the nation's indigenous majority, but its excessive emphasis on Indian ideological values was only a translation of the mestizo sector's own internal intellectual weakness, its unwillingness to assert its own values. The third indigenista generation inverted the terms of the older generation's paradox: having a much broader knowledge of indigenous culture, and placing a high positive value on it, this generation nevertheless contributed to the discovery of the mestizo and the description of their own culture, as distinct from the Indian culture from which it derived. This last indigenismo, the one most deserving of that name to date, has been able to highlight the central role that the mestizo should play in forming the long-envisioned integrated nationality of Peru, for its members were the first to have attentively studied that curious figure who had hitherto drawn more disdain than praise, especially from the passionate pro-Indian propagandists of the 1920s.

José María Arguedas was still very close to those propagandists at the outset of his intellectual career. We see this in his use of the dualist thesis; his close-minded defense of the Indian; his dichotomous view of society (Indians versus *mistis*);[15] and his distaste for mestizos, who always appeared in his stories in the service of the landlords, as schematic figures and mere ancillaries of power. It nevertheless fell to Arguedas to discover the positive value of the mestizo social strata; it was Arguedas who skillfully recounted their obscure and roundabout saga and who showed how they were reworking the artistic traditions that the Indians had safeguarded in a fixed folkloric state and were now introducing them to the nation.

The fundamental subject of Arguedas's ethnological essays was the mestizo and the interstitial mestizo class; he examined them through literature and sociology after discovering them with some difficulty. He paid more attention to them in his essays than in his novels (though he did give mestizo traits to the idealized Demetrio Rendón Willka of *Todas las sangres*), becoming their lucid and understanding analyst. When we referred above to the dialectic of the concrete in Arguedas's intellectual experience, we were thinking of this inversion in the terms of the conflict, which allowed him to overcome the limitations of the indigenismo of his elders, adapting it to the process that was transforming society.

It was no easy task. Arguedas did not draw close to the mestizo without uneasiness and suspicion. He felt repelled by the mestizo's disconcerting ambiguity and his seeming antiheroism. He saw him as closely dependent on the landlords and carrying out the lowliest chores; he also saw the speed with which he could shift from one side to the other without clearly committing to either, but above all, he was bothered by his lack of morals. It called for a great effort of understanding to take a realistic measure of the mestizo's social situation, his way of life in a land that belonged to everyone else but not to him, forcing him to develop conditions adapted to a hostile environment. These same traits explain the attention Arguedas paid to this character, whom he perceived as early as 1950 in these lucid terms:

> And what is the fate of the mestizos in those villages? Today they prefer to leave, to go to Lima, to support themselves in the capital at the cost of the most difficult of sacrifices; that will always be better than becoming the landowner's overseer, beneath the silence of the highest of skies, suffering the encompassing hatred of the Indians and the equally staining contempt of the owner. There is another alternative that only one in a thousand chooses. The struggle is fierce in those worlds, more so than in others where it is also fierce. To stand up, then, to both Indians and landowners; to place oneself like a wedge between them; to fool the landowner by honing one's ingenuity to an incredible sharpness, squeezing out even more of them, and at times conspiring with them in the deepest secrecy, or showing only the tips of the ears, so that the owner may learn of it and be induced to yield, whenever necessary.[16]

He articulated this interpretation in his report for the First International Conference of Peruvianists in 1952. Countering the negative views of Luis E. Valcárcel, who was trying to gather followers, Arguedas asserted that the mestizo represented a real, existing, and numerous social class, which could already be defined quite precisely, but which was as yet insufficiently studied despite its being the key ingredient in "the future possibilities and destiny of the country."[17]

In the critical thinking of the time, this redemptive role, which Marxism assigned to the proletariat, had been transferred to the pure Indian of the southern highland *ayllus*; Arguedas described him in the same way, idealizing him even more, if possible, and endowing him with the function of "sacrificial lamb." Bit by bit, he gave the same role to the mestizo—a character without the Indian's noble pedigree and with scant intellectual or moral prestige but whose know-how, energy, and capacity for adaptation made him more viable, the only one who could keep something of the Indian legacy safe through the difficult process of acculturation.

Before he could recognize the validity and virtues of mestizo culture, which most observers thought either nonexistent or very vulgar and crude, he first had to take a step that he resisted: letting go of the nostalgic evocation of the Inca era that might lead to a foolishly hoped-for purist restoration and recognizing instead the mestizo nature of post-Conquest Indian culture. This entailed acknowledging the Quechua people's extraordinary capacity for adaptation, which they demonstrated throughout the colonial period. Their cultural plasticity and their skill at preserving the key values to which they owed their existence and identity also allowed them to absorb enormous contributions from Spain (religion, clothing styles, musical instruments, crops, fiestas), which they refashioned through their own traditional channels.

By recognizing the value of indigenous culture under colonial rule and even after independence, which left it basically unchanged, Arguedas distanced himself from the indigenistas who were only able to value contemporary Indians for the ancient cultural traits that they were seen to preserve, such as their language and a few art forms, while considering everything they had incorporated from Spanish culture pernicious and impure. There are a number of instances that demonstrate this distancing. Arguedas used and defended the Quechua language as people spontaneously spoke it—that is, packed with borrowings from Spanish—and opposed the linguistic purism of the academics in Cuzco. He insistently condemned evocations and stylings of the Inca era as a parody—what he called a "monstrous bit of nonsense."[18] He always preferred the use of contemporary instruments, clothing, music, and so on, even when the Spanish influence on them was evident. These elements came together to form a living, contemporary culture, and nothing could justify eliminating them to benefit the idealization of a vanished past.

This attitude adjustment with regard to indigenous culture made it possible to recognize another culture derived from it that had incorporated many more foreign elements from Western civilization: mestizo culture. This was hardly an exceptional intellectual exercise; rather, it was the goal of many professionals—sociologists, anthropologists, folklorists, linguists, many with more polished academic credentials than Arguedas. During this third period of indigenismo, the human sciences were dedicated to a methodical study, using better tools, of Peruvian society in its totality. This meant paying closer attention to the mestizo classes. If the number of studies about this sector grew after 1950 (at the same time, there were attempts to reclaim the periods from the past when the opening lines of the saga of the mestizo were first being written), it was because of the intense migrations that had led to the massive incorporation of highland people into Lima and the other industrialized coastal cities. Paul Rivet lived to witness ("with special joy," according to Arguedas)[19] the invasion of the city of Lima by Indians who retained their original cultural formation and who entered a dizzying transculturation process as soon as they moved into its squalid slums. Through the analyses that the Instituto de Estudios Peruanos carried out under the direction of José Matos Mar, we can trace the history of this social earthquake, which blatantly altered the demographic composition of the erstwhile capital of coastal culture, the spear tip of Western dominion, long aimed at the rest of the national territory; in just twenty years, the population of Lima tripled. Arguedas told the same history in some of his articles on the so-called clubs of migrants from the highlands and their fiestas in the coliseums,[20] as well as in his last novel, *The Fox from Up Above and the Fox from Down Below*.

"The *Amauta* movement coincided with the opening of Peru's first highways," Arguedas asserted,[21] explicitly dating the transformations in his country that served as the background against which the third indigenista generation carried out their task. Arguedas viewed this problem less from a sociological angle than from the perspective of cultural anthropology; his concern was to safeguard the national identity, the moral and philosophical values of the indigenous tradition that he judged superior (notions of property, work, group solidarity, nature, humanism). It was not that he found mestizo culture superior to the shielded culture of the Indian communities in the department of Puno; rather, mestizo culture provided an effective conjuncture for preserving those values in part, whereas conservative indigenous groups were in a far less auspicious position. Incapable of resisting the assault that bourgeois capitalist Western culture was launching against their highland bastions from Lima, they were condemned to social and spiritual disintegration.

Arguedas's writings are full of accounts of the disintegration of conservative Indian communities that had lived on the defensive for centuries and, as a result, had been unable to develop antibodies for confronting the acculturation now unleashed upon them with all the technology of the twentieth century. He saw clearly that economically robust communities (which is as much as to say, communities that had already undergone a process of mestizo transformation, incorporating elements of Western economic culture) were capable of defending themselves with some chance of success, replacing their old Indian institution with more modern ones without losing their identities and possibly even forging original solutions. By contrast, poor communities—that is, ones that had not undergone any mestizo transformation at all—were rapidly disintegrating:

> Everything is beginning to change in the cities and nearby villages, and they can no longer even maintain their old organization. Many

heirs inherit no more than a single furrow of land. Nobody wants, or is able, to hold a political or religious office any more. Cooperative forms of labor, family organization, the whole colonial structure, all are disappearing, but that is turning the human group into chaos: they are left with no authority, no fiestas, no land. The only path left open to them is emigration.[22]

After this bitter realization, Arguedas developed his interest in the mestizo, which in turn led him to write about the region where he had spent his childhood and adolescence. There the harmonious evolution of Indian culture, through its absorption of the European message in a position of freedom, had resulted in an early mestizo transformation.[23] He based his optimism on the results of this research. As in the scriptural text of St. Paul, a proof of resurrection sustained his faith:

> We should note, however, that the Mantaro case is still an exception in Peru. But this happy event now serves us as a living example for the difficult study of the cultural differentiation that has always existed between the highlands and the coast, a fact that has grown ever more acute in the modern era. It will also serve us for our study of the possible process of harmonious fusion between the cultures that each region represents—a fusion that is possible, given that in this region it has been accomplished. Had the case of Alto Mantaro not appeared, our vision of Andean Peru would even now be bitter and pessimistic.[24]

If fusion has happened anywhere, it could happen everywhere, Arguedas might have said, paraphrasing Lévi-Strauss's citation of Tylor.[25] With this realization, academic research lost its seeming gratuitousness and became part of the "urgent anthropology"[26] that motivated Arguedas's polemics at the 37th International Congress of Americanists in 1966. This knowledge is the basis for establishing a politics of Latin American culture, and it is on this knowledge that such a culture—integrated, necessary, and joyously mestizo—can be constructed. The mestizo tinge that will be the sign of this continental culture has often been mentioned, particularly by writers from the regions of the "New Peoples" (to use Darcy Ribeiro's term)—for example, in the case of literary studies by Arturo Uslar Pietri. Nevertheless, this label has not been accompanied by a concrete study that might explain what this mestizo transformation consists of in our America; how a multitude of cultural influences have acted on it; what has been retained and what has been discarded of the many traditions that flowed into it; and what the principles and the dynamics of these operations might be. The history of mestizo transformation and how it works has not yet been studied.

However, it has been anticipated by José María Arguedas's essays, which have proved to be highly perceptive and useful studies in the sociology of Latin American art. This was not because of their theoretical dimension, though Arguedas never failed to use the teachings of the great Anglophone anthropologists (Melville Herskovits, Ralph Linton, Ralph Beals, and so on) effectively and prudently, but because of his highly empirical ability to trace the relationships between works of art, the real producers of those works, and their real consumers, examining the consumers' place in the social structure and ultimately determining the association among the themes, forms, and systems of making art in order to compare the works with their producers and social recipients. Arguedas's observations were astonishingly fine-grained, and they led to many of his most felicitous discoveries about the functioning of society, its diverse strata, and their interests and conflicts. He developed a consummate ability to read society through its artistic works, so his field studies devote more space to that aspect than to any other kind of sociological analysis—through artistic data he could interpret the society as a whole. His knowledge of folklore and his personal familiarity with art forms allowed him to grasp the similarity between a given aesthetic configuration and the very specific worldview of a given social group.

In his studies, he began to specialize in detecting the mestizo traits in art. His finest analysis of this theme was his "Elementary Notes on Popular Religious Art and the Mestizo Culture of Huamanga" (1951), in which he studied the art of the sculptor Joaquín López and the transformations he had introduced into his *retablos*, or "San Marcos" boxes.[27] Arguedas's analysis of the evolution of this religious object and folk art product throughout the period of transformations that Peruvian rural society had undergone, and the participation of the mestizo in this evolution as the only actor able to "realize this syncretic and harmonious representation of the symbols of such different and hostile religions, for one of them was officially persecuting the other with the aim of destroying it," is a model of sociological analysis worthy of Arnold Hauser.[28]

His studies of myth were in the same vein; it is a pity that Arguedas was unable to develop them further, given the excellence of his study of the Inkarrí myth, to which he devoted several articles. These were important not only because of the fascinating and rich meanings of the Inkarrí myth itself but also because of the intelligent way Arguedas linked the diverse formulations of the myth to the social structures of the people who generated them, establishing systems associating the myths and communities where they were created, which revealed those communities' most secret hopes while also deconstructing the hidden meanings that the myths carried. His final study of Inkarrí illustrates his free, empirical, and subtle exercise of the methods of the sociology of art,[29] but his spontaneous ease with sociological theory did not in any way diminish his appreciation of art. He could have said the same about his analysis of myth that he said of his use of socialist ideas: "How far my understanding of socialism went I really do not know. But it did not kill the magic in me."[30] His understanding of the social roots of art, the ideo-logical freight it bears and within which it is formed, did not cloud his aesthetic emotions. Social consciousness and art went together, neither harming the other but rather complementing and enriching each other, so that his essays in ethnology or folklore can, and should, be read from the holistic perspective in which everything merges harmoniously.

CHAPTER FIVE

Mythic Intelligence

Concentration and Reiteration

The intellectual works of José María Arguedas display a rare unity in the context of the literature of his time. Apart from his testimonial novel *El sexto* (1961), based on his experiences in the prison of the same name in 1937–38, and from a handful of pages on scattered topics, what unifies his works is their exclusive focus on a specific set of themes, centered on the Indians of Peru. His ultimate aim was to reflect, from a frankly nationalist point of view, the sociocultural totality of the country, whose central organizing principle, Arguedas felt, was none other than indigenous culture. Such a focus would not in itself have distinguished him from other social *indigenista* writers of that era such as Jorge Icaza of Ecuador. What accentuated the unity of Arguedas's works was his willful, stubborn insistence on seeing and interpreting his themes through the worldview of Peru's Indian communities. Early on, Arguedas made the indigenous communities' focus his own. He later expanded this focus by adding the viewpoint of the mestizo social strata, which he saw as a continuation, even a revival, of the Indian communities' worldview.

During a period when stylistic and thematic variety was becoming the norm for Latin American writers, Arguedas instead demonstrated an absorbed concentration, a powerful and exclusive fixation on a single aspect of reality, as well as an equally unified and consistent view of this complex thematics. This literary practice, which sidesteps the norms of modernism, can already be seen in his first book of short stories (*Agua*, 1935) and his first novel (*Yawar fiesta*, 1941, tr. *Yawar Fiesta*, 1985). His later books of prose fiction (*Diamantes y pedernales*, 1954; *La agonía de Rasu Ñiti*, 1962; and *Amor mundo*, 1967) and novels (*Los ríos profundos*, 1958, tr. *Deep Rivers*, 1978; *Todas las sangres*, 1964; and *El zorro de arriba y el zorro de abajo*, 1971, tr. *The Fox from Up Above and the Fox from Down Below*, 2000) confirmed this obsessive concentration, with only minor variations, in the sense that they aimed at attaining a register that more closely reflected the social totality of the nation. Their coherence and meaning become clearer when we place his literary work in the full context of his intellectual production, especially that of his closely related essays on anthropology and folklore. Not only did his essays cover the same set of themes and use the same focus, but the peculiarities of the genre forced him to rationalize them, using his intellectual talents to the fullest, constantly seeking to ground and explain the positions he had taken.

In contrast to the norm of mobility and variation through the incorporation of ever-new, ever-changing facts, Arguedas's works testified to his fixed concentration on a world that he took on time after time, in successive partly repetitive, partly differentiated waves — efforts that revealed both the profundity of the knowledge he was after and the impossibility of fully encompassing and exhausting it even after successive attempts. The norm of variation was based on a desire for sensations and their spontaneous vivacity; sensations blaze up in intense and dazzling brilliance, are rapidly exhausted, and constantly call for something new to take their place, so bourgeois industrial society valued them positively when it created modernity. Arguedas's norm, by contrast, was based on a desire for knowledge and led to his unflagging insistence on overcoming each of the levels that he progressively reached, a task that meant his advance was literally inexhaustible. This norm was diametrically opposed to the characteristics of the European (or Atlantic) civilization that expanded victoriously through Latin America during the twentieth century.

If we were to classify Latin American writers according to these opposing norms, we would have to draw up a table of the various nuances, the levels of influence, and the important transformations and commitments produced by the two poles of power that we have proposed: one centered on the permanent influence that flowed from foreign culture centers, using modern cultural precepts and with ready access to the corresponding information technologies for broadcasting them; the other centered on a retreat to the local traditions of societies consigned to the status of conservative by the advance of foreign cultural centers —

societies that endeavor to preserve the continuity and identity of a social group through the use of dry, traditional means of communication. If Jorge Luis Borges can be placed somewhere in the vicinity of the first of these two poles, José María Arguedas must be located very near the second.

These aspects of Arguedas's intellectual works can be traced to a broader and more complex set of questions of which they are mere superficial manifestations, skin-deep translations of a deep mental process in which the original components of the writer's worldview can be detected. The importance of this fact calls for closer examination, but we may anticipate the results with this superficial manifestation. It was not simply that Arguedas concentrated on a small number of topics; rather, he applied a reiterative system to them, taking them up over and over again, introducing small variations into them, putting them back into relationships with other elements that introduced further variations, and rearticulating them into structures that proved unstable and had to be replaced by new structures that were similar in part but were also composed of new elements.

This way of doing things can be compared with the workings of a mentality enriched by mythical thought, for it seems to us to be at least closely related to (if not prototypical of) the behavior of mythic thinking. We find distinctive overtones of mythic thinking in Arguedas that are characteristic of both primitive and traditional societies, though he integrated them on a different level while visibly struggling with other forms of thought. This admixture may explain the variety of ways in which he introduced them and the products of the changes he rang in them, making them seem like relics of the mythic mentality rather than constitutive articulations of it.

In any case, we may approach such manifestations by starting from Lévi-Strauss's definition of mythic thinking in *The Raw and the Cooked*: "The dual nature of mythological thought ... coincides with its object by forming a homologous image of it but never succeeds in blending with it, since thought and object operate on different levels. The constant recurrence of the same themes expresses this mixture of powerlessness and persistence. Since it has no interest in definite beginnings or endings, mythological thought never develops any theme to completion: there is always something left unfinished. Myths, like rites, are 'in-terminable.'"[1] Given that such a description runs the risk of applying not only to tribal communities but also to many people from the most highly developed societies—even to entire sectors of those societies (which shows us that mythological thought is a condition that survives in all societies today, particularly in still-unrecognized and newly emergent strata)—it is important to point out that mythic ways of thinking are not necessarily incompatible with other forms of thought, are not necessarily magical and irrational, and, as Lévi-Strauss argued in *The Savage Mind*, can be distinguished from other ways of thinking more by the subjects on which they are used and by the way they arrange information than by their specific mentality.

The Path to Transculturation

Arguedas worked from a clear spirit of political activism, almost militancy, in the service of the indigenous communities that had so long been oppressed and exploited, first by the Spanish in the colonial era and then by the Peruvians of the independent republic. At the same time, he was well aware of the problematics of the Andes, which he always strove to analyze with a critical eye, avoiding simplifications and partial explanations. The problematics of the Andes, for him, revolved around the central issue of the stagnation of indigenous culture. That was why he found it so important to study the social, economic, and political situation of the Indians and other social groups closely imbricated with indigenous people.

From his earliest writings, he lucidly perceived the rigidity of Peru's social stratification, though his first, dichotomizing schema of Indians facing off against *mistis* (mestizos) soon gave way to a more complex view of the social structure and the system of domination in which it was forged by creating distinctions between the country's diverse races and classes. He perceived the effects of that injustice on the downtrodden as well as their overlords, among whom he detected a kind of spiritual dissolution as a result of their exercise of domination. Finally, he kept an eye on the contributions of the middle groups, made up of mestizos. When he studied the tripartite structure of Indians, *cholos*, and whites—which, in the words of one current anthropologist, "operates more as three symbiotically organized strata than as one integrated society"[2]—Arguedas would write not only about the socioeconomic level, with critical digressions to diversify that too-narrow focus, but also about the most difficult cultural peculiarities of each group, specifying their functions and effects.

He never lost sight of the fact that the various elements of the social structure were mutually interdependent and that the key point about it was the oppression of indigenous culture. This fact was so forcefully evident that we can understand why Arguedas, while recognizing the social complexity of the situation, frequently returned to his dichotomized view: "How long will the tragic duality of Indian and Western endure in these countries descended from Tawantinsuyu and from Spain?"[3] Despite this, despite the fact that he sometimes lumped students, mistis, and mestizos together, his fiction, like his essays, blazed a trail through the complexities of society. His point of departure in his fiction was a conception of man (and, by analogy, of the narrator) based on the thinking of the *Amauta* generation of indigenistas, for it was they who introduced to Latin America the view of social class as an all-powerful category that subsumed and eliminated the individual, thus putting an end to the liberal conception, which modernism had perfected.

In both his anthropological theory and his narrative practice, there were three levels on which a person (or a fictional character) could be confronted: as an individual, the master of a subjectivity that was more or less circumscribed, but within which knowledge was produced (as an appropriation and reelaboration of objective reality) and from which arose a will to act that could be conflated with the ego; as a member of a social class, replacing individual traits with the generic traits of the person's group or position in society, especially those set by economic imperatives; or, finally, as a member of a culture, a concept that had a fluctuating relationship with that of social class, tending to encompass it due to the intensity of the traditions and customs that culture transmitted from the past.

Of these three conceptions, the second was the mark of the innovative thinking of the *indigenismo* during the 1920s (Mariátegui); in literature, it generated the norms of the social indigenista novels of the era, the most successful of which was by Jorge Icaza. Such novels favored panoramic collective scenes played by "the Indians"; when novelists took the time to deal with individuals, they endeavored to make them a synthesis of the generalizing traits of the social class to which they belonged and of their particular position within it. Though Arguedas claimed to support this class-conscious view in one critical essay,[4] his truly original contribution to the second indigenista movement (especially in his novel *Yawar Fiesta*) was his discovery of the concrete human being behind the collective concept of class (which he did not ignore): Felipe Maywa, whom he had known as a child; the *mak'tillo* Pantaleoncha; Don Mariano; his whole gallery of vivid characters, who became dear to his readers. His contemporary Ciro Alegría adopted the same position and, theorizing it, concluded that Latin America had not recognized any literary characters as individuals before the regionalist generation and that his generation was making up for this lack by unconsciously returning to the models of nineteenth-century European fiction.[5]

The view that Arguedas developed was more complex. He did not resurrect the established nineteenth-century character-as-individual, though that was the model with which he was most familiar through his readings. Instead, he took some traits from that model that he found useful for creating credible realist figures, and he reconstituted them within two frameworks: one that corresponded sociologically to the generic facts of the character's social class and another that was lined up more anthropologically with the character's culture, thus giving us both the fictional character and the class to which he belongs. In this way, Arguedas's fictional characters moved in two spheres, one of class and the other of culture, which do not entirely overlap. These give the characters an environment in which any excessively individualistic design disappears. They function like collective sounding boards in which actions can be justified or confirmed. These ideas can help us understand the confession he made in 1950: "In the highland towns the romance, the novel of individuals, has been blotted out, buried by the drama of the social classes. The social classes also have an especially heavy cultural base in Andean Peru; when they clash, and they do it barbarically, the struggle is not impelled by economic interest alone; other spiritual forces, deep and violent, fan the flames, arousing the factions relentlessly, with unceasing and inevitable urgency."[6]

If, for Arguedas, the starting point was political activism, demanding the legitimate rights of the oppressed Indian sectors of society, and if he got there through a focus on culture, then he could not avoid becoming involved in the problematics of transculturation from the moment his work centered on two cultures—one dominant and the other dominated—that belonged to two very different sets of conditions and situations. As a result, the role of protagonist in his works was gradually taken over by a specific type of mestizo—the sort we might call the pious heir (as opposed to the child who disowns his family), the one who bears his parents with him from one world to another, carrying out within himself the transformations necessary to allow them to survive.

This was the role played by Virgil's hero, Aeneas, in the first filial civilization in history, the first civilization that collected its inheritance and transmitted it with respect. This was the role that Arguedas assigned to Demetrio Rendón Willka in the transculturating Peru of the twentieth century, making him a magnificent American Aeneas, responsible for bearing his own father (the Indian cultural tradition) on his shoulders so that the tradition might take root in new soil (a new cultural structure, modern and efficient).

The writer, as Chekhov rightly declared, is under no obligation to solve society's problems through literature. It is enough to present them correctly, something that Engels had hinted at even before Chekhov.[7] Obviously, it was not up to Arguedas to put Peru's transculturation into practice; his only task was to describe it lucidly, revealing the exceptional moment when its longstanding and very slow development suddenly accelerated. For him, though, that task was not sufficient. He understood that literature can function like one of the exceptional zones of reality he had studied (the Mantaro Valley) where a happy sort of mestizo transformation had occurred—one that did not mean denying the Indian ancestors in order to progress, an attitude that gave birth to the "cheerful demon" who spoke both Quechua and Spanish, as described in his essay "I Am Not an Acculturated Man."[8] Given this attitude, literature served him as a scale model of transculturation, by means of which he could demonstrate and prove the prospect of its realization; if transculturation was possible in literature, then it might also be possible in the rest of culture. Arguedas—not being a government, political power, or revolution—could not set the transculturation process on an easy road to fulfillment; instead, he did what he could do or what he believed he could do if he put all his energy into it: display transculturation in fiction and realize it in his artistic writing.

His literature was all about demonstrating and proving that the fusion of cultures was possible. He did not carry this out on the level of subject matter alone (if so, he would not have surpassed the achievements of the best indigenista fiction, Ciro Alegría's), nor did he do it only on the level of explicit programmatic statements (if so, his best designs, such as *Todas las sangres*, would never have surpassed his overt statements in his anthropological essays). Rather, he did it through literature itself—through his literary art, his writing, his texts. Only by achieving transculturation there, in the very body of his creative work, could he give proof positive of its possibility.

If the task he had taken on was arduous, given the breadth and demands of the project, it also seemed to be too great a challenge, given the author's intellectual background. His schooling had been haphazard, his university years difficult and interrupted (he had to work, and he was thrown in prison), and only at a late date was he able to begin his systematic education. As an adult, he completed his studies in his academic specialty—folklore and anthropology—and, even though he humbly downplayed his training, in everything he wrote he demonstrated his intellectual aptitude and practical knowledge, which had more to do with the concrete functioning of culture than with theory. Writing at a time when functionalism reigned supreme, he was able to work around its inadequacies because he continued to develop a view of the world, the nation, and politics and because he was familiar with the major figures of Anglophone anthropology (Herskovits, Boas, Linton) through their books and the teaching of their students.

His knowledge of literature was admittedly spotty, unsystematic, and filled with the predictable gaps: there is no evidence that he read the Surrealists or that he had immersed himself in the fiction of the *vanguardistas*, but creativity does not depend on how much an author knows, so Arguedas's level of understanding may be examined from a different angle. Foreign artistic models had little influence on him, unlike other Latin American writers for whom those models ultimately made it difficult to see and enjoy their own reality. This reinforced his inclination to write about an inner world, humble and concrete, circumscribed, and little valued even by intellectuals who shared his political and social ideas. He was able to dignify that world artistically and judge its importance intellectually. This positioning as a national, or even provincial, writer (as Arguedas himself emphasized)[9] led him to fill his panoramas with local materials and to base his system of artistic values on them alone, with no need for direction from other kinds of values. Such an approach has its risks, for it often leads to the kind of dull-witted provincialism that undermines aesthetic judgment. Arguedas avoided this because he could call upon the great indigenous cultural legacy, its glorious past, and its truly impoverished present. He also could count on his native skill and aptitude for appreciating art.

On top of these difficulties, the educated circles of Peru were not broad enough to establish useful contacts between the clearly talented elites who had been trained and invigorated by the indigenista generations and the majority population who had been relegated to low levels of education and who in any case were little disposed to participating in an effort at integration. This massive sector, which had achieved some education merely as a consequence of some development project or other, whether bourgeois or proletarian, had only just begun to appear when Arguedas began his literary career; that explains why it took so long for him to be recognized nationally (it was almost twenty years before

Deep Rivers was republished) and why he lacked a dedicated audience to follow him throughout his career. As a result, the transculturation that Arguedas hoped for could only take root among the rebellious circles (intellectuals, students) of the dominant culture, finding no counterparts in the subjugated culture, which was spiritually impoverished and whose mestizo sectors, to whom the message was really addressed, generally still had no favorable prospects in the arts.

Speaking of his literary origins, he said, "To describe life in that village, to describe it so that its throbbing being would never be forgotten, so that it would pound like a river against the reader's consciousness! That was the ideal that guided all my efforts, from adolescence."[10]

It is clear here that his guiding focus was transcultural; he did not create his works for indigenous people but for readers who belonged to "the other side," in whom he sought to inculcate, persuasively, a set of values that they held to be inferior or spurious. Rather than pitying the Indian, rather than insisting (like the Lima cholos of *Yawar Fiesta*) that the Indian should integrate into the values of the dominant society, Arguedas sought, through literature, to make the Indian into a model that would win people's admiration. To this end, he reinterpreted all of the Indian's actions within his cultural structure, for only there would they be validated, and blamed his defects on the corrupting actions of the dominant classes (landowners, *gamonales*, priests, government authorities). Thus, we see a double movement of justification and exculpation, restoring innocence within a particular cultural structure whose laws, of course, would not necessarily coincide with those of any other structure.

The singularity of the transculturation process lies in its exceptionality. A white man takes on the status of Indian in order to undermine the culture of domination from within, so that the indigenous culture can join it. Strange as it may seem, this move is similar to Karl Marx's favoring the nineteenth-century European proletariat by distancing himself from the bourgeois class from which he arose. As Karl Mannheim observed, for a person joining forces with an emerging social group, such a move takes on the drastic quality of an intellectual conversion. Given that Arguedas could count on less support from indigenous groups than Marx found among the incipient proletarian cadres, he had to fulfill his mission exclusively from within the dominant culture, with no backing other than what he might garner from a group of like-minded intellectuals—in other words, the progressive avant-garde.

His works were thus pervaded by a defining trait of every vanguardista spirit: futurity. They were altogether a long-term bet, and their full payoff, their thinking, and their art were left for future generations that would already be marked by the substantive change he forecast.

Form: Language and the Genre of the Novel

Arguedas did use the regionalist devices in vogue at the time, but he substantially modified them, adding in a bit of postmodernist literary sensibility but especially (and this was his own personal inspiration) the artistic traditions of indigenous culture. This was his own contribution—and in my opinion, it was a great one—to an enterprise whose full scope has still not been fully grasped: to renew, which is as much as to say to strengthen, regionalist literature by reclaiming some of the hidden values that would give it unexpected power. In this sense, his works mirrored those of César Vallejo, for by remaining attached to regionalism, he enhanced it with new possibilities that he discovered at its very core.

The universalism/provincialism dichotomy—which had tormented Latin American writers for decades and made so many of them go astray, which so distressed Mariátegui and Vallejo that they ended up embracing both terms equally—continued to dominate the nearly four decades that witnessed the birth and development of Arguedas's aesthetics. Arguedas lived in a house of mirrors that kept shuttling him from one side to the other. On the indigenous side, he sought to join the dominant culture, to appropriate a foreign language (Spanish), and to force it to express a different syntax (Quechua), "to discover subtle ways to disarrange the Spanish in order to make it into the fitting mold, the adequate instrument of expression"[11]—in a word, to plant the indigenous worldview and the indigenous protest on enemy soil. Simultaneously, he was transculturating the Spanish-language literary tradition by having it appropriate an indigenous cultural message so it could bear both a specific set of themes and a whole expressive system. As if that were not enough, he always felt impelled to respond to the universalist demands that the early vanguardistas had bequeathed to the regionalist generation. It is interesting that he found his solution in a Gestalt theory that in some ways prefigures our structuralism. "Was and is this a search for universality through the search for form, for form alone? For form insofar as it means a conclusion, an equilibrium reached through the necessary mixture of elements seeking to constitute themselves into a new structure. . . . I aspired to and sought a universality that would not disfigure, would not diminish the human nature and terrain I attempted to portray, that would not yield one iota to the external and apparent beauty of the words."[12]

Form, as Arguedas perceived, functions as a balance of opposites. It resolves, on the symbolic plane of artistic creativity, tensions engendered by contradictions of which we are aware because they are the express manifestations of real, objective cultural conflicts. Along the same lines, form is a dialectic response to conflict; obviously, the term *form* is insufficient to cover the meaning of the process. As Arguedas correctly stated, form is a "new structure" that resolves the contradictions arising from a "mixture of elements," so that the particular structure of a work of art (a novel or short story, in this case) becomes a scale model of the macrostructure that would be generated by full-scale transculturation, giving us something more than a frustrating conjunction of disparate elements or the destruction of some elements and their replacement by others. This macrostructure, to be attained through neoculturation, should have room for integrating disparate elements (from diverse and distant sources) with an appreciable margin of harmonious functionality; in this way, the concrete, specific realities of one group's culture could articulate with the concepts of a culture that had arrogated to itself the right to represent universality as a consequence of the principles that yielded its historical triumph. Inversely, the macrostructure would also allow the products of the dominant culture to enter the structures of meaning in the indigenous society.

On this level, form should be understood as a freestanding literary system in which elements from diverse cultures gather in harmony to create a self-regulating structure. Thus, artistic creativity lies at the core of transculturation, declaring itself a privileged site where its possibilities can be tested. In his literature, Arguedas portrayed strictly individual experiences, neither supported by nor translating the collective experience of a people in the process of becoming integrated, so he inverted the terms of the process. As we have pointed out, he sought to create transculturation through his literary works, which he offered to us as symbolic models that had been validated as translations of an intermediate element in the sequence that was his own consciousness. He stated this explicitly in his acceptance speech for the Inca Garcilaso Prize: "I attempted to transform into written language what I was as an individual: a strong living link, capable of being universalized, between the great, walled-in nation and the generous, humane side of the oppressors."[13]

This allows us to measure his audacity and, at the same time, the solitude in which he formulated his project; no matter how fervent his proselytizing spirit appears to us, it was nonetheless aimed at only one of the contending sides — the side of domination. As an author, he filled the so-called contact agent role in a very sui generis way that I find rather unusual for such a culture-contact situation. He was from Peru's Hispanic culture, which, as the dominant culture, had introduced its values into the subjected indigenous cultures, forcing them to accept those values to the detriment of their own, though at the same time, it picked up a few crumbs from theirs. The values of this unilateral conversation were inverted in Arguedas. He was absorbed by indigenous cultures, made their intrinsic elements his own, and thereby turned himself into a white man acculturated by the Indians.

This would all be clear and simple if the process had ended there: a contact agent is swallowed up by a lower culture and ends up joining it. There have been many such cases in history. But the process went on: Arguedas returned to the dominant culture, and it was there that he carried out his intellectual task, working with his specific resources and the tools of domination at his disposal.

From what we can tell of his life in Lima during the early 1930s, his choice of the vocation of writer (obscure as that choice is for anyone) was related to, or conditioned by, his ideas about transculturation. Literature came to him at the point where several lines of force converged: his personal abilities or vocation, his desire to project indigenous culture into the heart of a society that rejected it, the fields that the dominant social structure left open to a man of his background and education, and the likeminded public that he might be able to influence and that was already being cultivated by the discourse of indigenismo.

Another force that could be included in this schema was the literary genre he turned to: the novel. During a historical period marked by the publication of César Vallejo's *Tungsteno*, the novel seemed like the right vehicle for an urban bourgeoisie in the midst of modernization, one they could put to good use in the expectation it would yield effective educational results. He might well have turned to poetry instead, a genre in which he had worked sporadically and the preferred form in indigenous culture. His message, however, was not meant for them but for the dominant culture; he was driven by a typically missionary zeal that could not be restricted to the field of folkloric and ethnographic studies. He had in mind a new social group that was arising interstitially within the petite bourgeoisie through intellectual means (university students, service sector employees, and so forth). For all these reasons, the novel seemed to offer him an ample expressive solution. Apart from what it represented as a vocation (and clearly, given the lyricism that characterizes his fiction, that vocation was none too explicit), there was a social ingredient in that choice, a weighing of the possibilities for making a greater impression and having a greater impact on a particular reading public.

Turning to the novel meant undergoing a fundamental transculturation. As a genre, the novel—which in Latin America has developed hand-in-hand with the middle sectors of society in their frustrated rise to power—revealed particular conditions that cannot be easily assimilated to the thought systems and artistic forms of Peruvian indigenous culture or to those of any rural society at all. No matter how Arguedas tried to base the organization of his novels on the lyrics of popular *huaynos* (Andean songs, usually with Quechua lyrics), no matter how he adapted the language to find Spanish equivalents for Quechua, he constantly came up against a literary structure that was radically hostile to his project. Hence, his first (and fundamental) battle was, as he himself recognized, against the form—against the novel itself. He undertook the conquest of one of the dominant culture's best defended fortresses—so entrenched, indeed, that every writer of pro-Indian social protest fiction had used it without hesitation, adopting the model that had already been institutionalized by the regional novel and limiting themselves to giving it a social spin that oversimplified its characteristics so it could bear meanings that diverged from its ideological foundations yet not alter them. This was a problem that Marxist critics hardly noticed (in Lukács, this lack of perceptiveness was almost criminal), nor was it a problem only in Latin American literary circles, for it has overshadowed the problematics of the survival of the novel genre all over the world, especially in socialist countries.

The Latin American social novel of the 1930s did not raise this issue as a problem, did not debate whether it was working with one of the favorite forms of Western bourgeois culture; at most, it twisted the novel into accepting an ideology that reflected the orientations of leftist thought (a mix of liberalism, progressivism, and timid forays into Marxism) with little overt modification of its forms beyond simplifying them into a more markedly denotative and logical/rational system. This school of thought was quite antagonistic toward the later forms of the avant-garde novel, which it interpreted as manifestations of bourgeois disintegration in the imperialist period; it never reacted like that to earlier forms of the novel, which actually belonged to the European bourgeoisie's era of triumph and expansion. It accepted those forms passively, not even utilizing them with the irony employed by one of the great disciples of the nineteenth-century novel, Thomas Mann. It is possible to discern a secret cultural connection in this behavior, the continuity of a certain notion of reality and of the literary forms that are appropriate for translating it, which accepts only variations of degree but not of substance, thus highlighting the contradictions presented by the rise of new social groups that nonetheless belong to the same cultural model.

Roland Barthes's observations about the socialist realism model of writing are apposite here, for the Latin American social novel sought to follow that model in the 1930s, following the projects of the Latin American regionalist novel, which was the manifestation of the ascendant petite bourgeoisie that had suddenly gained strength around 1910. "This lower-middle-class mode of writing has been taken up by communist writers because, for the time being, the artistic norms of the proletariat cannot be different from those of the petite bourgeoisie (a fact which indeed agrees with their doctrine), and because the very dogma of socialist realism necessarily entails the adoption of a conventional mode of writing, to which is assigned the task of signifying in a conspicuous way a content which is powerless to impose itself without a form to identify it."[14] A specifically proletarian culture had not developed in the Peru of the time; in its place were the radicalized sectors of the petite bourgeoisie that had arisen from within the dominant culture, but they questioned that culture and supported their rejection of it by appealing to the supposed values of the indigenous peoples. This would seem to confirm Bourricaud's observation on the ties between the indigenista movement as originally formulated and an emerging mestizo sector that found itself up against the interests of another, dominant mestizo sector and that wielded the Indian question as a weapon in its struggle for power. As a result, the Indian question was really not even touched upon in the arts, except as an argument in an internal debate within a single culture, when one social group found itself detained and paralyzed by the economic and social structures of the day.[15]

The proof that Arguedas's indigenismo differed from that of the social fiction writers of his time, that in his case we are witnessing a genuine effort to affirm the Indians' cultural values, can be found in the formal conflicts he dealt with as he endeavored to transmit those values to the official Peruvian culture. He found such literary forms as the regional novel and the social novel in that culture, but he could not use them without first modifying them, a fact that demonstrates how stiffly they resisted his efforts, clearly indicating the distance between the two cultural worldviews. Throughout his time living with indigenous communities and in his subsequent ethnological research, Arguedas observed the huge number of borrowings from Western culture in indigenous culture, attesting to the fact that such borrowings do not always change a culture substantively. For example, adopting new musical instruments did not necessarily lead to replacing the traditional repertoire of songs, dances, and melodies, and incorporating Spanish words did not modify Quechua syntax. In those cases, Indian culture demonstrated its strength and coherence by maintaining its basic trend line, keeping its borrowings from other regions within that line and using them in the service of local cultural conditions. In the case of loan words, as he accurately observed on one of the many occasions when he rejected the ideas of Quechua purists: "Well, there they are, deep down inside the Quechua context, morphologically untouched but transformed to fit Quechua semantics with the absolute rigor of a chemical conversion—preserving their elements and virtues, but forming part of a new function, a new universe."[16]

The inverse—borrowings from the lower stratum into the upper one—is more complex, especially with respect to artistic inventions. The official culture can accept and even encourage (as it in fact constantly does) the incorporation of bits of folklore such as pottery, woven textiles, dances, and songs or of their equivalents in literature: legends, folktales, poems, religious hymns, and so forth. They are not truly integrated into the dominant culture as dynamic components leading to a new semantics; rather, they are relegated to a lower, stagnant level in the dominant culture. This is mainly because, as Arguedas himself suspected in his review of folkloric literature,[17] this kind of material combines popular inventiveness with the impositions of the interest-driven model of education deployed by the dominant culture in order to further its imposition of authority. In this way, the dominant culture distorts the popular imaginary to its own benefit, though it must do so via a shadowy struggle over cultural trends in which the popular imaginary also seeks to express itself freely, whereas other cultures yield to the worldviews imposed on them and once more relegate the popular imaginary to the realm of folklore.

The original forms that Arguedas got from indigenous culture were the song and the folktale. The forms that the dominant culture put forward were the novel and the short story—the models established by both regionalist and social writers, descendants in turn of the realist writers of nineteenth-century Europe. Given that this was the line adopted by

Arguedas in his narrative fiction, we must infer that the battle over form, in its first assault—in other words, in the choice of genre—was decided in favor of forms determined by Western culture. After this choice was made, we observe that he treated those forms in a way that introduced profound changes in them, changes that he further intensified with elements from indigenous culture.

Folk songs were fully incorporated into his fiction, and they so pervaded his stories and novels that some read like illustrated versions of a folk poem. His use of folk song fulfilled a double function: the traditional function of the regionalist novel, in which folk songs or sayings serve as elements of realist staging and coloring; but also, as in Brecht, as an articulation of the story itself, furnishing it with an explanatory synthesis of its various sequences or of the entire work in the field of higher-level meanings, drawn from another level than its specific narrative discourse. This allowed the deeper themes of a story or novel to travel parallel to the plot line, through a series of intercalated huaynos that reinterpret the theme while translating it onto a symbolic level, thus allowing it to communicate with a world of different values. To invoke the "demon of analogy" that runs so delightfully through Arguedas's works, these songs serve as axes of translation to facilitate the passage from one cultural field, with its established artistic forms, to another field, more suggested than made manifest, in which they lack potentiality.

Finally, the songs enhance the lyricism of his presumptively realist fiction, supplying the high notes of his composition's tonal scale. Following other genres (Greek tragedy, Renaissance operatic tragedy), Arguedas also used three different dictions in the discourse of his fiction, balancing them along its harmonic scale. One was the realist plot; another was the peculiar recitative, represented by dialogue among the Indians or by their use of an artificial language that Arguedas constructed from Spanish, which he used to translate their thoughts in the dialogue and narrative. Finally, there was song, which he placed at the high point of this ascending line of tonalities, where it capped off the final composition and distinguished it as a "fabulous opera."[18]

There is an obvious musical equivalent to this way of organizing material; we can trace a hidden musical structure in the form of Arguedas's novels that would doubtless have pleased the Lévi-Strauss of *The Raw and the Cooked*. In chapter 9 of *Deep Rivers*,[19] the violent actions are divulged at measured intervals, in an order that does not obey the mere logical/rational sequencing of realist writing but follows instead the repetitive and evocative systems of music, using the song of the *calandrias* [mockingbirds] as a central part of the narrative syntax and concluding with this frank and truthful confession: "As I listened to its song, which is surely the stuff of which I am made, that nebulous region from which I was torn to be cast in among men, we saw the two girls appear in the poplar grove."[20]

Another reading of Arguedas's novels is possible, one not governed by the actantial advancement of the plot but rather by this mixed management of melodies and rhythms in which themes are repeated, contrasted, alternated, placed in dialogue, or joined together in chorus. In Arguedas's combination of plotted episodes, which may seem clumsy or disjointed to an eye trained by the norms of realism, one can recognize an adaptation of a covert musical scheme that does not judge situations, characters, or conflicts in terms of their direct logical/rational meaning but rather in terms of their contributions to the melody or rhythm, their musical demands.

The rich interspersion of folk lyrics in Arguedas's fiction has no counterpart in a similar use of folktales; he could find no use for their themes, stylistic devices, or structures. There is a precipitous distance between his compilations of folktales and his own creative works; even within his works, a text such as his retelling of the Quechua folktale *El sueño del pongo* [The Pongo's Dream, 1965] occupies a marginal position. It is true that his final, difficult attempts at fiction offer glimpses of his intention of finding a way to introduce mythical and folktale materials into the narrative; such is the case of the concupiscent foxes that he borrowed from the Huarochiri Manuscript and inserted in his posthumous novel.[21] The very structure of that novel, its assemblage of such disparate elements, only bears witness to the insurmountable difficulty posed by this change, the resistance put up to such incorporations by the fictional genre that Arguedas had elaborated. It is not a matter of some essential incompatibility between folkloric storytelling and Western bourgeois fiction, of course, for just as the novel was imposed on the folktale, so could the novel be swallowed right back up by its original structures: in the "First Diary" of *The Fox from Up Above and the Fox from Down Below*, Arguedas lucidly remarked on the links among the episodes of *One Hundred Years of Solitude* and the folkloric material collected by the priest Jorge A. Lira from the lips of his maid Carmen Taripha, and not only because of their similar novelistic motivations but also because of the ways they plot the narrative and their admirable ability to interweave the fantastic and the real on the same narrative plane of verisimilitude.

I think the explanation for this omission of folktales from Arguedas's fiction derives simply from the artistic norms of the time when he was being formed as an intellectual. The narrative models he had at hand when he got his start in literature meant that he could not avoid the reigning realism and psychologism, as García Márquez (writing twenty years later) or Rulfo (thirty years later) could when those were less coercive models and when European avant-garde forms had reached the Americas. Arguedas felt obliged by the underlying sociocultural claims of his era and his hypothetical audience to work with a notion of verisimilitude that had been rigidly imposed on him. The tools he employed to reduce this imposition was the trend of subjectivism, the use of a child as narrator, and the lyrical distortion of reality through the light it threw on a watchful consciousness.

He accepted the impositions of his times, seemingly situating himself as a regional novelist, but he had to soften the harshness and severity of the regional novel genre when he faced the greatest difficulty in his literary project, which, as I have explained several times, was its language.

Arguedas pondered the problem of language in the novel in a particularized, restricted way, considering only his difficulty in making his Indian characters speak in Spanish, something that struck him as discordant and contradictory to his experience as a Quechua specialist who knew and spoke the Quechua language. It therefore began as a question of realism—how to find a language for the Indian characters that would be literarily realistic but at the same time be a completely artificial invention, for among themselves the Indians spoke Quechua and not Spanish. The most complicated aspect of the problem—figuring out how to take an indigenous worldview, adapted to a Quechua syntax and lexicon, and translate it into a different syntax (that of Spanish)—was implicit in his initial framing of the question as one of realism, and it was masked by it. Given the characters he had chosen and the situations in which he imagined them, the primary problem was to decide the language they should use, for his readers would, for the most part, speak only Spanish. As we know, he managed to harmonize two seemingly contradictory elements. His first move, which he often mentioned, was to create an artificial language that combined quasi-Quechua syntax and a sprinkling of Quechua terms with a Spanish vocabulary. His second move, implicit in the first, was to use this literary linguistic invention to rearticulate an intellectual discourse (as well as an imaginary and a sensibility) that could bear witness to indigenous ways of thinking.

The result of this *ars combinatoria* was an economic yet effective Spanish style, a very communicative language with markedly literary connotations, which he used to deliver messages that were quite clear and rational despite their numerous and often ecstatically lyrical allusions to myth or superstitions; it was a language perfectly suited to the expression of powerful feelings and emotions. Given that Indians did not speak this way, not even when they used their broken Spanish, the result was a literary language specifically designed for certain characters in the novel in a way that seems to mimic the expressive systems of traditional theater (Chinese opera is a good example of the longevity of such devices), and it thus contributes to the effects of distancing and defining the characters.

By resorting to poetic discourse, by including folk songs, and by using linguistic structures that differed from everyday Spanish, Arguedas worked up an artificial language that, although not the Indians' own, was the expressive medium that fit them best in the genre of the novel. The world of representations that his literary works set forth was clearly distinct from the audience's real world, despite Arguedas's conviction that his words referred quite concretely to reality and despite the fellow human feelings that his Indian characters generate. Without taking away one iota from his novels' obvious verisimilitude and veracity, Arguedas made a crucial contribution to the regionalist novel, which at the time was still saddled with the doltish language of its stagnant realist conventions. His great innovation arose from his recognition that a novel's language is an invention specific to it, an artistic tool meant to serve its verbal nature.

In a rarely cited text from one of his essays, Arguedas covered the problem of translation from Quechua to Spanish, and he stated the following about his sufferings in this regard:

> I should mention that I am a fiction writer whose mother tongue was and still is Quechua. In the few novels and short stories that I have written, the reader will find a style that differs (quite clearly, no doubt) from the very original style of the Quechua folk tales that I have translated. This may demonstrate that I have remained faithful to the content and form of the stories I have translated. I have tried for a faithful, not a literary translation. For example, more than once the narrator uses a characteristic Quechua turn of phrase to describe the dimly lit hour of twilight: *pin kanki hora.* The literary translation of the phrase would be: "The who-are-you hour," or more strictly: "Who are you hour." I have translated it as: "The hour when it is not quite possible to see people's faces

and one must ask, Who are you?" Those who speak Quechua will understand that this is an exact version, for the phrase *pin kanki hora* contains this thought.[22]

If it is obvious that, as we have noted, one cannot discover the style of Arguedas's folktales in his fiction, and if it is likewise obvious that in the translation example given here Arguedas intended to convert a Quechua form into Spanish syntax and semantics while avoiding a literal (or what he called literary, letter-by-letter) equivalence, it is at the same time blatantly true that his fictional language absorbed forms peculiar to Quechua syntax, which are doubtless more blatant in the dialogues than in the narrative sections produced by the narrator character. These structures are what carry the modern poetic effect that pervades the language of the novel, which, without Arguedas's noticing it, was well illustrated in his translation example. Readers can agree that the phrase "Who are you hour" has a certain intensity, a way of calling up unexpected associations with distant things just as Réverdy and Breton wished poetry to do, that is lacking in the long, expository Spanish phrase.

Mythic Intelligence

The transformation of the narrative model that Arguedas carried out cannot be restricted to the limited problem of how the Indian characters spoke in his fiction. If that were the case, it would just be another iteration of the alternating and contradictory system of the Latin American regionalist novel, placing author and protagonist in adjacent watertight linguistic compartments—just one more case of leaping incessantly between two expressive forms, two cultures, declaring the author's own culture to be the superior one, the one that follows academic norms, and the lower-class protagonist's culture to be inferior, fit only for what is defined as corrupt speech. This is not the reading we glean from Arguedas's fiction.

The generalized subjectivization of his fiction (often written from a child's point of view and transmitting the mental operations typical of a child, which escape rational normativity) and his inclusion of lyrical passages that range on various occasions from poetic descriptions to popular songs are two effective tools that Arguedas employed to unify his fiction through a new narrative language. This artificial language, created for the expression of the Indians in his novels, spread more leisurely to the rest of his works. On one hand, it enlivened his fiction with its tense, halting, rapid prose, in which reality was translated into a set of varied brush strokes and events burst forth without prior warning like sudden flashes of lightning, only to become lost rapidly in the welter of their immediate effects. This process explains the difference between the stories in *Agua*, where Arguedas recognized that he had managed to capture a reality, and his earlier short stories, which he left unpublished even though they covered practically the same topics and characters.[23] On the other hand, it refracted and dissipated reality in fragments of lyrical prose, which, through the gimmick of a veristic child's worldview, give us access to a mythical worldview in which reality is animated by latent ideas that can only be made manifest in symbolic form.

Of all the transculturating operations that inspired the invention of new literary structures for Arguedas, none was more singular yet more akin to those that are the sign of the other writers of transcultural narrative in Latin America than the way he ordered his materials along the diachronic axis of his fiction. It seems that, in his novels, we are witnessing an accumulative system in which various fragments succeed one another. Occasionally, they are taken up by a character who experienced them; at other times, they do not have such grounding but are tied to the setting or to the unforeseen consequences of actions scattered in the story.

This behavior is related to the problem of narrative unity, a late development in the history of the novel. It came about in phase with the development of the structures of modern industrial civilization. Thus, we went from the scattered pattern of the medieval novel to the accumulative pattern of the Renaissance novel (a single character's dramatic crises), and finally, after passing through the peculiar vicissitudes of the eighteenth century and the various directions that were attempted then (didactic, epistolary, and so on), we arrived at the structure that has been taken as prototypical, though it is merely the Romantic-realist solution put forward by the nineteenth century, in which unity was achieved around the organic life course of one character, on which the setting, action, other figures, and so forth depend. Later extensions (families, social groups) are nothing but applications of the nineteenth-century principle of organic unity to broader groups, over which social law begins to hold sway as a substitute for the psychological law of the individual.

This last conception of narrative was the one inherited by the Latin American regionalist and social novels, and it can be found once more in some of Arguedas's short stories, especially his early ones. He attempted to return to this pattern in *Todas las sangres* in order to present a vast sociological panorama of Peru, though it was not the source of the best qualities of his work. In most of his short fictions, and in his novel *Deep Rivers*—in other words, in the defining center of his original contributions—it is not this conception that we observe but rather a sort of return to the accumulative system that recalls the earliest stages in the development of the genre. I have indicated the extent to which the demands of musical composition outweigh those of an ordered (and causal) development of narrative events. However, even on the actantial level, we find discrepancies with the prototypical nineteenth-century realist conception of the novel, in which the third-person narrator and the chain of autonomous events related in the simple past tense "presupposes," in the words of Roland Barthes, "a world which is constructed, elaborated, self-sufficient, reduced to significant lines, and not one which has been sent sprawling before us, for us to take or leave."[24]

The contradictions in this model—his handling of apparently independent kernels of information, from his description of an Inca wall in Cuzco with no apparent causal link to the plot to the attention he pays to an almost magical child's top (the *zumbayllu*),[25] which he halts the action to dwell upon—are related to the workings of a different level of culture, different psychic mechanisms for perceiving reality: those found in narrative structures exclusive to realism. Adolf Jensen, among others, pointed out the affinities between the poetic experience and the mythical experience characteristic of primitive peoples: "Obviously, poets make statements about reality that cannot be resolved through causal logic: the root of poetical communication consists of just this."[26] The characteristics of mythical thought do not necessarily entail their irrationality, as Lévi-Strauss has shown,[27] but they do entail dealing with the materials at hand in a way that concedes a broad freedom of meaning to many aspects of reality and, concomitantly, an extreme use of analogy. This allows explanations of the world to be built from kernels of meaning that are repeated, amplified, and modified in a variety of cases where they are applied practically to other fields or topics.

The way these operations are put into effect in an Arguedas novel can be seen in the accumulation of intense, sudden illuminations—synchronic and structured views of a perception of the real that involves all of its possible manifestations. These illuminations are repeated in other contexts where they are partly emended and used particularly to demonstrate the law of analogies so that seemingly very distant zones are placed in contact. The first chapter of *Deep Rivers*, "El viejo" [The Old Man], is an example of the way one of these illuminations turns by various circumstances into an application module: the entire novel is right there in the first chapter, just as, in a sense, all the deep meanings of *Todas las sangres* are present in that novel's stunning, Dostoyevskian first chapter. The intensity of the experience that the nineteenth century would have called divine inspiration is what fuels these first, sudden attempts at an interpretation of the world, establishes a model for understanding its factors, and fulfills cognitive expectations. Based on this, we witness a double process: on one hand, a causal chain of actions and characters is set in motion, in keeping with the traditional requirements of realist narrative; on the other hand, new illuminations arise, which may or may not be connected to this actantial level but which allow for another kind of development and another kind of interpretation that are more profound for the author and more effective as literature.

The resulting novel straddles two methods of composition, between which, despite their dissimilarity, it is possible to recognize a formal balance. Indeed, at the level of literary forms, we once again find two different cultural configurations that try to harmonize with each other but that instead flow parallel to each other, creating two simultaneous readings. The richer of the two, from the artistic point of view, is the one that draws on mythical thinking, though such a reading seems unable to structure, on its own, an entire novel, at least as we understand the novel in our Western tradition. This is where the realist models of social regionalism come in; their presence is greater in *El sexto* and in *Todas las sangres* than in *Deep Rivers* or, certainly, the short stories, which belong to a genre better suited to the joyous outburst of illuminations.

Those illuminations, though, are what vouchsafe the originality of Arguedas's work. Their strength, but also their enigmatic quality, resides in their association with a cultural configuration that is not our own. We perceive them as literary values, incorporating them into our habitual cultural text, but we might suspect that their meaning is only realized in full when they are seen in relation to the component elements of another cultural text—rather like the function of myth as Lévi-Strauss imagines it when he sees in myths a "matrix of meanings" that always, ceaselessly, refers to another matrix: "And if it is now asked to what final meaning these mutually significant meanings are referring—since in the last resort and in their totality they must refer to something—the only reply to emerge from this study is that myths signify the mind that evolves them by making use of the world of which it is itself a part."[28]

Part III

CHAPTER SIX

The Novel, a Beggar's Opera

Je devins un opéra fabuleux.
G. Apollinaire

Studying Art, Studying Ideology

Deep Rivers is a major work of contemporary Latin American fiction. It took Peruvian critics twenty years to appreciate its place in their country's literature; it has taken critics from the rest of Latin America even longer to recognize its exceptional nature, and they have still not granted it the stature that they now unquestioningly give *Pedro Páramo*, *Rayuela*, *Ficciones*, *Cien años de soledad*, and *Grande sertão: Veredas*, among the works of recent decades.

The problem, from a continent-wide perspective on Latin American literature, is that the national sociopolitical framework and the autobiographical framework, through which *Deep Rivers* has been alternately read, need to be set aside in favor of an aesthetic framework. That would allow us to evaluate it as an original artistic invention within the competitive field of contemporary Latin American literature.

There are multiple motivations behind almost any literary work, just as all literary works bear multiple messages. Some works, as Hermann Broch lucidly observed, may not have even been motivated by an explicit aim of producing a work of art. Their importance and longevity nonetheless depends on the artistic meaningfulness with which they were constructed. It is this aesthetic extra, on top of the author's basic motivations—whether religious, moral, political, or simply confessional—that articulates the work's messages and endows them with meaning, which may clash with the author's own motives. Then we begin to touch on the deep sources of ideological perspectivism, those that imbue and unite the work, beyond any explicit doctrinaire discourses it may contain or any voluntary intentions of the author.

Ten years after his novel was published, Arguedas recalled how concerned he was when he read the first responses from the critics,[1] worrying that they had not detected "the intention of the novel," until César Lévano published an analysis in which he emphasized the revolutionary content of the scene in which the Indians braved military repression in order to hear a midnight mass and save their souls.[2] Arguedas's overt attempt to show that even the meekest and most submissive individuals, the *colonos* (Indian workers) on the great rural haciendas, could count on a hidden strength that would let them stand up to the unjust and coercive legal order, enlivens the novel's shocking final chapter. Without belittling its importance, it should still be recognized that this intention was a commonplace of *indigenista* fiction: the earliest indigenistas flaunted it with utopian idealism; later, in the five novels of Manuel Scorza's Silent War series on the recent revolutionary struggles of the Indians of Peru, it was grounded in historical facts. The recognized originality of Arguedas's novel could not be a result of such doctrinal motives, though they were obviously a factor in the novel, and our perception of them lends it a special flavor in comparison with the works of other writers of the era, such as Ciro Alegría.

Another reason why the novel's aesthetic singularity was not appreciated early on was that it came out of a literary school that defined itself in positivistic terms, centering on a concrete social topic and sociopolitical position. With the author's consent, it was subsumed into a preestablished general framework, which, on top of everything else, was dominated by the teaching of two undisputed masters: Mariátegui for theory and Vallejo for narrative praxis.[3]

Though not ignoring the debate that raged in Peruvian intellectual circles from 1920 to 1960,[4] nor the culturalist corrections that Arguedas introduced into that debate,[5] I feel it is crucial to tackle *Deep Rivers* from a strictly artistic point of view, subjecting it to a double analysis.

First, we will analyze it for signs of formal inventiveness comparable to what was achieved during the 1950s and 1960s by the writers who renewed Latin American fiction, and we will counter the dismissive reactions of some critics who consigned it, within Vargas Llosa's gross dichotomy, to the category of "primitive novel," which preceded the supposedly new "creative novel."[6] This became a point of sharp tension in the First Diary of *The Fox from Up Above and the Fox from Down Below*, when the author himself declared that he was alienated by the modernist literary techniques of Carpentier, Cortázar, and Fuentes. In our analysis, we will have to study his formal inventiveness—not only at the level of his handling of the language of his Indian characters, which was where Arguedas himself obsessively located it (as Vargas Llosa was quick to appreciate),[7] causing many of his critics to pay the same exclusive attention to that aspect of the novel, but also at the level of the novel's organizing narrative structures. Our analysis will insist on drawing a clear critical distinction between the materials an author uses—which in Arguedas's case were as humble as the old boots that Van Gogh took as the subjects of his clearly original paintings—and the intellectual and literary means by which the author constructs a work, which are what give it its particular significance. The handling of rural themes and characters, the honest social perceptions corresponding to doctrines that were articulated during the 1920s in Latin America, the use of many traditional realist techniques: these are traits that Arguedas has in common with Rulfo, though neither of their works resembles the social or regional novel that flourished in Latin America alongside the avant-garde. The perverse thematic classifications of regionalist critics (Luis Alberto Sánchez, Manuel Pedro González) have led to this delusion, which must now be cleared up.

Second, our analysis will look into the ties between Arguedas's artistic inventiveness and his intellectual, cultural, and political positions, both as explicitly put forth in his many essays and as implicitly borne by his particular worldview. This part of our analysis will be based on the hypothesis that forms are generated along the channels of ideology, even if they eventually outgrow and detach from ideology, and therefore there exists a link between artistic forms and ideological perception, making it possible to skip back and forth between one and the other. Discovering what is specific to a literary form—what is irreducibly its own—means finding a valid path to the inner core where the author's ideology is at work in a particularized way, within the ideology of the movement to which he belonged or the era in which he lived. Both aesthetic inventiveness and the corresponding ideological conceptions frequently hide behind the overt appearances of a fictional work; just as the subject matter might make it difficult to grasp the structures into which they are artistically translated, so an author's programmatic discourse in his essays or fiction may hinder our grasp of the key focus point of his ideology, which, for that matter, may not have been clear even to him.

If we grant that the structural articulation of a work is the locus where narrative materials acquire their full aesthetic sense—where those materials (which may be collective, ownerless) achieve a dialectic, communicative precision that precisely expresses the work's orientation—then we must acknowledge that the same operation fully settles the matter of its ideology. That is the conclusion this essay will reach: in the end, what we find in *Deep Rivers* is the invention of an original artistic form, on a level with the most important figures of Latin American literature today. It is, in fact, unprecedented, given the audacity with which it was created from humble materials of a sort scarcely acknowledged by the world of letters. This form was created patiently over the course of a full decade,[8] during which Arguedas wrote many articles on folklore and ethnology, feeling that he had become sterile for writing literature, swallowed up by the conflictive milieu to which he belonged, for we refuse to see the ailments he suffered from after 1944 as a purely personal, individual matter. The aesthetic form that he invented for *Deep Rivers* was the solution to the dilemma around which his thoughts revolved, as witnessed by the number of essays he wrote during those years. It obviously offered an appropriate response to an ideological question by combining quite disparate tendencies and making them function in a disciplined way in the service of spiritual and social change. Yet I cannot say for certain whether ideology guided artistic form or whether his breakthrough in artistic form clarified his understanding of ideology.

Word as Thing in Quechua

Unlike a certain recent brand of Latin American literature, Arguedas conceived of his narrative as an exact verbal depiction of reality, whose self-evidence he never doubted. This was reality, this was exactly the way to tell it in words, and for all practical purposes there was no distance between these distant registers. The joy he referred to in his essay on writing *Agua*,[9] which in his own interpretation arose from his happy discovery of a means of transposing Quechua syntax into Spanish, speaks even more clearly of another matter. It speaks of his private discovery that reality lives in all its splendor in the world of words, perhaps in even greater splendor than it does in the world of things themselves. Arguedas was never bothered by problems with the referent, such as those we might note in the solipsistic trend of current Latin American writing.[10] He was not even aware that such a conflict could exist, as witnessed by his astonishment at Sebastián Salazar Bondy's critical pronouncements on the distance between word and thing.[11]

For him—as, at root, for most poets—the word *was* the thing, not merely its meaning represented in a sound. This inextricable relationship was the basis for his meditations not only on literature but also on culture. This can be seen as the pre-Renaissance stratum of European thought as analyzed by Foucault, but it can also be linked to a concept that is widespread in primitive or archaic societies, and in rural communities more generally, from the most diverse cultural areas on earth. From his key childhood experiences, from his mature work in folklore and ethnology, Arguedas was intimately linked to communities that did not use writing, where the word, as the privileged instrument of cultural elaboration, was used with a reverence and terse style befitting its high value, with a recognition of its capacity for enchantment, its supernatural power, and its sacralizing significance. Given Peru's hostile bilingualism, on the borders of which he lived, and given the fact that he was a writer—that is, a man who worked with words—his attention to words could have been predicted, though perhaps not to the superlative degree that made them the key point around which his creative endeavor revolved.

An awareness of language in literature has of course been on the rise over recent decades among writers of fiction in Latin America—a statement not meant to validate certain ingenuous theories about the "novel of language" that have been circulating without any linguistic precision, whose triviality is shown both by their ignorance of literary history and by their overlooking the risks taken in this area by José María Arguedas and João Guimarães Rosa, who had some points in common.[12] Where the Brazilian writer worked with different dialects of one language, examining them in the light of the foreign languages he spoke, the Peruvian writer was limited to two languages spoken within Latin America, superimposed on, yet alien to, each other.

A good portion of the linguistic problems that faced the international writers of the moment, such as Borges and Fuentes, also arose from invidious comparisons between Spanish and foreign languages—specifically English, which replaced French during this period as the language that challenged Spanish-language writers. Their own language, their Spanish-American mother tongue, was put into question by the English they learned and used as their second language, just as the modernist poets had done with French, a trend that in some cases (Octavio Paz) led to groundless theoretical pronouncements on the possible referential unfitness of Spanish. Though this was the model of a generalized conflict, several different situations cropped up within it. Arguedas worked with a centuries-old situation, internal to Latin America, that set the language of the conquest against the indigenous language of the conquered. His problem was therefore more similar to what Unamuno faced in Spain: adopting the dominant language (Castilian) in place of his conquered regional mother tongue, a fact that Ortega y Gasset found sufficient to explain the Basque writer's obsession with etymologies and his constant scrutiny of the words he had learned and therefore observed from a distance, delving into their meanings and clothing them in their signifiers. Unamuno exercised his obsession with Spanish—tracing it back through its lines of derivation to the original Latin and Greek—in a tenacious effort to appropriate his acquired language; Arguedas, instead, turned inquisitively to his mother tongue, not daring to carry out the same task with Spanish, which was nevertheless the language in which he wrote practically all of his literary works. Where Unamuno appropriated the instruments of his adult life, working to clarify them through analysis, Arguedas turned back to the ways of his lost childhood, a practice that calls up contrasting descriptives: childish or devout, questioning or militantly political.

Though almost all of his linguistic observations referred to Quechua rather than to American Spanish, the latter was obviously his reference point for detecting the singularities of Quechua and for making it the intellectual objective of a consciousness that was transformed from the merely existential to the analytic. This is an example of what I have always taken to be the central thread of his thinking, having arisen from his tattered life experience: his perception of difference. Few Latin American writers of his era had life experiences as radical as his, even though most of them were marked by similar problems in an era rocked by sudden international contact and rapid deprovincialization.

The most surprising thing is that Arguedas—having acquired, by 1958, full command of a disciplined and rhythmic Spanish, devoid of rhetoric, as dexterous, flexible, and terse as the Portuguese of Graciliano Ramos, and warily poetic in the oft-censured manner of Ricardo Güiraldes— kept silent about the concrete problems in his handling of the Spanish language, which, as he once recalled, he had struggled tenaciously to make his own. Because all of the linguistic problems he spoke of were also problems of Spanish, not of Quechua alone.

The initial dilemma he faced was more arduous but no different than what the regionalists had to bear in mind during the early decades of the century, and the solutions he came up with were likewise similar to theirs. It was a matter of projecting a veristic voice for the speech of lower-class characters in realist writing: realist authors from Latorre to Gallegos, from Rivera to Azuela achieved this by stylizing their characters' dialectal speech in a way that allowed their urban readership to understand their novels without detracting from the desired illusion of reality. However, neither the regionalists nor Arguedas in his early period perceived the need to unify their works linguistically, whether by perfectly harmonizing a work as a whole, absorbing it all into a single dialectized rural speech (the approach Rulfo would take), or by adopting another veristic, but urban, speech for the narrator, running parallel to the speech used by lower-class characters (Cortázar's approach). Therefore, the regionalists' works, like Arguedas's early short stories, display a curious linguistic imbalance between the speech of their rural characters and that of the narrator—a translation, on the level of language, of the cultural and class imbalance that underlay the movement.

In his early stories, Arguedas tried to find a stylized veristic speech style for his characters—something that must have proved difficult, for they were Indians and mestizos who spoke Quechua, not some Spanish dialect. He focused his efforts on just two of the many aspects involved in language, though they were undoubtedly two of the most important aspects: syntax and lexicon, each of which presented different problems.

As for syntax, he tried importing the Quechua structure into Spanish. On the literary plane (but not the linguistic), this effort involved a sort of dialectizing similar to that of the regionalists who were his closest models in the 1930s. As was also the case with the regionalists, neither his first-person narrators (who presumably also spoke Quechua) nor, more reasonably, his third-person narrators (who might be expected to be Spanish speakers) were subject to the laws of linguistic verism that were strictly enforced on lower-class Quechua-speaking characters. In *Agua*, in *Yawar Fiesta*, and in *Diamantes y pedernales*, we find once more the familiar imbalances of the regionalist texts: a fluid, sometimes rather rigid Spanish, always strongly Latin American in accent, as the ruling norm[13] and, emerging from it, dialogues in a language that seem less dialectal than simply artificial, and which serves as a signal, a sign that the character speaking is Indian or mestizo.

According to Arguedas, he discovered a way to translate Quechua syntax into Spanish. It matters little, however, whether or not that is really true once the text is in the hands of a Spanish-language reader who, in principle, knows no Quechua. For such a reader, these dialogues are merely a convention, and any other convention would have served as well, even the simple use of a graphic sign in front of anything said by a Quechua speaker, which could then have been written in standard Spanish. Arguedas's invented language will always be perceived as rudimentary Spanish (a Spanish that eliminates articles, overuses gerunds, avoids reflexive verbs, conjugates verbs poorly or forces them into awkward syntactic positions) or as an artificial language such as the priestly tongues common in sacred texts. Given the militantly political and idealizing context in which these characters appear, within the movement's generalized indigenista ideologization, the sacralizing perception is the one emphasized by this use of language, as well as by its strategic incorporation of a few ritually significant Quechua words (*yawar, danzak', layk'a*).

Conscious of the imbalances in this system yet unable to find a persuasive solution to the veristic literary problem he faced, Arguedas abandoned it in his later works. He thus followed the same path taken by the other writers of his generation mentioned above (Rulfo, Cortázar) who sought a linguistic integration that could perfectly harmonize the voices in their fiction. This is the path that the fiction writers of following generations would take and insist upon. The language of *Deep Rivers* is a flexible Latin American Spanish, into which Arguedas occasionally inserts Quechua phrases or words, translating them in parentheses or footnotes. Its dialogues use Spanish liberally, indicating in asides that the participants are speaking Quechua. The initial project of transposing syntax had failed. It had neither fulfilled its veristic goal nor preserved the linguistic unity of the text, though it had carried out its function as a multivalent cultural indicator as intended by the authors who used it, in the case of Arguedas by pointing to high, almost sacred, traditional values. Henceforth, the two paths forked: he could use Spanish or, alternatively, Quechua. Arguedas would take both paths, the former for his novels and the latter for some of his poetry, reinforcing the literary dignity of the Quechua language.

Nevertheless, something of the failed project remains in the writing of *Deep Rivers*. The experience of transposing Quechua syntax was arguably displaced from the level of linguistics to that of literature, given the features that distinguish this novel from its predecessors: its extraordinarily rapid rhythm, a precise use of ellipses, an introduction of poetic modes reminiscent of folk poetry, intercutting plot line sequences, indirect forms of dealing with plot development, and so on.

The other linguistic aspect to which Arguedas paid close attention was lexicon. There was no way he could resolve this issue, even in the partial way he found for syntax, given the contradiction between his choice of Spanish as his literary language and his exclusive interest in Quechua words, which he did not balance with any similar attention to words in Spanish. This fact corroborates his own claims and removes any doubts that may have arisen: Spanish was, for him, a language that he learned late and accepted as a necessary instrument for intellectual communication, whereas Quechua was his innate language (by which I mean the language you have no memory of having learned, the language that seems to have been born in your voice when you were born) and thus was surrounded by emotional associations and endowed with rich polysemy. Everything that Arguedas had to say about Quechua words, a Spanish-language poet could have said about Spanish words. The semantic links and homophonic transfers that he noted (as in his exposition of *yllu* and *illa*) referred exclusively to words from his mother tongue—the language he used exclusively up to the age of puberty—making it predictable that those words would retain a vivid network of the emotional and intellectual associations with which they were used during his childhood and that their sounds would pick up not only other analogous or simply contiguous sounds but also images, scents, tastes, and even concepts of the world that we grasp through just such means. Everyone experiences this with his or her own language regardless of the abstract discipline imposed later on by educational systems and adult intellectual life, so we can imagine how fresh his language's powers might remain for a man who switched to another language in adolescence and experienced much of his affective life in that second language.

Arguedas's case is the typical sociolinguistic situation that occurs when one language despotically dominates a society and forces all others out of the public square. Those others then become personal languages—family, group, neighborhood, or professional languages—and are thereby imbued with the sort of emotional load that public languages tend to lack. This is why speakers of a public language are constantly forced to resort to lexical, semantic, and even syntactic invention in the private sphere in order to make their language more flexible and more conducive to family or group emotionality.

The words of one's childhood tongue hold an overwhelming associative force that can easily jump the gap between the most distant points of reality, stirring up unforeseen associations of images and retrieving old times that seemed not just forgotten but obliterated. Three traits explain this force.

1. These words continue to function by a system of analogies that emphasizes their component sounds or phonemes—qualities that we, in our adult lives, think of as secondary (given that we use words to communicate meanings) but that are primary for children. This has been abundantly revealed by Freudian analyses of linguistic displacements and overdeterminations, which are active in dream work. Signifiers float free in this childhood language, hooking up to form the kind of couplings found in tropes, bringing about unforeseen connections of meanings. This is exactly what Arguedas carefully stated in his exposition on the *zumbayllu* in chapter 6 of *Deep Rivers*; he first establishes the obvious phonetic connection between illa and yllu, and then goes on, with less assurance, to suggest an uncertain connection between their meanings: "The term *illa* has a phonetic relationship and, to a certain extent, shares a common meaning with the suffix *yllu*."[14]

2. Moreover, the world of the child treats the energy of words with greater respect than the adult world does. We think that this is owing to the fact that the child's world recognizes the presence of the "thing" in the word, though the nature of this recognition runs a curious gamut, from a sensation that the word is a doppelganger summoning the thing to a conviction that the word engenders the thing directly. Even in adult life, this childish association lingers, as seen in the use of obscene language. This well-known potential for an insult, by itself, to cause an unbearable wound is something we only find fully in the mother tongue; it dissipates in languages that are not our own, where insults melt into Daliesque rubber guns. It is understandable, then, that when the characters in *Deep Rivers* trade insults, they use Quechua, not Spanish. This can be cumbersome for the Spanish-speaking reader to whom the text is addressed, but words meant as insults only attain their power to wound, both for the characters and presumably for the author, when Quechua is used: *atatauya, k'anra, k'echa.* The same is true of words that excite hysterical horror: we read *apasanka* and *apank'ora*, Quechua words for varieties of tarantulas, but never *araña*, the Spanish word for spider.

In his essay on *Ollantay*, Arguedas explained why he found some Quechua terms so difficult to translate into Spanish: "It is impossible to translate with equal intensity the painful tenderness that the Quechua text communicates. By repeating verbs whose phonetics bear a sort of material reflection of the movements produced in the depths of one's being by grief, suffering, weeping, or collapsing beneath the blows of an implacable enemy, a penetrating effect is produced on the reader, because the same terms are fraught with the essence of the tempestuous and ornate Andean landscape and with the way this external world lives, blazes, inside the Quechua man. Man, world, and language form a single unity."[15]

In several texts, with a variety of nuances, Arguedas referred to his conviction that the Quechua language is linked to the subjective life and objective reality of the highland Andean habitat; in its most extreme expression, he spoke of a material bond (*Fox*, "First Diary"). In the text quoted above, he was more careful and precise; he did not assert an equivalence of consciousness, object, and language but rather a harmonization that allowed them to reach unity in much the same way that a variety of instruments do in an orchestra. His arguments here were descendants not of some magical conception peculiar to traditional societies but of the European movements of Purismo in art and symbolism in poetry, particularly the lessons of Baudelaire's "correspondences." When he turned to the more extreme position, he had to bring up onomatopoeic examples, which are not exclusive to Quechua. It was no coincidence that Arguedas emphasized, beyond the bounds of credibility, the supposedly onomatopoeic character of Quechua or that his own exposition on the zumbayllu hardly constituted a proof, not to mention the fact that, of course, onomatopoeic animal sounds are transcribed differently in different languages.[16]

In the text cited above, he tells us that the phonetics of Quechua verbs materially reflect not the feelings but the movements that feelings produce and that Quechua words "are fraught with the essence" of the landscape — not with the landscape itself. Rather than a system of univocal transpositions, what is produced is an approximation of diverse orders (or diverse structures) through the equilibrating intermediation provided by the rhythmic or melodic schemes of the words, something that Matila Ghyka would doubtless have approved of. Arguedas's observations apply better to César Vallejo's poem "Los heraldos negros" [The Black Heralds, which was written in Spanish] than to *Ollantay* [written in Quechua]. The semantic development of Vallejo's poem is accompanied by markedly rhythmic periods, with the verbs *ser* [to be] and *saber* [to know] repeatedly and strategically set in the stressed syllables of the meter.

No matter by what means he produced that harmonization (and we will try to show that he did so through rhythm and melody), the first thing is to prove that, for Arguedas, language played a central role in it.

He did not simply yoke subjective consciousness to objective reality; instead, he constructed a triad: being, world, and language. Implicitly, he granted language a station equal to that of subject and object. I understand that this key point is due to the peculiar duality of the linguistic sign, for if he seems to have rejected the Saussurian concept of the sign in some of his writings, in others he unconsciously returned to it, for it was indispensable to the harmonization he sought.

3. There remains a third link between word and thing: metonymy. This is not about bundles of free-floating signifiers or the power of words to reconstitute objects in the imagination, infusing them with the full intensity and emotion with which they were lived in the past (Breton's *vécu*).[17] Rather, it is about the fact that words dredge up the heterogeneous contexts in which they were once heard and that they can magnetically attract things that were spatially contiguous or associated with them, however distant in time and space. The word functions like a focal point—an aleph—that takes up a wide range of facts or images. Newly recalled, it radiates them over the verbal space where it has reappeared, imbuing the rest of the statement with its accumulated treasure hoard. Because these Quechua words are, moreover, spoken rather than written, their evocative capacity is similar to that of music, although, of course, music exercises that capacity more freely, as it is not tied to the specific meanings that the linguistic sign entails.

There are dozens of examples in Arguedas's novels: "As I accompanied the melody of the singing in a low voice I would think about the fields and stones, the squares and churches, and the streams where I had once been happy" (46). Melody was what allowed him to call up these visual images. Similarly, he recounted an episode from his adolescence in one of his essays:

> In the small valley where the town of Pampas, the capital of the province of Tayacaja, lies, bordering on Huancayo to its south, I would listen at night to the pea threshing songs; I would walk near the threshing grounds, and for a few minutes I could watch the labor: a group of women, singing around the edges of the threshing field. [Here he transcribes the song.] The men were grinding the dry pea pods with their feet to the beat of the song. It was a moonlit night, and in the clarity the figures of the trees and people stood out, almost shone. The women had the voices that are characteristic of all Indian women who intone ritual songs, piercingly high. I was sixteen then and could not stay around to see how the threshing process worked. But I learned the lyrics and melody to the song.[18]

He did not see them threshing, but the lyrics and melody, which he recorded exactly, invoked their images as precisely as if they had been spread across a screen.

Here, again, the word is music; it is song, which, as he wrote in *Deep Rivers*, "is surely the stuff of which I am made, that nebulous region from which I was torn to be cast in among men" (149).

The word is not seen as writing; rather, it is heard as sound. In an era when poetry had already become writing, Arguedas continued to perceive it as phonemes, linking words intimately with their musical frames. A trace of his upbringing in the heart of communities without writing, a passion for songs in which the word reclaims its fullness of sound: in Arguedas, the word is not dissociated from the voice that utters it, intones it, or sets it to music. It might be said, then, that his narrative itself is not so much a work of writing as of speech.

The Function of Music and Song

When Arguedas sprinkled songs throughout his novel, he was not simply incorporating beautiful folkloric poems, even though he was aware that "the lyrics of the Quechua songs that I learned as a child were as beautiful as the finest erudite poetry I studied and assimilated in books, astonished."[19] He was incorporating sung words, a symbiosis of signifiers and signifieds that adapted and improved itself through actions that followed the rules of music. Those rules fulfill a function in both the strictly linguistic sense and the semantic sense, for they lend tone and timbre, intensify some sections, repeat those sections in choruses, harmonize different texts by giving them the same musical phrasing, and so on. They are even more effective at moderating poetry than the matrices of meter or musical rhythm.

Arguedas highlighted the close association of music and the word in his essays, speaking of the *haravec* or poet of the ancient Inca Empire, who, like the troubadour, was also a musician. "The literal translation is: 'he who creates songs for himself, in order to sing them himself'; both must have been common terms for ancient poets and musicians, for composers; because in those days music, poetry, and dance—especially music and poetry—formed a single world, were born at the same moment, like Quechua folk poetry today, where beautiful words arise girt in music, owing their aesthetic value to their tender, throbbing naiveté, far from all formal devices, from anything extra- or anti-poetical."[20]

Every time a song appeared in the book, it imposed an obligation on the author that he had dodged in the narration and dialogues: that of transcribing it in the original language. He always provided the Quechua text and its translation into Spanish in parallel columns. If the devices of avant-garde writers had been available to him, he probably would have added the musical score, a practice that he followed in his essays on folklore. Even without the notes, the reader is not being cheated; he knows that at these moments the novel is singing. The narrator says so explicitly, surrounding the songs with facts that underlined their radically musical condition and remarking on the instruments, the rhythmic characteristics of the composition, how it is interpreted, and so on. Arguedas was clearly aware of the difficulty that the reception of transcribed music in a literary text would pose for the reader, and he tried to overcome it. He wanted the reader to hear the song as he heard it.

All the songs are traditional-style folk compositions, anonymous for the most part, but still in current use. They are the spontaneous songs of the people. The most common ones are *harawis* and *huaynos*. The two harawis transcribed in the novel appear at moments of high emotional intensity: one when Ernesto recalls his departure from the ayllu where he spent his childhood and the other when the women defy the soldiers. According to Arguedas, under the Inca Empire, the harawi was considered "the most sublime form of poetry and music," as he wrote in an article just before the publication of *Deep Rivers*:

> They are songs of imprecation. Men do not chant them, only women, and always in chorus, at farewell or reception ceremonies for very dear or very important people; during sowing and harvesting; at weddings. The women's voices reach high notes that are impossible for men's voices. The vibrato of the final note pierces your heart and sends the message that no particle in heaven or on earth has escaped being marked by that last cry. Even today, after residing for more than twenty years in the city, where I have heard the pieces of the great Western composers, I still believe that it is not possible to give greater power to human expression.[21]

But most of the songs are huaynos, both ancient and modern, from different regions of Peru. Their predominance is due to the principle of verism, for the huayno is the most popularized form of music in the country and it is to be expected when people get together at *chicherías* or when schoolmates hold competitions where they are said to sing up to fifty huaynos.

Moreover, Arguedas had a predilection for the huayno because of the song's attractive rhythm, which lends itself so well to dancing. He wrote in one of his essays of "the *pasñas* dancing gracefully, swirling their *polleras* and *rebozos* to the beat of the *huayno*, in rapid twirls, but always to an ardent rhythm, in never-failing harmony with the *huayno*."[22] Even more, because he saw it as holding a power for forging Peruvian nationality, "the *huaylas* and the *huayno*, much more than these decorative objects, are on their way to becoming our common cultural heritage, a nation-building link among all Peruvians."[23] This is music that ties all Peruvians together while also tying them all to their pre-Hispanic roots, fulfilling the two basic conditions of national cohesion: "just as it was four centuries, five centuries ago, the *huayno* is the power, is the voice, is the eternal blood of all the fiestas of Andean Peru."[24]

These songs carry out a central function in the story, for they are engaged in the narrative discourse—sometimes in its surface argument and sometimes in its deeper currents. These are moments of intense emotional and artistic concentration, veritable arias, which, within a short space and in a single musical tessitura, encode the meanings that every work of fiction must develop at length.

However, they are not meant to disrupt a stream of words unlike them in kind, the way Bertolt Brecht uses songs to produce distancing. On the contrary, they appear within an extraordinarily broad and varied gamut of musical references that allow us to speak of a generalized musical cacophony or harmony. These materials have many sources: first and foremost, there is nature, which Arguedas, a fine connoisseur, presents as a spectacular musical sequence full of rivers, wind, trees, insects, and birds; then there are the artifacts of popular culture, such as the zumbayllu; then the thousand sounds that form the backdrop of everyday life, from the peeling church bells to gunfire; and above all, there are the voices in their thousand registers. All of these join in such an insistent, complex, alternating fashion that I can only compare the resulting multiplicity of sound devices to an orchestra that plays through the course of the novel, accompanying the characters' public and private lives, duplicating their habitual visual references through melody.

What we have here, I think, is a realist perception of working-class behavior, especially of the rural working class who show a clear preference to feel surrounded by a wave of sound in which they participate, rejecting the forms of silence and individual solitude. I also think that this is an effective literary technique for endowing a text, more spoken than written, with a luscious display of sound correspondences. The novel sets up a musical double, which is the privileged agent mediating between the human community and the kingdom of nature—between subjective consciousness and the objective world, given that both are always singing and that they can sing in unison. To the degree that their songs keep rhythm and melody, they build an unforeseen path so that both spheres can come to mutual agreement, join in harmony, and attain, at last, the longed-for universal order.

In the kingdom of nature, each object possesses its own voice, just as each human being does. These natural voices can harmonize with just one another, but they can also combine with human voices in a broader concert. "The soft noise of the dry wheat field, rustling in the wind, even reaches inside the huts; it is like a song that might last all night long. And when the river is nearby, the voice of the water joins that of the wheat fields."[25] "The voices of the boys, the voice of the Rector, the voices of Antero and Salvinia, the song of the women, and the song of the birds in the poplar grove of Condebamba echoed and commingled in my mind, falling upon my dreams like an uneven rain" (110).

Every natural element, object, or being has its own voice (or "sings its own song," as Darío put it). That voice proclaims its singularity and is the privileged bridge to the possibility that many or all voices may begin to sing in unison. Due to its double nature, song holds an exceptional place within such a homogeneous totality, similar to that of the linguistic sign. It is an ordering of metered words, and it is an ordering of likewise metered musical notes, but this strict correspondence does not hinder the clear autonomy of each part, for they can bear distinct and sometimes temporarily discordant messages, as we will see.

Indeed, the function of music is similar to that of meter. It establishes a strict, almost immovable pattern interconnecting two aspects: the imperceptibly distant time from which the music hails, linking us to the past, and the collective quality that distinguishes music, for it is shared and even molded by many sectors of society, especially the working classes. Lyrics are introduced into this immovable pattern and fitted to it; as they are adapted to the pattern's fixed rhythms, lyrics can also set free new meanings that express the contemporary situation of whomever invents them. Balance is thus established between components that often seem in conflict: on one side, the past and the collectivity; on the other side, the present and individuality. Describing the *cholo* singers of Namora, Arguedas explains, "They sing in Spanish, almost always improvising the lyrics, and all of them play guitar. They are *cholos*; the only thing that is still Indian about them is their music and its meaning."[26]

The privileged position of song in transculturation is thus obvious: it saves the traditional (Indian) past and permits the creative (cholo) freedom of the present.

It is within this orchestra that the words circulate, and if they are not sung in the book, then they are spoken, intoned, perceived as sounds, and rarely seen as written. Orality, so much a part of the greater Spanish American poetic tradition, surrounds *Deep Rivers*, albeit without the playful homophony that Miguel Ángel Asturias used to the same ends in another cultural area of the Americas. Such spoken words can be found in both the dialogues and monologues that occupy nearly half the text and in the narrative that covers the other half.

Interestingly, these dialogues and monologues, with their correct yet flexible syntax, almost always bear clear messages. They are patently utilized for intellectual communication, and they can even slip into discursive grandiloquence, as in the curious wisdom that occasionally possesses the protagonist. This is a legacy of nineteenth-century European realism and its tenacious practice of rationalization, but if we can avoid falling into the trap of our exclusivist cultural perspective, we should also perceive here a legacy of the precise, terse, and parsimonious handling of language that is characteristic of communities without writing. Nevertheless, writing alone does not contain the full meaning of these dialogues and monologues; their meaning also depends on the intonation with which they are uttered, and sometimes they can only be understood when they are heard in context. Young Ernesto soon discovers that signifiers are sensitive registers of sentiments beyond their univocal meanings and that terms can become so tinged with passions that they mean different things depending on how one's voice imparts the sounds. This is how he discovers Padre Linares's duplicity—comparing the way he speaks Quechua with the *colonos*, in order to subjugate them, and the way he speaks Spanish to the authorities and to his students, with the aim of developing their destinies as the dominant ones (122). This is how he is able to perceive the differences in the adults' verbal behavior, observing how hatred inflames their words. "I was aware of the inflections people used when they spoke; I understood them very well. I had been brought up among people who hated one another and hated me; they could not always brandish clubs, or strike with their hands, or set dogs on their enemies. They also used words, injuring one another with these, imbuing their tone of voice, rather than their words, with their mild or virulent poisons" (199).

Arguedas paid the same attention to the music of these voices in the novel that he did to musical instruments, for he saw voices as instruments of meaning:

> The priest spoke in Quechua, in his high reedy voice. (112)
> His throat swelled as he pronounced the words gravely and
>   solemnly. (203)
> Those who sat up with the dead sang hymns in a falsetto. . . . (206)
> He spoke with a coastal accent, pronouncing the words with
>   incredible rapidity. But there was a lilt [*cantaba algo*] to his
>   speech. (183)
> She was speaking Quechua. The soft *c*'s of the sweet Quechua of
>   Abancay now seemed to have been chosen especially as notes
>   of contrast to make the guttural sounds that carried to all the
>   walls of the square harsher. (91)

The multitude of songs, music, sounds, and human voices that make up this orchestra is subsumed within another voice that spreads throughout the greater part of the novel: that of the narrator, who is speaking, rather than writing, the story. Despite the logical precision of his storytelling, it is articulated at a hectic pace with an uncommon alacrity and variability that imparts constant motion to it. The process is similar to what Rulfo did by reintroducing all of the voices in his novel *Pedro Páramo* in the voice of the narrator/son, though Rulfo gave his narrator a markedly rural form of speech, whereas Arguedas developed a speech form for his own narrator that was more educated but at the same time more Indian. From the sentence "We entered Cuzco by night" (4) in the first chapter, the principal (but not the only) narrator offers his reminiscing voice to gather up the dispersed voices that follow, one after another, interweaving. This literary solution is more fitting and more unifying than those Arguedas found for *Agua* or *Yawar Fiesta*.

To sum up, the words of *Deep Rivers* appear to exist on superimposed strata: an explanatory, rationalized Spanish prose on the lower level; songs in Quechua on the upper level. Between the two levels, there is a varied array of intermediate cases: realist narrative, nimble dialogues, effusively lyrical prose, and so on. Throughout the book, there are rising and falling movements that run the gamut of verbal and musical strata, responding to an uplifting impulse that ceaselessly propels the material up to the levels of lyrical prose or directly into song, passing from Spanish into Quechua. The episode of the letter in chapter 6 models these movements; it opens on a level dominated by conventional, dead writing—mere words on paper. It continues to a second level, still one of writing, but in an urgent rhythm, communicating its emotionality. It then moves to the living speech of a monologue, spoken out loud, before it finally jumps to the highest level, in which the insufficiencies of the prior verbal styles are made up for with song: "Writing! Writing for them was useless, futile. 'Go; wait for them on the roads and sing!'" (74). Hardly has this been said than the text bursts into Quechua, with an exhortation to the young woman to listen and not read: "*Uyariy chay k'atik'niki siwar k'entita* . . . Listen to the emerald hummingbird who follows you; he shall speak to you of me; do not be cruel, hear him'" (74–75).

The swelling orchestral movement one hears over and over again in the novel is resolved at the highest level by transforming sound into song, in which all the voices join in unison. What this culmination meant for Arguedas was stated in his description of funeral hymns: "The women keep on shouting. The voice of the chorus crosses the heavens, vibrates in the earth, like the greatest effort the human voice can put forth to reach the limits of the unknown world; the song makes its intention felt in all its power."[27] Indeed, only such a chorale is capable of perfectly harmonizing the world in its entirety and even transcending it, making contact with the beyond—from which, however, Arguedas was cut off by his fundamental agnosticism. Nostalgia for universal order, which society's injustice and confusion have only encouraged to the point of hysteria, finds expression in this chorale.

Music, especially in the form of songs (sung by the characters mentioned), thus fulfills a central ideological function, which could send us back to an unanticipated Neoplatonism. Music appears as the model of a higher order (though natural rather than divine) that establishes agreement and balance among a massing crowd of factors, due to the fact that they can all partake of the same rhythmic and melodic structure. It reestablishes unity within diversity. It is the model for the natural beauty that Arguedas revived. Arguedas demonstrated its ability to integrate diverse forces in his analysis of the title of Andrés Alencastre's book of Quechua poems, *Taki Parwa*:

> The title captivates a reader with indigenous sensibilities. *Parwa* is the proper name for the maize flower, the mottled white-grey plume that tops the plant. The adoration that Indians, and other men of the highlands, feel for this bland, lusterless flower is based not only on the particular beauty of *parwas* dancing so lightly and

musically on the hilltops, their music harmonized by nature with the rustling of the leaves; their adoration for the flower is part of their adoration for the ancient grain itself, the age-old grain that has nourished the man of the Americas since his origins. We know what *taki* means: singing and dance. The phrase *taki parwa* is almost untranslatable. It can be explained, as I have attempted to do, but an exact and faithful translation is not possible. It does not mean a song to maize, but rather a song that is like the maize flower; but "maize flower" is the poorest possible translation of *parwa*. *Parwa* is the only proper name for the flower in Quechua, and it is fraught with musical and religious meaning.[28]

The Poor People's Opera

In view of all the elements that are in play and the particular uses to which they are put, I have proposed that rather than reading *Deep Rivers* as a novel arising from the regionalist and indigenista tradition (while obviously rising above it), we should read it as a very special type of operatic score, for it can evoke both the forms of traditional Beijing opera and the Florentine Renaissance origins of Western opera, when it first emerged as a modern transcription of classical Greek tragedy.[29]

The importance of musical elements in the novel and their power as signifiers are not typical of the novel genre, according to the Western canon that has taken shape since the eighteenth century as part of the headlong prosification of literary genres that has characterized the aesthetics of the bourgeois age. The dominant trend in bourgeois society was to abandon poetry in favor of prose, abandon the lyrical world in favor of realist and psychological worlds, and replace orality with writing; during its period of ascent, bourgeois society did away with magical/religious concepts and replaced them with analytical/rational ones, and, extracting narrativity from popular and collective folklore, it placed narrative in the service of the individual at the heart of society.

Interestingly, Arguedas's inventive prose took off from the ultimate realist, rationalist model of the novel — the critical social novel — during the period when the rising lower sectors were taking it by siege. The great narrative tool of the bourgeoisie was taken over by antiestablishment groups, which introduced such indispensable modifications as adopting collective parameters and turning the main characters into representative types of their social classes — traits that remained important in Arguedas's works. He began an unconscious rebellion against the model—one with points in common with interwar avant-garde literature, though Arguedas never read those works and, indeed, worked in the enclosed precinct of Peru's internal working-class cultures, so he never really followed the avant-garde trajectory. The middle sectors inherited the realist model, and they lent it a peculiar and delightful gruffness; Arguedas returned the social novel to the hazy origins of the genre, moving backwards to recover its popular forms. This backward movement, too, could be called a revolution, in the etymological sense of the term, which implies that any inventive advance into the future must rely on a return to primordial sources. It apparently arose from the ambivalence peculiar to the author's cultural situation: standing in a courtyard of the university in Lima, Arguedas read, fascinated, the novel *Tungsteno* by César Vallejo, a writer he called his teacher to the end of his days and whose political beliefs he shared; at the same time, he was enthralled by a traditional rural society that had conserved ancient, pre-bourgeois forms. *Deep Rivers* is located at the intersection between the social novel and the folk opera, and it is this unique hybrid character that constitutes its originality.

Earlier critics have perceptively analyzed the elements in *Deep Rivers*, both literary and ideological, that derive from the social novel. What must be added are the elements derived from this unconscious operatic source, from the mother lode of folk culture in which half of the author was immersed, whereas his other half accepted (while inverting its polarity), a form that arose from bourgeois rationality and that was shared by the intellectual cadres of the middle and lower classes who were trying to seize power.

Alternating between Individual Characters and Choruses

From their origins in agricultural rituals, Greek tragedy and modern opera have conserved the balance between individuals and the chorus, putting forth progressively plural individuals and plural group choruses, among whom the dramatic conflict became more complex and richer. We find the same alternation in Arguedas's novel, whose most striking feature is the scale and the skill with which it incorporates choral groups (the *chicheras*, women who sell *chicha*, Andean corn beer; the colonos, Indians who work under serflike conditions on the haciendas; and the soldiers), given their flagrant absence in the best Latin American novels of that era, which focused exclusively on individual conflicts. Vargas Llosa's reproach—to the effect that Arguedas had made an innovation in

Peruvian literature by introducing "a world where individuals are eliminated and replaced as characters by human groups"[30]—does not apply to *Deep Rivers* or, for that matter, to *Todas las sangres*. The individuality of the students in the school is captured by a subtle use of composition; the same is even true of quickly sketched episodic characters (the priest, the school rector, the black priest), though Arguedas was careful to join the specific, personal traits of their individuality to their qualities as representatives of finely distinguished social groups. In addition to this range of characters, Arguedas deployed enormous chorus groups, brilliantly handled, which act on their own. There are three basic groups: the chicheras, led by their coryphaeus, Doña Felipa; the colonos; and the *huayruros* [soldiers], with their military band. Each of these groups is treated differently: the colonos collectively, with a single, homogeneous outline; the chicheras in unison but with differentiating nuances; the soldiers in greater detail and more individually, emphasizing their martial hierarchies and the resulting social strata. However, they all fall under the rule that covers operatic choruses: they are grouped together, bedecked in fantastic vestments, where imaginative, surprising, even unreal tones can be freely struck. This vibrant, coloristic presentation imparts a distorted, almost expressionistic dimension to them within the narrative. The narrator first perceives this dimension when he discovers that the soldiers are "wearing costumes," and that the clothes they wear make them even more terrifying than the *danzak'* (193). The distortion takes on a phantasmagoric, sepulchral tone in the "epode" of the novel, which is left to the colonos, walking through darkness to hear the midnight mass before they die of the plague, improvising demonic verses to the "dismal tune used for funerals" (232). The chorus of chicheras receives the same treatment but with a note of jubilation: their brightly dyed dresses are described in detail; we hear them repeating their leader's orders in unison; and they undertake a march through town to the beat of "a carnival *danza*," at which, Ernesto notes, "the troop was transformed into a *comparsa*" (96). Each of these choruses is accompanied by rowdy music, whether sung a cappella or reinforced by a fascinating brass band, as in the case of the soldiers.

Although the choruses become more important in the second half of the novel—chapters 7 to 11 (five chapters that are much longer than the first six)—this does not detract from the individual characters, whose personal dramatic crises reach their culmination in the same chapters. Arguedas alternates between the individuals and the choruses, bringing them together through Ernesto and drawing contrasts among them through almost all of the other individual characters in such a way that the protagonist carries out a mediating function in the construction of the various episodes, whereas the other characters have oppositional functions to different degrees.

Consecutive Scene Sequences

Arguedas's narrative composition style evokes not only the distinctive lineal, consecutive order of tragedy and opera but also the early form of scene sequencing in film before D. W. Griffith's revolutionary innovations. The chapter divisions after the protagonist's arrival in Abancay are purely decorative, for they cloak a different organization—an organization of the novel into scenes marked off by blank spaces. Beginning with chapter 6 ("Zumbayllu"), temporal continuity links each chapter to the next through a series of chronologically ordered scenes, most of which begin by imparting information about the date or time of the events that will be described. In chapter 6, following Arguedas's theoretical introduction about the Quechua suffixes *yllu* and *illa*, we find this sequence:

1. "In the month of May, Antero brought the first *zumbayllu* . . ." (67)
2. "'Hey, Ernesto, they tell me you write like a poet. I'd like you to write a letter for me,' said Markask'a, a few days after the debut of the *zumbayllus*." (71)
3. "Next morning after school . . ." (72)
4. "The little bell that was rung for a long while to tell us it was time to go to the dining hall . . ." (75)
5. "At eight-thirty they rang the little bell which announced the hour to go to the dormitory." (81)
6. "The next day I got up quite early." (86)

Immediately after this, chapter 7 ("The Insurrection") links up with the previous scene and continues the system:

1. "That morning, during recess . . ." (88)
2. "At twelve o'clock, when the day-pupils went out into the street . . ." (89)
3. "Late in the day, as the sun was setting . . ." (99)

The novel is thus constructed in fragments that acquire their relative autonomy by three means: first, because they take place at a specific time, rigidly located on a timeline in such a way that one fragment follows another with scarcely any lapse of time between them; second, because all the fragments relate exclusively to what can be known, seen, or heard by a single protagonist who has little mobility (and who, even when evoking some event in the past, does so from a particular circumstance in the present that the narrator emphasizes); and third, because most of these fragments are scenes in the theatrical sense of the word—that is, they are set in a single physical space where a given number of characters have gathered and to whom something will happen. Only rarely does the narrator follow the protagonist Ernesto as he shifts freely from one place to a different one (such is the case with chapter 10, "Yawar Mayu"). What we usually get is a stage—the chichería, a schoolyard, the dormitory, the plaza of Abancay—where an episode develops in relative autonomy.

The detailed, lineal chronological sequencing; the succession of scenes in fixed settings; the scope of vision reduced to that of a single character: these manifest a primitivism in narrative technique that becomes blatantly incapable of expressing the simultaneity of actions that occur at the same time. We are not even dealing with ironic guilelessness of a Lezama Lima's manipulation of nineteenth-century novel conventions ("Meanwhile, what was happening with . . . ?"); this is simply a strict, ascetic expository linearity, reminiscent of what almost every genre (from plays to fiction to film) went through in its first attempts to organize literary material. An elemental aura—as in the *laude* of Jacopone da Todi; as in the succession of scenes in ancient tragedy; as in popular opera— upholds narrative material in which psychological, sociological, lyrical, and realist perceptions are hectically stirred up and replaced, almost in contradiction to the simplicity of the sequencing.

Variety of Expressive Forms for Human Voices

An inalienable legacy of the modern opera form that sprang from an imitation of Greek tragedy is the variety of its oral registers, accompanied by simpler or more expansive musical arrangements. Between the aria (both individual and choral) and declaration (which could almost be mistaken for a simple reading aloud of the text), we now had a third, intermediate form: recitative, defined in the sixteenth century by one of its inventors, Girolamo Mei, as "un altro modo di cantare che l'ordinario" [a manner of singing different from the usual one]. Its function was to supply the need for a progressive mediation between dramatic declamation and full-blown song; in Greek tragedy, this need was filled by the introduction of double flutes to back up the actor's rhythmic diction, from which he could transition gradually into song without jumping into it brusquely from declamation. These three vocal strata overlapped, facilitating the voice's ascent into song; they were accepted as canonical by modern opera and in a more irregular form by the popular manifestations of opera, such as operetta and zarzuela, which gave preference to arias and the spoken word, to the detriment of recitative.

It is these popular manifestations that Arguedas's novel resembles: its general tessitura derives from the reading out loud of its characters' many voices, which are all incorporated into the voice of Alberto, who narrates and describes; at special moments, song breaks out, whether as individual expressions (arias) or as chorales. Despite this tendency, the use of recitative is also notable: in some of Ernesto's wistful monologues, in his lyrical effusions at perceiving the spectacle of nature, in the magical exorcisms through which he endeavors to communicate at a distance, in his imprecations against the enemies of the Indians, and in his fiery discourse when possessed by passion or fervor.

The vocal strata of opera thus have their literary equivalents in the distinct forms used in the novel. On the lowest level, corresponding to speech, we have a realist narrative that can cover the varied expository connections of the plot and the characters' interchanges in dialogue form. On the middle level — the equivalent of the rhythmic modes of recitative and its relative freedom from the practices of regular spoken language — we find a poetic narration that consists of prose electrified with similes and metaphors, applied mainly to the lyrical description of subjectivity or of the impeccable beauty of the universe. On the highest level — that of song — music bursts forth, and voices with it, in both monody and polyphony. The novel's essay sections occupy a specific space; their informative function places them on the lowest level, but they frequently join the middle level due to the poetic burden they sometimes carry.

These three operatic modes course through a novel of clear social import, establishing a counterpoint in which we can begin to perceive the work's ideological focus, which is what we seek to reveal through this analysis of artistic form.

Musical structures are closely related to poetic rather than narrative structures; Jakobson's arguments about matrices of meter are therefore relevant. With vocal music, we simultaneously perform two readings or, more precisely, two listenings: of the linguistic signs that transmit well-codified meanings and of the melodies or rhythms that do not, in themselves, bear such precise dictionary definitions. These two orders of communication are coordinated, but they do not repeat each other, and it could even be said that they act on different, non-overlapping zones. The linguistic sequence (in fiction or theater) works on the principle of succession; the melodic sequence works on the principle of repetition.

Let us examine this in two aspects of opera, as examples of a more generalized behavior: overture and aria. An operatic overture will often use musical themes that come up later in the work, expressing the themes without lyrics (the linguistic sequence of words with which they will reappear) so that when we meet them again in the arias we will have an exclusively musical memory of them, to which we will then add entirely new verbal meanings. Moreover, these themes might reappear at several points in the opera, applied to a variety of linguistic messages, thus generating musical associations that inevitably lead to or impose other verbal associations.

The opening chapters of both *Deep Rivers* and *Todas las sangres* clearly function as musical overtures. Scarcely connected to later plot developments, they are independent and extraordinarily vivid kernels that present to us, in concentrated form, the set of profound themes that will reappear periodically in the text and fuel the narrative episodes, for they form the deep links among somewhat disconnected events that are organized by melodic repetition. These kernels tell us everything in a concentrated, highly poetic way: these are the deep themes, the veritable deep rivers that will irrigate the comings and goings of human lives. Strictly speaking, the novel, as story, begins with the traditional narrative ventriloquism of chapter 2; there, the narrator tells us who the father was, what kind of relationship he had with his son, how he wandered around the highlands, and how he felt obliged to enroll his son as a boarding student at a school in Abancay, which will become the setting for the rest of the novel. As a musical structure, *Deep Rivers* calls for a sumptuous chapter 1, with an entrance into Cuzco, a recollection of its Indian origins, the stone wall of Inca Roca (that river of stone), the tolling bells of the María Angola echoing eternally throughout the valley, and the oppressive social stratification (from the Old Man to the *pongo*) that translates into the spatial distribution of people through the system of multiple, intercommunicating courtyards, which we will find again at the Abancay school.

As for arias, we have already pointed out that the virtue of traditional melody is its ability to simultaneously link us with the past and update it by changing the melody's verbal contents. Every era has used this double process, conserving an almost mythical identity and reintroducing history into it, yielding novelty and invention. Every man in my generation knows a repertoire of Spanish folk melodies dating back to the fifteenth and sixteenth centuries. We used to sing those songs with newer topical lyrics referring to the Spanish Civil War of 1936–39. Arguedas did much the same: recall that he contributed enormously to the expansion of folkloric music through modern adaptations that enriched the middlebrow music of Peru. In chapter 10 of *Deep Rivers* ("Yawar Mayu"), a provocative mestiza woman turns a traditional Christmas *jaylli* song into an insult aimed at the soldiers who had gathered in the chichería; they hesitate to respond, disconcerted by her alteration of traditional elements. The phrase with which the novel announces this song is highly significant: "By now the girl was improvising new words to the song; like the dancer and the musician, she was equally launched forth into the unknown" (177). Exactly: launched forth into the unknown, inventing the history of the present, incorporating herself as an actor in history in her own circumstances, but within a musical structure that conserves the past, that even recovers myth.

This is the double reading that resolved the conflict of transculturation for Arguedas; the double reading that explains the headstrong rejoicing he expressed in his famous acceptance speech for the Inca Garcilaso Prize. He was quite familiar with the mestizo character of Peruvian culture, and he also knew his own role as an agent of transculturation, so the whole problem consisted in finding forms that the ongoing transculturating process of becoming mestizo could adopt that would not destroy the roots of rural communities or provoke anomie in them but that would also not dry up their creative sources and prevent their full incorporation into history.

As for literary form, the equivalent of this double reading is the extraordinarily original structure of *Deep Rivers*. Arguedas established multiple readings of the text through his use of varied levels, which sometimes split only to suddenly converge. These levels correspond to the musical, poetic, and realist strata through which the action zigzags, but they also correspond to a double and antithetical formulation: the mythic and the historical. Arguedas had not read Godelier's lucid arguments,[31] but he knew enough about myths to steer clear of the traps that have beset Latin American writers from Miguel Ángel Asturias to Carlos Fuentes. He was familiar with the virtues but also with the traps of myth, and he was always a man of his time, of his history, with a spotless social democratic consciousness. Myth appears in *Deep Rivers* on the levels of recitative and song, and history does so on the lower levels of declamation and narrative, but the lower levels can suddenly join the higher levels without distorting the values of either. It is a rare feat in the history of literature.

If it is not a so-called beggar's opera, like John Gay's eighteenth-century production, it is at the least a poor people's opera, like the interwar efforts of Kurt Weill and George Gershwin, because it is constructed from the humble materials that make up popular culture. At times, one might say it is constructed from the ruins of great cultures, both Incan and Spanish, conserved and elaborated through the bricolage that rural communities undertake with the crumbs that fall from the banquet table of the rich. All of the action takes place in poverty, rubbish, rags, Indian kitchens, muddy paths, dirt-floor chicherías, school latrines, wastelands, and tumbledown dining halls. There is no hint of higher education, not even among the teachers in Abancay; no presence of the greater cultures, of which these teachers are the last forsaken heirs; and no more than the provincial caricature, in one character (Valle), of an effort to appropriate those cultures mimetically.

The orchestras that play here are Indian bands (harp, violin, charango), military regiment bands, or simply a harmonica played solo—or even less than that: the sound of a spinning top. The songs are hymns, harawis, huaynos, or carnival music. The environmental features are those of the region: rural birds, flowers, animals—hardly the top priorities of art and literature. There are not even any literary devices beyond those found in the provincial stylings of the 1920s.

Nevertheless, there is an unequaled energy and beauty that sets all of this poverty in motion. This is a violent world, in constant struggle, whose dynamics never abate, impressing its rhapsodic rhythm on the narrative. The tension and energy of the text, as Ariel Dorfman has observed,[32] is the precise equivalent of the tumultuous world that it expresses. Indeed, that tension and energy are what create it and take it beyond the level of history and its various dramatic crises. Two great virtues complement this energy: precision and transparency. The acuity of the gaze and the speed with which the elements of the composition are arranged go hand-in-hand with the precision with which they are cut and distributed. Everything becomes lucid, rapid, clear, and sharp.

None of the work's parsimonious components have been masked by cosmetics; on the contrary, the hopelessness and horror have been highlighted. They are all accepted in their naked corporeality and set to serve a rhythm and a melody. This silent acceptance of material that lacks all prestige, yet has great strength, is precisely what gives the works its spiritual splendor. It gives rise to a sumptuous artistic invention, making this poor people's opera a magnificent jewel.

CHAPTER SEVEN

The Crisscrossing Rivers
of Myth and History

Narrators in Counterpoint

We argued in chapter 6 that *Deep Rivers* is thoroughly operatic, suffused with the sensibilities of folk and popular opera, but we should not lose sight of the obvious: such operas basically belong to the narrative genre. The novel is, therefore, a narrative opera, which brings us back to its narrators and their function.

The author uses two narrators, who, like a pair of interpreters sitting on either side of the imaginary stage where the action transpires, make it their business to tell us what is happening. Two narrators—not one, as critics have repeatedly asserted, confused by the seeming homogeneity of the narrators' locutionary function. Indeed, the two narrators are easily confused because their profiles are not explicitly defined, their entrances and exits are not announced by any metalinguistic references, and their special autonomy can only be detected by modulations in the handling of language and the narrative point of view.

The first is the main narrator, an adult man recalling his childhood at a distance of three decades or more. As in the classic model established by the *Divine Comedy*, we must distinguish between this principal narrator and the child Ernesto, the protagonist of the events in the novel: the latter is at center stage and is simply a character (playing the obvious role of protagonist) to whom things happen that are completely beyond his powers of foresight and control, not only because the future is obscure and unforeseeable for all human beings but also because his youth and lack of power make him an excellent witness—but not a mover—of

events. The principal narrator, presumably Ernesto as an adult, is someone who remembers, reclaiming from the past a series of actions whose
sequence and consequences he must naturally know, given the place he
occupies on the timeline. He describes the dramatic crisis from outside
the developing actions, and from a perspective that, though privileging
the character Ernesto's point of view, is always free to adopt other characters' viewpoints as well. It seems that we should be allowed to perceive
the basis for those viewpoints; the principal narrator does this by employing a non-explicit sociological frame, according to which the characters' independent actions are situated in class or cultural coordinates.

This principal narrator uses the prototypical verb form for narrative: the simple past tense. He sometimes slips into the past progressive;
in the vast majority of cases, however, he sticks with the simple past,
which guarantees him the greatest possible distance from the events he
remembers, for that tense conveys the fact that the events in question
are definitively concluded. Whether he uses the simple past or the past
progressive, though, he is working from the "retrospective point" (to
use William Bull's classification system[1]), with a preference for the zero
vector, the "retro-perfect" of the simple preterit. This tense dominates
the narrated actions and encircles the dialogues in which events recover
their historical present through stage directions—in the first case, using
mainly the conventional third person, and, in the case of dialogue, using
both the third and the first person (he said, he told me, I told him).

Before him, however, there is another narrator who can be distinguished by his academic tone and his wider culture, which encompasses
everything the principal narrator knows but extends beyond it due to
his systematic understanding of the realities of Peru. This narrator fulfills a more restricted function, for he does not participate as often in
the storytelling; instead, his function is cognitive, for he gives readers
the general information they need in order to round out their understanding of the events of the novel. The principal narrator is Ernesto's
double, distanced and enriched by the passage of time, a fact that restricts
the story's scope; the second narrator, on the other hand, has access to
much broader intellectual resources and takes on the task of educating
the reader. As we have said, his presence is never announced; he appears
abruptly in the novel, almost snatching the words right out of the principal narrator's mouth whenever there are facts that he finds indispensable
and unknown to the readers or listeners of the tale. This means that the
second narrator's contributions presuppose those readers and listeners,

whereas the principal narrator simply constructs an autonomous world without addressing his tale to anyone in particular.

The arrival of this second narrator, whose contributions mark him as an expert ethnologist, is signaled on the linguistic level by a change in the tessitura of verb tenses.[2] In contrast to the principal narrator, he prefers to use the present tense so he can be assigned to a different tense orientation: the "point present." Although both narrators unavoidably depart from the "me, here, and now" and both "speak" rather than "write" their contributions, there are some basic distinctions between them. First, the principal narrator sticks to a single point in the past in order to recount something that happened at that point, which has been annihilated by the subsequent passage of time; the second narrator, on the other hand, concentrates on an aspect of reality that is much less determined by the vicissitudes of time—one that can therefore be perceived as a constant and thus be rediscovered, without any perceptible differences, in the present. Second, the principal narrator does not necessarily presuppose a reader, as we have observed, taking advantage of the seeming neutrality of the third person simple past tense; whereas the second narrator, given the didactic quality of his contributions, exerts an informative pressure that implies the existence of a concrete reader to whom the message is addressed. Third, they each use radically different prose styles: the principal narrator's style is narrative; the second narrator's is highly discursive, as if drawn from a classroom lecture—so much so that eliminating his contributions altogether would not affect the storyline in the slightest, though it would impinge on our deeper understanding of many terms and situations.

The author has shuffled the two narrators' voices in various ways. On some occasions, he has neatly separated them by leaving a blank space between them, just as he did between the different scenes of the novel. In chapter 2 ("The Journey"), the second fragment belongs to the second narrator, whom we should perhaps call the ethnologist. He proceeds to explain, with complete independence from the action of the novel, the behavior of birds in highland villages, putting all his verbs in the present tense: "In the small towns, at certain hours, the birds *can be seen* flying toward accustomed places. To the stony fields, to the orchards, to the shrubs that *grow* on the shores of the ponds. Their flights *vary* with the time of day."[3] In chapter 4, ("The Hacienda") and chapter 6 ("Zumbay-llu"), the second narrator gets the introductory fragment: "The small-town landowners *contribute* huge earthenware jars of chicha and big pans

of peppery food for the community work projects. When there *are* fiestas they *dance* and *sing* huaynos together in the streets and squares. Ordi-
narily they *go around* wearing . . ." (38). As for the much-cited text on
the *zumbayllu* with which chapter 6 opens, it had actually been published
separately as an ethnological article ten years before it became part of the
novel.[4]

On other occasions, the Ethnologist abruptly jumps in with a parenthetical comment, after which the action is rejoined as if there had been
no interruption, though these abrupt insertions often give us the information we need to properly evaluate what is happening. Two examples:

[Primary Narrator] The sun was heating up the courtyard. From the
shadow of the archway and the porch we looked out onto the
blazing paving stones.
[Second Narrator] The sun instills silence when it shines into the
depths of these rocky, bushy ravines at midday. There are no large
trees.
[PN] Several bumblebees crossed the porch, from one end to the other.
The slow flight of these insects . . . caught my eye. (141–42)

[PN] The *calandrias* were singing in the mulberry bushes as if they had
been trained.
[SN] Usually they perch on the highest branches.
[PN] They were also singing and swinging in the tops of the few
weeping willows that grew among the mulberries.
[SN] The native word for the calandria is *tuya*. A flashy, strong-beaked
bird, it flies to the highest part of the trees. In the tops of the
darkest ones . . . [and so forth].
[PN] As I listened to its song, which is surely the stuff of which I am
made, that nebulous region from which I was torn to be cast in
among men, we saw the two girls appear in the poplar grove.
(149)

Linguistically, the distribution of the novel's material between the two
narrators corresponds to the two systems of time defined by Émile Benveniste,[5] which he has called "history" and "discourse," assigning the
simple past tense, progressive past, conditional, past perfect, and pro-
spective aspect to history and the present, future, and *passé composé* to discourse, though the latter also uses the imperfect and past perfect. With
some variations, this is the same division of tenses into two groups that

Harald Weinrich proposed,[6] arguing that the present, passé composé, and future tenses correspond to the "commented world," whereas the simple past, progressive past, and past perfect correspond to the "narrated world." This distribution of tenses provides a basis for two different modes of linguistic communication, defined very appropriately by Benveniste's formula as history and discourse, but it does not necessarily mean that whenever a single text switches from one type to the other we should recognize a shift in narrators. There are, indeed, two different linguistic registers on a first, objective reading. Given the author's occasional use of blank spaces to demarcate the discursive texts, we can deduce that he was aware of the different natures of history and discourse and the different functions they played in his novel. We might add that the appearance of discourse, almost always marked by the use of the present tense, often brings in its wake a modification in the verb forms used by history. History tends to use the simple past, both in narrative passages and in the phrases that introduce dialogue, but in the immediate vicinity of discourse it tends instead toward the progressive past, thus generating a kind of gradation—I saw, I was seeing, I see—that does not derive from rules of tense agreement but rather from progressive slippages between the prototypical literary forms of history and discourse.

On a second reading, we believe that the two linguistic systems referred to here do fit the novel's two parallel narrative situations, allowing us to bring back the concept of two alternating narrators but with an awareness that the author is not rigorously separating them but handling them with more spontaneity than calculation, at times letting the borders between them blur. Since the protagonist of the novel is a boy named Ernesto, and not José María, the principal narrator must of course be an Ernesto who has reached adulthood and is recalling some episodes from his past. José María Arguedas, like any other novelist, lent this character some of his own perceptions and used a lot of autobiographical material to construct his history, but these devices hardly contradict the fact that he obviously avoided autobiography and strove to create an autonomous character whom he named (and I have always wondered why) Ernesto. The fictive independence of the character Ernesto from the author has its repercussions on the adult narrator, on the subject of whose circumstances, life, habits, and education Arguedas is utterly silent. He never tells us anything at all about the adult Ernesto who narrates the story; the silence, the void within which the adult Ernesto is presented, means that he is, simply and austerely, the Narrator, a fictitious, undelineated character invented by Arguedas to carry out the function of telling the story. He is distanced in time from the protagonist, and at the same time he is, still, all of a piece with him. He is simply Ernesto as an adult, and even his one defining function—his ability to tell a story—is foreshadowed in the child, who is begged by his schoolmates to write little love letters and considered a bit of a poet.

Nothing in the negligible bit we learn about the adult Ernesto could justify the assumption that he was responsible for the discourses, nor can any explicit references in the text confirm such a supposition. The contributions of the second narrator do not appear subject to the same obligations of narrative fiction nor to the same obligatory continuity that we find between Ernesto the Protagonist and Ernesto the Narrator. They generally assume a neutral, impersonal tone that contrasts strongly with the personal focus of the principal narrator. As objective sources of information, they discourse on the ethnological reality of Peru, at times with subtle hints of poetry. They resemble the contributions of a professor or essayist, someone who is quite familiar with all the material in the narrative but also capable of making interpretations, generalizations, and articulations that seem beyond the principal narrator's scope. On some occasions, this narrator casually cites essays that were in fact written by José María Arguedas, or he paraphrases results of ethnological research that Arguedas published in specialized journals. Interestingly, it is the second narrator who is most recognizably similar to José María Arguedas. Despite the objectivity of his explanatory discourses, he sometimes makes personal references, as in chapter 6, and then establishes the point he has in common with the principal narrator:

[PN] I *began* to feel more cheerful, to get up my courage, by *commending* myself to the great mountain, just as the Indians of my village *used to put* themselves under its protection before rushing into the plaza to fight the brave bulls which had condors bound to their backs.[7]

[SN] K'arwarasu *is* the Apu, the regional god of my native village. Around it there *are* many lakes, where pink-plumed cranes *live*. The kestrel *is* the symbol of K'arwarasu. The Indians *say* that during Lent he *emerges* from the highest peak in the guise of a firebird and *pursues* the condors, breaking their necks, making them whimper and humiliating them. Flashing like lightning, he *flies* over the planted fields, across the cattle ranches, and then *sinks* down into the snow. The Indians *invoke* K'arwarasu only in

times of great danger. They *have* only to pronounce his name, and
the fear of death *vanishes.*

[PN] As I *left* the chapel I *was* unable to control my feelings any longer.
As soon as the Father Director and the other priests *had gone up*
to the second floor, I went over to Rondinel and *nudged* him with
the toe of my shoe, by way of warning. (80)

The linguistic and literary independence of the two narrators converges
on one unifying point: "my village," where, if they are not a single person, they are at least cousins.

The significance I find in Arguedas's use of these two narrators parallels the significance I noted in his use of song in the novel. Songs consist of melodies, which conserve tradition with their air of eternity, and
lyrics, which can relate the circumstances of the moment when they are
created. Both narrative and song seem able to unite two currents that can
be analytically divided. They are devices that join separate, even antithetical, modes: the historical component—that is, the unique, original
happenstance that creative freedom brings about but which, by the same
token, can never be repeated in the same way once it ends; and the mythical component, as Mircea Eliade understood it—the remote past, situated in the realm of origins, constantly reenacted without ever producing any notable modifications, a cultural substitute for eternity.

These modes, history and myth, correspond at the level of narrators
to the modes of history and discourse, as employed by the adult Ernesto
and José María Arguedas, respectively. Ernesto recounts a series of episodes that occur just once, in the precise tense of the simple past, and will
never be repeated; Arguedas prefers to discourse on birds, mountains,
the meanings of Quechua words, popular music, and religious celebrations—all the fixed elements to which he devoted many anthropological
articles—delightfully recording their permanence rather than change.
These are their contrasting aims, which call for their use of the specific
tenses that identify them: history, the narrated world, corresponds to the
past tenses; myth, which is fundamentally a contemplated world, corresponds to the eternal present (as well as the passé composé and the
future) that shores up its unwavering longevity.

Both narrators deal with specific fields in the novel; one narrates
everything that cannot be resolved more directly through dialogue and
song, whereas the other explains everything he considers necessary for
the reader to understand the story that his companion tells. The translations of most of the Quechua language texts can also be attributed to the

latter narrator. Nevertheless, neither enters into the action proper, which remains entirely autonomous. The field of action belongs to the character of Ernesto, the child, alone.

The Shadow Line

"I was fourteen years old," he says (103). No longer a child, he is now an adolescent. More precisely, he is entering puberty, situated on a border as keen as a knife blade, one that has often been compared to a second birth. This is the moment of metamorphosis, when, according to his school's classification system, a minor comes of age; it is a metamorphosis that takes place through the exercise of sexuality. This is the moment when an adolescent qualifies as a man and enters the manly world. Ernesto has reached this point, and he is terrified, wavering uncertainly between a decisive step forward and a withdrawal to his old familiar world. He shares the rare wisdom found in the prepubescent girls of Juan Carlos Onetti's tales, though he lacks their peace and security, their confidence and firm sense of belonging. Quite the contrary: he lives in a state of vertigo, of despair, of horror. In the case of Arguedas, as in Onetti's, the Dostoyevskian lineage of this theme is obvious, though it had spread widely enough through the nineteenth-century European novel that we can find many other points of diffusion; *Le grand Meaulnes* (1913) was one of the most widely read.

The all-too-well-known autobiographical source of some episodes in *Deep Rivers* has distracted readers and critics from looking at how Arguedas used personal materials—as any novelist does—to serve a meaningful literary project. He was not stringing together specific, restricted events from one period of his life; he was organizing them so they would serve his narrative design and, by the same token, help establish its meaning.

Choosing a character from the borders, one who moves between two spheres and is aware of the violence of that transition, suggests a certain willfulness on the author's part and must arise from his unconscious notion (inherited from the regionalists and the ideological *indigenista* movement) that there is a link between individual and society, that an individual might function as a representative of a much larger group, and that an entire sociological panorama might be found in concentrated form in an individual. In this view, man and the world are not simple antitheses, as in the Romantic style; rather, they are communicating vessels. In the individual, we find social conflict reproduced on a rich existential level. Biography and sociography are dealt with in a balanced way, with the problems raised in the former being more widely developed in the latter. Given this sociological perspective, the successive framings of the novel can be seen as progressive enlargements of the scale model we are given in the protagonist. His internal tensions are reproduced and distributed among several other characters in the school, and those tensions are enlarged again and redistributed among the social groups (rather than mere characters) in the town of Abancay. Finally, as if through a hazy aura, we can foresee that the town of Abancay is itself a scale model of how Peruvian society functions as a whole. This view had been embedded in Arguedas's thoughts since *Yawar Fiesta*, and it reached its fullest expression in *Todas las sangres*. Within this process of adjusting his concept of the novel, *Deep Rivers* represents the midpoint, the balance point, where biography and sociography play equal roles.

The character of the borderlands, torn between two spheres, is society itself, maintaining a precarious balance and securing that balance through ruthless violence. On the individual level, the protagonist wavers between childhood and puberty; on the social level, an enormous portion of the population—basically the Indian *colonos* who work on the haciendas—are brutally kept in an infantilized state by the mestizos and *mistis* who occupy the dominant positions, as Ernesto observes: "In the towns where I used to live with my father the Indians aren't *erk'es* [young children]. Here it's as if they wouldn't let them grow up. They're always frightened, like little children" (146).

In some of his reportages and in the stories of *Amor mundo*, Arguedas told of his own conflictive dealings with sexuality, which critics have rightly viewed through the perspective of his obsolete conservative Catholic education;[8] critics have also recognized that in some of his stories ("El ayla"), he was able to offer a free and joyous vision of sex.[9] I think that the same vision can be traced, somewhat less explicitly, in *Deep Rivers*, in the distinct combinations in which sex and violence appear.

The border that Ernesto must traverse is that of sex, but this is no neutral entity, devoid of cultural connotations. For Ernesto, as for all of the students at his school, sex is violence and disdain, an uncontrollable force that arises from a despotically *machista* view of life and that resolves into a rigid dichotomy: on one side, the physical exercise symbolized by the students' couplings with "the idiot" (the "feeble-minded woman" who works in the school kitchen); on the other side, the spiritualized idealization represented by the polite young girls—Salvinia, Alcira, and Clorinda. On either side of the divide, sex is a matter of violent appropriation, of becoming the master, and thus is a translation into amorous relationships of the system of domination that governs society. Sex, violence, and property are one and the same thing, according to the cultural values of the social group to which Ernesto and most of the boarding students belong, though the behavior of each student varies for both individual and social reasons.

At the Abancay school, students are classified as either younger or older, creating two groups with distinct modes of behavior. The rector recognizes this division: "Besides, he's just a boy. You are almost young men" (198–99).[10] All students experience this division when they arrive at the borderline that gives them access to the adult sphere; this line is their relationships with women, whether sexual or emotional. The character nicknamed Wig offers "the idiot" to Ernesto: "And now I'd give her to you, really, for sure. It's time you learned to be a man" (186). Sexual initiation is the preferred way to guarantee one's status as an adult. Several characters (Lleras, Añuco, and Wig) already belong to this sphere when we first meet them; they are defined as "the bad guys" (145) because of the vile sexuality they use with "the idiot" as well as their constant, despotic brutality in their treatment of the younger students. Other students, represented by Valle, also belong to the adult sphere, but their emotional relations with the "good young girls" of Abancay do not necessarily imply sexual relations and therefore do not entail disdain for the younger students. Where Ernesto sees the former as "brutes," he sees the latter as phonies: "He gestured, moving his hands and fingers affectedly, putting them, and even his mouth, right up to the girls' faces. They must have felt his breath" (185).

There are also differences among the members of the boys' sphere, though these are not defined by their relations with women. Nevertheless, they all share a more or less self-confessed expectation of sexual experiences in the future. The Ernesto who pronounces fervent moral judgments is constantly tempted by his memory of seeing "the idiot" naked: "How I trembled on those evenings when she would fall to the ground, and heaven and earth were unable to swallow me up despite my supplications!" (189). His distant, mental relationship with her is stained with shadowy eroticism as well as with a desire to appropriate her—which he finally does, after her death, by turning her into a spiritualized figure like the polite young girls of Abancay.

Therefore, if the border that must be crossed to reach manhood is the presence of women, that new territory appears in two neatly dichotomized versions, which we might define as sexuality and sentimentality, working separately, not only according to the individual case but also according to the social strata to which the students belong, as seen in the difference between "the bad guys" and the "phonies." In this series of divisions and subdivisions, we see Arguedas's deft handling of the society's cultural values, but we also see, at the same time, his characteristic way of working with differences and contrasts, leading him to find illustrative examples.

In the novel, Ernesto never crosses this shadow line, but one of his spheremates does: the oldest of the young students, his friend Antero. Antero joins the older group and goes on to view his former friend as a "baby," becoming friends instead with the strong, frank, and healthy Gerardo. This transformation takes place simultaneously in two registers, sex and violence, thus linking them as forms of gaining access to manhood. Women come to be seen as prey to be hunted and progressively dominated: "Gerardo already had one over at the Mariño River. He made her cry, the bum. He sampled her" (196). The lower strata, the Indians, are viewed through the eyes of a master who has the power to repress them by force: "As for me, brother, if the Indians rebelled, I could go and kill them easy" (146). Both registers are closely linked to property, as Antero spells out when he justifies himself to Ernesto: "But the Indians must be kept down. You can't understand because you're not a landowner" (147). Thus, a boy assumes the triad of sex, violence, and property in all its fullness when he enters the adult sphere.

This is one cultural concept of sex; obviously, it is not the only one. Ernesto refuses to accept it, despite the desire that agitates him. He then falls into the other side of the dichotomy: the spiritualization of non-native models (blue-eyed blondes), which is simply the counterpart of sexual brutality—and which therefore contains brutality, the awful other side of its coin. He also falls into thinking in vertical terms derived from religion (Catholicism, in particular), seeing purity as lofty and materiality as base.

There is, however, another concept of sex and life, similar to the one Arguedas revealed in "El ayla," though it has never been made explicit enough with regard to this novel. We see it in *chicheras'* free relations with their customers, imbued with deep, delightful sensuality and relaxed good cheer. In the third scene of chapter 10 ("Yawar Mayu"), which revolves around Papacha Oblitas and is one of the happiest portraits of working-class life in the book, there is a profile of one of the young women who serve as waitresses when Doña Felipa is away from her bar. All of the evidence points to Ernesto's sensual excitation at the girl's physical attractiveness, with a few sudden shows of timidity on his part but no sensations of sin or disgust. "'Damn, you're a tough kid!' said the waitress. She had a dirty face; her high, round breasts showed jubilantly through her pink blouse. . . . Her handsome hips swayed rhythmically; her bare legs and feet looked youthful against the dusty ground" (169).

The harpist notices Ernesto's enthusiasm and gives it his ironic approval. Then the corporal says "something sensual and coarse" to the waitress, but it leads to a jovial scene in which "we all laughed" (169). The two divergent paths of sex and sentiment, which so plague the school-boys' entry to the adult sphere, are here intermingled, topped off with *chicha* and dance and, above all, established as a relationship between men and women in which there seems to be no domination or appropriation but rather free consent of both parties: the chicheras accept or reject the requests they get, and one picturesque fragment, a statement we can attribute to the second narrator, affirms this female independence, which has reduced more than one man to tears.

> Several mestizas served the public. They wore shawls of Castilian cloth trimmed with silk, whitened straw hats, and wide, bright-colored sashes. Indians and *cholos* stared at them with equal inso-lence. The *chicha* bars often owed their popularity to the beauty of the mestiza waitresses, and their gaiety and availability. But I knew that the struggle for them was long and arduous; it was not easy to get to dance with them. The women who ran the bars watched them and taught them with the help of their long experience in trickery. And many men from other towns broke down and wept on their way home through the mountain passes because they had wasted their time night after night, drinking *chicha* and singing until dawn. (44–45)

This alternative approach would have made a more noteworthy solution, but there is no doubt that the adult world is defined in this novel in the same way as in Onetti's novels: it is a form of degradation, which can be summed up in a single word—power. The power to oppress or humiliate Indians, the poor, women, the weak, blacks, and rebels, turning them all into subjugated minors. This conglomeration is much greater than the mere sexual theme, which the novel explores extensively, and it explains not only Ernesto's withdrawal but also his choice, in the words of Martí's verse: "Con los pobres de la tierra / quiero yo mi suerte echar" [With the poor people of the earth / I mean to throw in my lot].[11] In Arguedas's work, as in Martí's, the Christian flame burns brighter than any other political or social inspiration of his time.

Ernesto's yearning to share lacks any objective basis, given his character's weakness and youth. The resulting mismatch between desire and actions leads to his imbalanced behavior. He does not carry out any actions of importance; the most he can do is to refract and thus give meaning to the actions of others. His role cannot be called passive, for his is a consciousness teetering on the edge, participating emotionally and intellectually in the dramatic crisis, but his actions do not change what really happens in the slightest. The result is a divide that runs through the entire novel; in the background, one episode after another takes place, some of them partially linked (such as the uprising of the chicheras, which leads to the intervention of the army), others disconnected from the plot (such as those concerning the various school characters or the events surrounding the sudden, unforeseen plague). In the foreground, separately, a torrential, confused continuity arises from the consciousness of the character Ernesto and his function as bearer of witness. It is up to this consciousness to tie together the basically unrelated incidents (the Old Man, his father, Cuzco, the chicheras, Abancay, the colonos), articulating them so they form a subjective, meaningful discourse. The components of the dramatic crisis are clearly not integrated; they follow one another like independent kernels, with little plot connection: the wall of the Inca Roca's palace, the courting rituals of the adolescents, the uprising of the chicheras, Ernesto's father, the black Brother Miguel, the river Pachachaca, the zumbayllu, and so on. Among these scattered incidents, one can only just make out an attempt to put a social whole on display. This fragmentary quality has something in common with the episodic narration of popular tales, which focus on one kernel without establishing causal connections to other kernels near or far, endeavoring to reach a more general articulation of the action. It is in Ernesto's consciousness that these episodes are subjected to the task of analysis, sometimes rational, other times magical, allowing them to interlock like necessary portions of a demonstration. Thus, they come together to create a message.

This is Ernesto's fundamental function in the novel. For him to carry it out, he is given some traits that at times seem jarringly arbitrary.[12] The external violence is matched by a very different internal violence, which is loving and lyrical; the confusion in the surrounding social reality that is sowed by chaos is compensated by Ernesto's almost hallucinatory clarity of vision, which sometimes evokes the insights of Alyosha in *The Brothers Karamazov*. From his first talks with his father in Cuzco to his adult conversations with Father Linares at school, which surprise the priest, Ernesto is endowed with a lucidity that does not derive from his intellectual powers of reasoning or from his accumulated knowledge of facts but from a stunning insight into things. At times he speaks and acts as if he were "possessed." Insofar as Arguedas is intent on bringing the novel to a frenzied conclusion, accentuating and exaggerating his realist literary devices to outrageous proportions, he moves his character frenetically and makes him unstable and violent; in fact, it is inside this character's consciousness that this expressionist projection takes place, much more than in the events described in the final chapter.

Father Linares, a provincial version of Dostoyevsky's Father Zossima, anxiously observes the strange, alienated condition of this character and describes him as a "lost creature" (211), a raving "madman" and a "wanderer" (229), and as frankly "demented" (230). Stationed on an instable border, the character Ernesto alternates between his emotion and his reason, his eroticism and his idealism, his rebelliousness and his impotence, his tender feelings and his hatred. This innermost imbalance and demented violence, propelling him more and more, give him the operatic quality he needs as the protagonist of the action. He is at center stage of actions through which secondary characters and masses of chorus members pass in response to their own, unforeseen, unprepared-for actions, emerging from them without warning. The dramatic crisis is fragmentary not only because the kernels of action remain unresolved but also because they lack antecedents; actions burst forth brusquely, transformations are unannounced, the characters have unpredictable moods, whirlwinds kick up suddenly, knock everything about, and then abate without warning.

This set of circumstances has an effect—a constructive one—on the character Ernesto, forcing him to struggle to encompass everything that is going on, but his characteristics are the ones that determine the dramatic crisis. His heightened tension, his exaggerated reactions, his agitation and confusion set the pace for the novel's action. Witnessing the barrage of howitzer shells falling on the trenches in the First World War, the poet Guillaume Apollinaire exclaimed, "Je devins un opéra fabuleux" [I became a fabulous opera].[13] It is Ernesto who becomes a fabulous opera within the grand operatic score that is this novel. It is he who dances, sings, hates, screams, and loves, ceaselessly chasing the other characters and groups so he can tie them all together with an interpretation that is, in the end, the interpretation of himself that he is seeking through the darkness.

The Levels of Mythical Concepts

Mythic thought is, clearly, an important component of the narrative project in *Deep Rivers*, as the author himself acknowledged. There has also, clearly, been far too much conventional analysis of this aspect of the novel, mainly because the critics have ignored its three distinct levels as a literary work: that of the materials, the consolidated myths, which the author has brought in from external social sources; that of the characters the author has created for the narrative fiction, as well as their functions; and that of the novel's general structure, over and above the invented characters—a level we can connect with, though at times also distinguish from, the author himself, and one that always reveals connections with the thinking of contemporary social groups.

To this can be added the imprecise usage of the word *myth* or the phrase *mythic thought*, depending on the currency of various anthropological concepts. Here, we will generally follow the line of argument that Claude Lévi-Strauss has developed,[14] setting forth a synthesis of the basic principles we follow before we begin our analysis.

Mythic thought is not an exclusive property of archaic or primitive societies or of non-Western cultures; it can be found even in the most advanced societies, both on its own and in combination with forms of thought that we call scientific, from which it is distinguished not by its mechanisms or abstract form (those being identical) but by the different fields and materials with which it operates. At the same time, the fact that most societies include sharply differentiated human groups, belonging to diverse educational and social strata, leads us to expect that we will find diverse manifestations of mythic thought in them. José María Arguedas proved this when he observed that, within any given Indian or mestizo group, the meaning of a myth will vary according to the social strata of the group's members.[15] On the other hand, Arguedas did not attempt to examine the mythical concepts at work in the various non-indigenous strata. That task is generally left to sociologists who sometimes frame it within the field of ideology, though there is no essential difference between the intrinsic falsity of myth and that of ideology, at least if we follow Karl Marx's view of the latter.

Any society—primitive or developed, ancient or modern—develops its thought through stories, beliefs, and doctrines; these are systems for interpreting the world that the society understands to be legitimately based on the reality it has come to know and dominate. Insofar as "human experience divides spontaneously and necessarily into two domains—that which, in Nature and in Society, is controlled directly by man, and that which is not,"[16] these stories, beliefs, and doctrines depart from the known in order to forge explanations of the unknown and the uncontrolled. These stories, beliefs, and doctrines apply the same methods they use for known reality to the unknown reality, transposing to it their materials, their knowledge, and their systems of relationships. Reading primitive myths tells us as much about the societies that generated them as reading modern myths about life in outer space (developed by the most voluminous contemporary literary genre, science fiction) tells us about the society that gave rise to them. For primitive men as for moderns, these stories function as truths. They reject the label of "falsehood" that has been pasted on myths since the Greeks condemned them, contrasting them with their discoveries in geometry. Ancients and moderns alike have dealt in myths, but that is not what they call them; for them, myths are what others—the less civilized—have.

For this very reason, myth, as myth, is transparent to those who use it and never experience it as falsehood, in the same way that no one experiences his own ideology as a false consciousness or a false rationalization but rather as a legitimate doctrine firmly based on objective values. The texts of myths—which, as Barthes has said, are nothing but stories, and thus comparable to literary texts—record both the social system that serves as the necessary point of departure for elaborating any myth and the intellectual work that articulates the data into a coherent interpretive discourse. This allows us to adopt Godelier's definition of myth: "myths are born *spontaneously at the intersection* of two complexes of effects: the effects *in* consciousness of the relations of men among themselves and with nature, and the effects *of* Thought on these data of representation, which it inserts in the complex machinery of reasoning by analogy."[17] The functioning of mythic thought and its products, the myths themselves, appear differently in *Deep Rivers* at different levels of the literary text.

The most obvious are the myths that emerge from Peru's Indian culture, like contemporary survivals of a vast traditional mythology in the heart of rural communities. These are the so-called consolidated myths we learn about from the discourses of the novel's second narrator, from what the characters say they have learned back in their social groups at home, or from the (carefully explained) behavior of some of the working-class characters, such as the colonos. None of this material was invented by the writer, and although he obviously selected the most appropriate materials for the development of his fictional work from among a large repertoire, he confined himself to transposing them into the novel's reality. In each case—a good example being the myth of K'arwarasu in chapter 6, mentioned above—the myth is retold briefly and didactically and, thus, is submitted to a rational analysis that lays bare its ideological armature. The myth is explained from an analytical, not an existential, perspective. The novel represents Ernesto as believing existentially in the myth; thus, something changes within him when he invokes the mountain, but the narrator's discourse situates it at a distance, as an Indian belief, and with that he ceases to participate in it. It is not a shared faith.

The second level consists of the characters' mythical concepts, especially those of the young students at the school in Abancay, and above all those of the protagonist, Ernesto. Though some of these concepts come from the indigenous source mentioned earlier, they cannot be entirely reduced to it. First, because they are heavily mixed with other mythical sources, particularly Catholic Christian ones; second, because they are affected to one degree or another by corrections imposed by the educational process, the social backgrounds of their bearers, or the bearers' experience in civil society. This is the level that has been studied most closely and most insistently by critics, especially in relation to Ernesto. Rowe has produced an excellent analysis of this theme, from a Lévi-Straussian perspective similar to our own, in his excellent book.[18] The risk of these analyses lies in the extrapolation from Ernesto's childish/mythical perspective to the novel as a whole.

Even on this level, it is striking how characters can transform the elaboration of mythic concepts in a way that evokes the confessions of shamans, as recorded by anthropologists and analyzed by Lévi-Strauss,[19] regarding the interpretive role that myths play when a community's realm of knowledge is widening. In two scenes in chapters 8 and 9, we witness two instances of messages being transmitted at a distance through magic; these are both clear examples of childish mythic concepts, perhaps with Indian roots but also familiar to Western societies where they have recently been adopted, like so many other magical concepts, under the scientific guise of telepathy. What is singular in both instances is the way the characters argue over the means they should use to communicate at a distance. In their arguments, they reject some methods and accept others, depending on the scientific knowledge they have assimilated. The magical act is carried out with complete faith, but it is adapted to their widening knowledge of the world via scientific data. In the first example,

Antero insists that the zumbayllu's singing and its message will rise up to the sun, at the same time that he corrects an Indian belief:

> It's not true that the *pisonay* blossoms on the sun. Indian beliefs! The sun is a red-hot star, isn't it? What flowers could be up there? But a song can neither burn nor freeze. A *winku layk'a* that's well wound and has an orangewood tip! First you speak to it, into one of its eyes, giving it your message and telling it which way to go. And then, when it's singing, you blow, you blow it carefully in the direction you want it to go, and keep on giving it your message. And the *zumbayllu* will sing into the ear of whoever is expecting you. (117–18)

In the second example, Ernesto and Romero debate using Romero's harmonica to send a message over the mountain peaks to Ernesto's father. Ernesto insists that "Abancay has the weight of the sky on it" (137) and only the music of a zumbayllu or a harmonica can cut through it; Romero argues that a message could also be sent through water or blood. Palacitos then adds his own advice, which is to remove the "strip of tin on which the factory trademark appeared" from the harmonica (138), in order to make its music travel farther. These are the workings of childish magic and cannot necessarily be traced to any Indian sources. They demonstrate how the characters elaborate their concepts right up to the limits of their knowledge, which they take as objective proof of reality.

Given that myths translate the sociological frameworks of the groups that invent them, it is to be expected that, in the indigenous myths found in the novel, we should discover a system of personal relationships where the higher forces appear in anthropomorphic form. This is the rural community's own system, the one it knows and uses, and therefore the one that it superimposes on the unknown social sphere by analogical thought. On the level of the characters, however, though we find vague personifications, their shadowy presences are far less striking than the notable absence of the gods. The absence, that is, of both the gods of the Indians' mythological world and (even more surprising among Catholic school students) of the Christian gods. What gives way in these young mythographers' mythmaking are the sociological frameworks of the Indian and Catholic worlds. With regard to them, what they produce is an agnostic slippage, which never reaches the point of negation, and the replacement of their superhuman characters with very powerful natural forces, whose meaning is obscure. The best example is the Pachachaca River, revered as a power but at the same time endowed—especially by Antero and Ernesto—with multiple meanings and behaviors. I would say that the children's mythifying concept is on a level with their perception of the reality that surrounds them, from the viewpoint of these characters' youth and weakness; it is a matter of their recognition of the Power that is above them and that rules over them in every way. The trio that will lead them to the adult sphere—sex, violence, and property—is nothing but a recognition of the forms of power in society.

This power, however, is not restricted to a single person, as it is in indigenous myths; rather, it is usually diluted among several people who act as equal repositories of force. The effects of power, its ability to coerce and create suffering, are more perceptible than the people who wield it. For a novel written in the tradition of indigenista narrative, it is always surprising that it omits any appearance of the owners of the haciendas where the colonos work (except the paradigmatic Old Man of chapter 1, who conducts the overture to the novel), of the local civic authorities, or of the *comandante* of the troops sent to repress the uprising. The personal embodiments of power have been diluted and expressed in collective forms (the hacienda owners) or through the servants of power (the soldiers), who also form a heterogeneous collectivity. There is one power that is personified, however: the school's rector, as Father Linares is habitually called. In the way everyone else behaves toward him, in the students' relations with him, we clearly perceive the ambivalence in their feelings. As for personifications, they provoke conflicting reactions: hatred and love, repulsion for their devious and despotic actions but attraction for their paternal protectiveness. The same occurs with the personification of a natural force in the dialogue between Antero and Ernesto about the Pachachaca River in chapter 9:

> "Let's go to the river, Markask'a!" I begged him in Quechua. "The Pachachaca knows the spirit in which the little children come to him, and why they come to him." [. . .]
>
> "Not if you get into him. Not if you go against the current. He'll want to sweep you along and break your bones on the boulders. It's not the same at all as when you speak to him humbly from the bank or look down at him from the bridge." [. . .]
>
> "But out in the middle of the stream is scarier; what I mean is that the Pachachaca's like an evil spirit there. He's not the Lord you imagine him to be when you're just watching him. He's a demon; when you feel his full strength, you're in the clutches of all the spirits that peer out from the cliff tops, from the caves, from the

mine shafts, from the Spanish moss that dangles from the trees, swaying in the wind. You must not go in; you must not! As for me, I'm like a son to him." (148)

This ambivalence extends to the various appreciations of rivers in a novel that uses the word *river* in its very title. It even gives rise to this reflection on the disconcerting contradictions of rivers, trying to account for the multiple connotations of the word. "Why, in the deep river beds, in those abysses of rocks, bushes, and sun, did the songs have such a sweet tone, when the powerful torrent of the waters was so wild and the precipices looked so terrifying? Perhaps because on those rocks the most delicate of tiny flowers frolicked with the wind, and because the thundering current of the great river flows through flowers and vines, where the birds are fortunate and joyous, more so than in any other part of the world" (171–72).

Despite these cases of personification, the dominant tendency in the mythic imagination of the students at the school is toward a recognition that natural forces work according to the system of laws with which they are endowed; according to the enigmatic higher channels of power. Therefore, when the students turn to magic, it is usually in order to make up for their own weakness, or for the weakness of other helpless and persecuted people (Doña Felipa), and to counteract the violent exercise of power. In all these operations, we can see a substantial change in the cognitive structure on which magic operates; these are not Indian myths — they are the myths of people who might be Indians, mestizos, or whites but who have, to various degrees, gained a greater understanding of society and of nature and who speak from the viewpoint of a different sociological framework.

Finally, we have the third level: that of the significational structure of the novel, its author, and his social environment. The arrangement of characters and situations, as well as the narrator's labor, present another form of interpretive agency that cannot be passively assimilated to that of the characters by, for example, turning Ernesto into a mouthpiece for José María Arguedas. Many narrators have worked with myths; many characters have been based on magical beliefs. Suffice it to mention Miguel Ángel Asturias and Alejo Carpentier, but no one ever suggests that the characters of Carpentier's *The Kingdom of This World* believe in lycanthropy because such beliefs were shared by the author or by the novel itself. Nevertheless, exactly that sort of slippage is often seen in appreciations of Arguedas's *Deep Rivers*.

Surveying the complete works of Arguedas, it seems almost unnecessary to state that he always worked from the perspective of realism, even verism, for all that he inflected it with his sensitive and restrained poetic accent. At the same time, his realism was aimed at a social understanding of Peruvian nationhood, culminating with the broad sociological overview of *Todas las sangres* and with the profound spiritual interpretation of the conflicts that have stirred the Peruvian people from their origins to the present in *The Fox from Up Above and the Fox from Down Below*. His constant dealings, as an ethnologist, with the Indian and mestizo and with the popular and traditional cultures of Peru enriched his understanding of mythmaking among the people of his country. He naturally called on those perceptions in creating his characters. In fact, in his essays and novels, we can trace his recognition of the energy contained in the worldviews that were disdained by the dominant rationality of the ruling ideological and political groups of the era and his loving support for their potential. There is, however, quite a difference between this support and actually sharing such beliefs. Even in his most admiring passages on Indian customs and beliefs, we find no trace of his identification with those beliefs; rather, we find respect and understanding.

This does not mean that he eschewed the processes of ideologization and mythification. A character such as Demetrio Rendón Willka of *Todas las sangres* is a good example, but those processes arose from a separate source, and they operated on a different field of knowledge — one that could be transferred to the zone of the obscure and unknown. If we grant that any philosophy or doctrine, even one that seems firmly founded on objectivity and scientism, is susceptible to ideological inflection and even mythification, we may wonder whether something along those lines might not have occurred to Arguedas with the cognitive systems he picked up in the intellectual milieu of the university during his youth and also from the environment promoted by the ideas of Amauta and its editor, Mariátegui. In his final years, when he received the Inca Garcilaso Prize, he recognized this guiding influence in his thought, but he also recognized the rough form in which he made it his own: "It was by reading Mariátegui and later Lenin that I found a permanent order in things; socialist theory channeled not only my whole future but also whatever energy there was in me, giving it a direction and making it flow even stronger by the very fact of channeling it. How far my understanding of socialism went I really do not know. But it did not kill the magic in me."[20]

Even more important than his affinity for socialist thought was the personal, experiential way he made it his own, the way he transformed it into personal energy by describing the order of the world and human action and the fact that this so-called scientific concept of society did not affect his inclination for magic. One possible reading of the above text, in light of many passages in Arguedas's fiction and essays, is that socialist theory was something he incorporated into a magical conception of the world through one of those transformations that are familiar in the history and evolution of socialist thought in our time. There is no need to invoke Karl Kautsky or research the ideological behavior of working-class strata around the world in order to discover that socialism has often been transformed into a religion or syncretic belief system, mixed with the most unlikely and even contradictory historical survivals. The spread of socialism through Latin America, Africa, and Asia is rife with such examples.

I think this is what happened to Arguedas. For him, socialism was not merely a theory or a method; it was above all a belief built upon a persuasive explanation of how society functioned. Thanks to socialism, he understood the world and saw clearly how it functioned, the forces that were at work in it, and the preordained utopian outcome in which he believed most of all, because it would bring about the liberation of the Indians who had been subjugated and abused. I would note that all of his personal tendencies found a perfect fit in socialism: his populism, his eagerness to right wrongs, his rage for justice and the good of all, even his sense of love, the roots of which were probably Christian. Socialism flowed through the channel of his personality and was molded by it. He worked it freely, existentially; he shaped it to reflect his deep impulses, and, having transformed it, he saw it as faithfully mirroring his innermost desires. Socialism thus functioned as an effective mechanism for linking the two cultural spheres in which Arguedas moved. It could form a bridge between the advanced people of the Western sphere and those who continued to live in the traditional sphere under horrible conditions of subjugation. The cultural concepts of the two spheres were diametrically opposed, but they agreed on concrete social and economic demands that would open up a path to liberation for the subjugated masses and the eventual integration of a divided nation. I think that Arguedas was not the only Latin American who experienced socialism in this way, though few did so with his refreshing innocence, enthusiasm, and hopefulness.

This is what underlies the mythic concept that is revealed by the novel itself, quite apart from the characters in the novel. There is a mythic concept molding the narrative materials, making one kind of selection and not another, articulating events and conferring meaning on them. This mythic concept has little to do with Indian concepts or with the notions of Ernesto and his schoolmates in Abancay; it deals with a different realm of known reality and different interpretive doctrines. Similar to them, it applies those doctrines to the unknown realm where compulsive forces are at work, exorcizing them and appropriating them through what it does know. This concept is this mythic transposition of socialism by Arguedas and, in a way, by his intellectual circle, the first group to incorporate Marxist thought into the national life of Peru.

From this perspective, the explanation that Arguedas always gave of his novel becomes comprehensible and persuasive: he viewed it as a social novel of immediate, hard-knuckled activism.[21] From his perspective, the novel's rich incorporation of magical perceptions in its characters was simply a realist recognition of the function of Peruvian folk culture, and it did not alter the clear social concept projected by its author, which rested on his use of Marxist social categories and the predetermined mechanisms of the transformation of social structure.

Each character in the novel is obviously portrayed with great representational skill, over and above being given his or her own class consciousness. The characters rarely assume their class consciousness, but the author takes care that his readers perceive the link between each character's social background and the ideas he expresses or the sentiments in play. To highlight this link, he gives detailed information on the class positions of each of his narrative creations while making sure that this doesn't detract from a character's personal autonomy, except in the overly idealized example of Ernesto. He only pays attention to a handful of the boys at the Abancay school, individualizing them by giving their names and narrating their actions extensively enough to allow us a clear perception of them as individual personalities. In each case, he adds information on their origins in a way that builds class resonances into their particular behaviors. Their personal behaviors express not only their particular personalities but also the behavior of the class or social group within that class to which each character belongs. The personality and ideas of Valle, Lleras, or Añuco are different from those of Markask'a, Palacitos, or Romero because the former are older and the latter are younger; beyond that first division, though, we can draw a second line that clearly demarcates one group from the other with regard to the class they belong to. Because the rule establishing equivalences between individual and class is never made explicit, and because it is possible to foresee the weight of the author's subjective views of these links, there will always be behaviors that the reader cannot comprehend clearly. One finds that Valle, Antero, Palacios, and Romero clearly tend toward certain class functions, but the reader might wonder to what degree Añuco's irregular behavior is tied to the landowning class from which he descends, albeit as an illegitimate son.

However, despite these scruples, the balance between individual and social class can be detected among the schoolboys. This balance disappears when we look at the role of the choral masses in the novel; their position as representatives of wide class groups predominates, whereas among them the individual note diminishes to the point of disappearing. Here we find the direct, frank action of a single social class, whether it recognizes itself as such or not, and therefore the individuals never achieve enough autonomy. In the best example, Doña Felipa of the chicheras, we find pigeon-holing rather than personality. The class concept behind the work thus becomes obvious.

Moreover, in addition to this classist substrate, there is another one, likewise general in form and drawn from an interpretation of Peru's regional diversity. Arguedas inherited not only a theory of social class but also a geocultural theory of his country. With this, the vertical coordinate system that allows him to place the classes according to their position in the social pyramid is complemented by horizontal coordinates that rearrange them by the contrasting degrees of modernization among the regions (coastal, highland, jungle) into which Peru is divided. Ernesto's cogitations on the odd cultural situation of the Indian Prudencio, a friend of Palacitos who shows up as a clarinet player in a military band (165–66), highlight the unexpected distortions that can occur when the social and geocultural coordinate systems are combined. This is true of Gerardo, the boy from the coast befriended by Antero, who drops his friendship with Ernesto but whom Ernesto can only perceive through his confused and conflicted emotions, which Romero shares. Both Ernesto and Romero waver between dropping Gerardo for class-based reasons and admiring him for his frank and completely straightforward behavior.

The system by which individuals are consigned to social entities derives from Arguedas's sociological framework, though we have seen that he did not treat that framework as a rigid rule book; it allowed for modifications among various possible distributions, and it blatantly did not apply in the case of the protagonist, Ernesto, who functions as an exception with respect to his class origins. If the sociological framework perceptible behind the Indian myths emphasized personal relations and interpreted higher forces anthropomorphically, endowing them with total, capricious freedom to grant or deny people aid; if the sociological framework perceptible in the schoolboys' own mythmaking recognizes the presence of natural forces that were sometimes personified but that, especially in the social sphere, were diluted among many distant beings; then the framework we find in Arguedas is clearly the structure of social classes whose power derives from their violent appropriation of the means of production and leads directly to the class struggle in which only the disciplined association of the members of the lower strata can make their future triumph possible.

This is the origin of the violence that dominates the panorama of the novel. It arises from one class's subjugation of the other classes, from their systematic exploitation, and it is this violence that incites the subjugated to rebel, relying on their strength in numbers. In keeping with the novel's reiterative composition, in which a kernel of meaning is approached serially, round after round, until it is fully attained, the book constructs two parallel lines, two growing series of uprisings by the subjugated against the dominators. The uprisings in the school plot line are carried out by the younger students against "the bad guys," that is, the abusive older students, and they culminate not only in the overthrow of the abusers but also in a recognition of their wickedness and misconduct, as revealed by their miserable fates. In the Abancay regional plot line, the rebellions are those carried out by the chicheras and by the colonos suffering from the plague; these uprisings, however, do not end in triumph, yet they do prophesy a future triumph, in keeping with the utopianism that Arguedas derives from his concept of socialism. We might point out he also turned Luis Valcarcel's teachings on Peruvian culture upside down here; instead of restoring the Indian Golden Age of the past, we have an expectation of its historical realization in the future. Arguedas's reading of the versions of the Inkarrí myth that he learned in those years can be found in his adoption of socialist utopianism.

The two sets of plot lines are laid out in parallel, and, in Ernesto's consciousness, both are animated by a bristling desire for revenge. The boy who bears witness to his earthshaking love for the helpless is the same boy whose heart brims with implacable hatred for those who exercise repression and cruelty. Their disappearance isn't enough for him; he also demands their demise, as we see when he imagines the fate of Lleras. The plague that strikes the colonos acquires the symbolic value of a power against which the disinherited must struggle, in the same way that Ernesto and the young students have struggled against the power of "the bad boys." The novel's final sentence compares Lleras and the plague as defeated enemies whom the river will sweep away to the country of the dead, thus establishing the convergence of the two forms of struggle and insurrection.

In each, disparate elements remain detached. In the social form, it is the colonos; in the schoolboys' private struggle, it is Ernesto. Ernesto will fervently accept the rector's suggestion that he should move to the hacienda of his uncle, the Old Man, when he discovers that the Old Man wields power over hundreds of colonos. The utopianism that unites the diverse episodes of the novel's final chapters returns here to link the separate plot lines; Ernesto will go incite the colonos to rebellion, and in that capacity he will take up the cosmic combat against the Old Man and against the power that subjugates, tortures, and murders. Like Balzac's Eugène de Rastignac confronting the power symbolized by the entire city of Paris that he wishes to conquer, Ernesto seems to be saying, "A nous deux, maintenant!" [It's between us now!] This is also the battle between David and Goliath, the established model for substantive power change in the world.

A utopian fever runs through the excitement of the last chapter. It is the moment when the narrator seems carried away by the main character's frenzy. The emotional temperature of the storytelling bears witness to the participation of the narrator (and, behind him, of Arguedas) in an exhilarating mythical image; it is the dazzling vision of a future combat in which history, the endless repository of injustice and suffering, is defeated by a radiant myth that establishes order, harmony, justice, and free will. Through social theory as deployed by a mythmaking thinker, the dark sphere of the unknown, which is both power and its future, has revealed the correct solution and succumbed to the vital, magical energy that forms the faith of the rebels.

Notes

Chapters 1 and 2 expand on ideas that I presented in "Los procesos de trans-culturación en la narrativa latinoamericana," *Revista de Literatura Hispano-americana* 5 (Universidad del Zulia, Venezuela, April 1974).

Chapters 3, 4, and 5 are updated versions of the following previously published essays: "El área cultural andina (hispanismo, mesticismo, indigenismo)," *Cuadernos Americanos* 33, no. 6 (November–December 1974); "La gesta del mestizo," introduction to *Formación de una cultura nacional indo-americana*, by José María Arguedas (Mexico City: Siglo XXI Editores, 1975); and "La inteligencia mítica," introduction to *Señores e indios*, by José María Arguedas (Montevideo: Arca, 1976).

Chapters 6 and 7 were written especially for this book.

Introduction

1 Noé Jitrik, "Ángel Rama: Una imagen," *Texto Crítico*, no. 32–33 (1985): 105–6. All translations are by David Frye unless otherwise noted.
2 Ángel Rama, prologue to *La novela en América Latina: Panoramas 1920–1980* (Bogotá: Procultura, 1982), 13; my translation. It is characteristic of Rama's cosmopolitanism that he assumes his readers' familiarity with Greene's novel *England Made Me* (1935) and casually incorporates the English phrase "made me" into his Spanish text.
3 José Emilio Pacheco, "La generación crítica," *Proceso* (January 2, 1984); quoted in Rosario Peyrou, prologue to *Ángel Rama: Diario 1974–1983* (Montevideo: Ediciones Trilce, 2001), 11.
4 Ángel Rama, "La Biblioteca Ayacucho como instrumento de integración cultural latinoamericana," in *Latinoamérica: Anuario de estudios latinoamericanos* (Mexico City: UNAM, 1981), 325.
5 Fundación Internacional Ángel Rama, "Cronología," appendix to *La crítica de la cultura en América Latina*, by Ángel Rama (Caracas: Biblioteca Ayacucho, 1985), 391.

6 Fernando Ortiz, *Cuban Counterpoint: Tobacco and Sugar*, trans. Harriet de Onís (Durham: Duke University Press, 1995); translation of *Contrapunteo cubano del tabaco y el azúcar* (Havana: Jesús Montero, 1940). Ortiz introduces and defines transculturation on pages 97–103. Fernando Coronil notes that Rama was the most prominent intellectual outside of Cuba to develop this concept, adding: "Perhaps through the influence of Rama's work, Ortiz's ideas have received some recognition in literary criticism and cultural studies." Fernando Coronil, introduction to Ortiz, *Cuban Counterpoint*, xxxvi.

7 Ortiz, *Cuban Counterpoint*, 102.

8 Ibid., 103.

9 Ibid., 98.

10 An English translation of the talk, "I Am Not an Acculturated Man," appears as an appendix in José María Arguedas, *The Fox from Up Above and the Fox from Down Below*, trans. Frances Barraclough (Pittsburgh: University of Pittsburgh Press, 2000), 268–70.

11 The Andean political-artistic movement of *indigenismo* should not be confused with the later development of indigenismo as a political institution of the postrevolutionary state in Mexico, as represented by the Instituto Nacional Indigenista (founded in 1948), which aimed to incorporate the country's marginalized indigenous peoples into full citizenship by acculturating—not transculturating—them into a homogenized "mestizo" society. The Mexican state abandoned this project after the Chiapas uprising of 1994, adopting in its place the vocabulary of multiculturalism.

12 José María Arguedas, *Fundación de una cultura nacional indoamericana*, ed. Ángel Rama (Mexico City: Siglo XXI, 1975). José María Arguedas, *Señores e indios: Acerca de la cultura quechua*, ed. Ángel Rama (Montevideo: Arca, 1976).

13 Ángel Rama, *Diario 1974–1983*, ed. Rosario Peyrou (Montevideo: Ediciones Trilce, 2001), 136, from the entry for March 8, 1980.

14 Rama, *Diario*, 145, from the entry for March 25, 1980.

15 Rama and Traba met at a literary conference in Chile in 1969, around the same time that he and his first wife separated. Traba's life story—immigrant Galician parents; literary youth in the Plata region; involuntary exile from her native Argentina; life in Colombia, Venezuela, Spain, and the United States; a combination of literary writing, criticism, and an ability to found and manage cultural enterprises (she was a well-received novelist as well as an art critic, and she helped found the first museum of modern art in Colombia); a first marriage to the Colombian journalist Alberto Zalamea, from which she had two children—paralleled Rama's life in uncanny ways.

16 Fundación Internacional Ángel Rama, "Cronología," 392.

17 See "Catch 28," *The Nation* (November 20, 1982): 515–16, and Bell Gale Chevigny, "A Latin American Odyssey Ends," *The Nation* (February 4, 1984): 126–28.

Chapter One: Literature and Culture

1 One of the most recent analyses of this behavior is Claudio Véliz, "Outward-Looking Nationalism and the Liberal Pause," in *The Centralist Tradition of Latin America* (Princeton: Princeton University Press, 1980), 163–88. [Throughout the text, Rama uses "America," "American," and "the continent" to refer to Latin America; he refers to the United States as "North America." — Tr.]

2 For English literature, this point has been studied by W. Jackson Bate, *The Burden of the Past and the English Poet* (New York: The Norton Library, 1970). [Rama's comment on the absence of a "modernizing dynamic" in Spain and Portugal was written in the 1970s, before the fall of the decades-long Fascist dictatorships in those countries. — Tr.]

3 [Andrés Bello (Caracas, 1781–Santiago de Chile, 1865) was a poet, philosopher, and educator, active during and after the Independence period. Citations in the text and notes are taken wherever possible from published translations, which are cited in the notes; otherwise, as here, all translations are mine. — Tr.]

4 Ignacio M. Altamirano, *La literatura nacional* (Mexico City: Porrúa, 1949), ed. and foreword by José Luis Martínez, 1:10. [Simón Rodríguez (Venezuela, 1769–Peru, 1854) was independence leader Simón Bolívar's tutor. Bello and Ignacio Manuel Altamirano (Mexico, 1834–Italy, 1893) were leading transnational literary and political figures in nineteenth-century Latin America. — Tr.]

5 See José Emilio Pacheco, *Antología del modernismo (1884–1921)* (Mexico City: Universidad Nacional Autónoma de México, 1978), 1:5. [The journalist and short story writer Manuel Gutiérrez Nájera (Mexico, 1859–1895) was an early promoter of the literary modernism movement often associated with Nicaraguan poet Rubén Darío (1867–1916). — Tr.]

6 [Rubén Darío (Nicaragua, 1867–1916) was the first great modernist poet of Latin America. The phrase "mental Gallicisms" is from Spanish writer Juan Valero's review of Darío's *Azul* (1888), which brought the Nicaraguan poet to the attention of the Spanish reading public. — Tr.]

7 [These were prominent schools and trends in literature and the arts from 1910 to 1940. In this chapter, Rama focuses primarily on regionalism (which emphasized the distinctiveness of Latin American regions, often in a rural-centered, folkloric vein, as key to the uniqueness of Latin American culture) and vanguardismo (the mainly urban avant-garde movement). — Tr.]

8 Alberto Zum Felde, *Índice crítico de la literatura hispanoamericana: Los ensayistas* (Mexico City: Guarania, 1954), 9. [Domingo Faustino Sarmiento (Argentina, 1811–1888), José María Samper (Peru, 1828–1888), and Eugenio María de Hostos (Puerto Rico, 1839–Dominican Republic, 1903) were influential politicians, writers, and educators in their respective countries. — Tr.]

9 For Mexican readings of Alarcón, see Antonio Alatorre, "Para la historia de

un problema: La mexicanidad de Ruiz de Alarcón," *Anuario de Letras Mexi-canos* 4 (1964): 161–202. [Here, Rama underlines a tendency among Latin American critics of the era to emphasize the "national character" of writers who happened to be born in their countries, regardless of where they produced their best known works. The writers: Alarcón (Taxco, 1581–Madrid, 1639) was a playwright born in colonial New Spain who wrote his plays after moving as a young man to Spain. Lautréamont (pseudonym of Isidore Ducasse, Uruguay, 1846–France, 1870), a Romantic precursor of surrealism, was born in Montevideo as the son of a French diplomat but was raised in France and wrote in French. Ricardo Palma (1833–1919) was a Peruvian essayist and journalist. Alonso Carrió de la Vandera (Gijón, 1715–Lima, 1783) was a Spanish functionary and merchant in colonial South America and the presumed author of the travel narrative *Lazarillo de ciegos caminantes* (1773), though recent scholars have leaned toward identifying its pseudonymous author as Carrió's indigenous Peruvian secretary Calixto Bustamante Carlos. The critics: Pedro Henríquez Ureña (Dominican Republic, 1884–Argentina, 1946) was a professor and essayist in Mexico, the United States, Dominican Republic, and Argentina. Alfonso Reyes (1889–1959) was a Mexican poet, critic, and essayist. Twin brothers Gervasio and Álvaro Guillet Muñoz (1897–1959 and 1897–1971, respectively) were Uruguayan poets and essayists. José Carlos Mariátegui (1894–1930) was a Peruvian writer and politician whose influential book *Seven Interpretive Essays on Peruvian Reality* (1928) is discussed below. Ventura García Calderón (1886–1959) was a Peruvian essayist and diplomat who somewhat coincidentally was born and died in Paris.—Tr.]

10 [Marcelino Menéndez Pelayo (Spain, 1856–1912) was an influential philologist, historian, and critic of Spanish and Spanish-American literature.—Tr.]

11 [Costumbrismo was a literary and artistic approach in Spain and Latin America that emphasized the depiction of everyday life and customs, usually with little or no social commentary or analysis. Regionalism (as used by Ángel Rama) was a literary movement that emphasized the cultural and linguistic uniqueness of regions within Latin American countries. Vanguardismo was a general term for early twentieth-century avant-garde literary and artistic movements in Spanish America, seen as linked to European movements and artists from the Surrealists and Dadaists to James Joyce; a separate but parallel movement was modernismo in Brazil. Mariano Azuela (Mexico, 1873–1952) was a writer best known for *Los de abajo* (1915) and other novels set during the Mexican Revolution.—Tr.]

12 Horacio Quiroga, *Sobre literatura*, vol. 7, *Obras inéditas y desconocidas* (Montevideo: Arca, 1970), 135. [Horacio Quiroga (Uruguay, 1878–Argentina, 1937) was a writer, poet, and playwright.—Tr.]

13 Gilberto Freyre, *Manifesto regionalista*, 6th ed. (Recife: Instituto Joaquim Nabuco de Pesquisas Sociais, 1976). [Freyre (Brazil, 1900–1987) was an influential writer, sociologist, anthropologist, and painter. He studied anthro-

pology at Columbia University under Franz Boas, who had founded the first anthropology department in the United States there in 1900. Mário de Andrade (Brazil, 1893–1945) was a poet, art critic, and musicologist. In his native city, São Paulo, he was one of the organizers of the Modern Art Week (*Semana de Arte Moderna*), February 11–18, 1922, which launched Brazil's modernista (avant-garde) movement.—Tr.]

14 Freyre, *Manifesto regionalista*, 52–53. [In the published Spanish text, the word *lyrical* is replaced, whether as a translation or as a printing error, by the word *historical*.—Tr.]

15 Ibid., 76.

16 Ibid., 54–55.

17 Ibid., 58.

18 José Carlos Mariátegui, *Seven Interpretive Essays on Peruvian Reality*, trans. Marjory Urquidi (Austin: University of Texas Press, 1971), 171. [Urquidi translates *indigenista* as "pro-Indian"; I have changed it back here to the original word.—Tr.]

19 [Enrique López Albújar (Peru, 1872–1966) was a novelist. Jorge Icaza (Ecuador, 1906–1978) was a novelist and playwright.—Tr.]

20 Alejo Carpentier, *La novela latinoamericana en vísperas de un nuevo siglo* (Mexico City: Siglo XXI, 1981), 12.

21 Vittorio Lanternari sees this modernizing impact as a factor in cultural disintegration: "A third factor in cultural disintegration results from the process of modernization in the independent countries, and may interfere with the process of urbanization and migration. As L. Wirth has indicated, for many societies the sacrifice of their cultural integrity appears to be the heavy price they must pay for progress. The sociological process parallels that of urbanization." Vittorio Lanternari, "Désintégration culturelle et processus d'acculturation," *Cahiers Internationaux de Sociologie* 41 (1966): 126. On the urban inflection of the process, see Ralph Beals, "Urbanism, Urbanization and Acculturation," *American Anthropologist* 53, no. 1 (January–March 1951): 1–10.

22 Gilda de Mello e Souza, *O Tupi e o Alaude: Una interpretação de Macunaíma* (São Paulo: Duas Cidades, 1979), 75.

23 Freyre, *Manifesto regionalista*, 28. [On Andrade, see note 13 above.—Tr.]

24 The three categories are outlined by Lanternari, "Désintégration culturelle et processus d'acculturation," 123, who adds: "In the innumerable cases of acculturation founded on 'cultural plasticity,' the elements of crisis and of disintegration are closely associated, in reality, with the elements that express or orient reintegration."

25 The initial problems in defining the concept led to the article by Robert Redfield, Ralph Linton, and Melville Herskovits, "Memorandum of the Study of Acculturation," *American Anthropologist* 38 (1936): 149–52. Expanded and systematized in Melville Herskovits, *Acculturation: The Study of Culture Contacts* (New York: J. J. Augustins, 1938). For a non-anthropological perspec-

tive based in the German philosophical tradition, see the essay by José Luis Romero, *Bases para una morfología de los contactos culturales* (Buenos Aires: Institución Cultural Española, 1944).

26 Fernando Ortiz, *Cuban Counterpoint: Tobacco and Sugar*, trans. Harriet de Onís (Durham: Duke University Press, 1995), 102–3. Translation of Fernando Ortiz, *Contrapunteo cubano del tabaco y el azúcar* (Havana: Jesús Montero, 1940).

27 Bronislaw Malinowski, introduction to Ortiz, *Cuban Counterpoint*, lix. "It is a process in which both parts of the equation are modified, a process from which a new reality emerges, transformed and complex, a reality that is not a mechanical agglomeration of traits, nor even a mosaic, but a new phenomenon, original and independent." Ralph Beals observed that Malinowski did not use the Cuban anthropologist's concept in any of his subsequent works; see Ralph Beals, "Acculturation," in *Anthropology Today*, ed. A. L. Kroeber (Chicago: University of Chicago Press, 1959), 628.

28 For a discussion of these terms, see Gonzalo Aguirre Beltrán, *El proceso de aculturación* (Mexico City: Universidad Nacional de México, 1957). Aguirre Beltrán concludes with this synthesis: "Going back to our terms: *ad-culturación* denotes the union of or contact between cultures; *ab-culturación*, the separation, rejection, of cultures; and *trans-culturación*, going from one culture to another." Following this definition, we rightly prefer the term *transculturation*. In favor of Fernando Ortiz's proposal, apart from the standard semantic reasons that he puts forward, there is the expressive felicity of the word itself. Ortiz's sensitivity toward the spirit of the language is what makes his books, unlike so many Spanish American texts in anthropology and sociology, a creative linguistic experience.

29 Gabriel García Márquez, "Los problemas de la novela," *El Heraldo*, April 24, 1950. Reprinted in Gabriel García Márquez, *Textos costeños*, vol. 1, *Obra periodística*, ed. Jacques Gilard (Barcelona: Bruguera, 1980), 269.

30 Gabriel García Márquez, "La jirafa," *El Heraldo*, April 27, 1950. Reprinted in García Márquez, *Textos costeños*, 273.

31 Edmundo Desnoes, "A falta de otras palabras" (paper delivered at the conference "The Rise of the New Latin American Narrative, 1950–1976," Washington, DC, October 18–20, 1979).

32 This talk, under the title "Yo no soy un aculturado," was included at the author's request as an epilogue to his posthumous, unfinished novel *El zorro de arriba y el zorro de abajo* (Buenos Aires: Losada, 1971), 297. English translation, "I Am Not an Acculturated Man," in José María Arguedas, *The Fox from Up Above and the Fox from Down Below*, trans. Frances Barraclough (Pittsburgh: University of Pittsburgh Press, 2000), 269.

33 George M. Foster, *Culture and Conquest: America's Spanish Heritage* (New York: Wenner Gren Foundation for Anthropological Research, 1960).

34 Ángel Rosenblat, "Lengua literaria y lengua popular en América," in *Sentido mágico de la palabra* (Caracas: Universidad Central de Venezuela, 1977). See chapter 4, "La novela social del siglo xx," 191–98.

35 Gabriel García Márquez and Mario Vargas Llosa, *La novela en América Latina: diálogo* (Lima: Carlos Milla Batres, Ediciones UNI, 1968), 15–16.

36 Alfredo Bosi, *História concisa da literatura brasileira* (São Paulo: Editora Cultrix, 1972), 481–82.

37 Roberto Schwarz, *A Sereia e o desconfiado* (Rio de Janeiro: Editora Civilização Brasileira, 1965).

38 Both texts are reprinted in João Guimarães Rosa, *Estas estórias* (Rio de Janeiro: Livraria José Olympio, 1969). [*Sagarana* was actually first published in 1946 and *Com o Vaqueiro Mariano* in 1952.—Tr.]

39 Guimarães Rosa, *Estas estórias*, 73–74.

40 Walnice Nogueira Galvão, *As formas do falso* (São Paulo: Editora Perspectiva, 1972), 70.

41 [René Etiemble, "Un homme à tuer: Jorge Luis Borges cosmopolite," *Temps Modernes* 83 (1952): 512–26.—Tr.]

42 Julio Cortázar, "Del sentimiento de lo fantástico," in *La vuelta al día en ochenta mundos* (Madrid: Siglo XXI de España, 1970), 69–75.

43 Jorge Rivera, "La nueva novela argentina de los años 40," foreword to *Las ratas*, by José Bianco (Buenos Aires: Centro Editor de América Latina, 1981), iv–vi.

44 Mircea Eliade, *Myth and Reality*, trans. Willard R. Trask (New York: Harper & Row, 1963), 4.

45 Pierre Chaunu, *L'Amérique et les Amériques, de la préhistoire à nos jours* (Paris: Armand Colin, 1964), 43.

46 Marx Horkheimer and Theodor Adorno, *Dialectic of Enlightenment*, trans. John Cumming (New York: Continuum, 1972).

47 [João Guimarães Rosa, *The Devil to Pay in the Backlands*, trans. James L. Taylor and Harriet de Onís (New York: Knopf, 1963), 132.—Tr.]

48 Benedito Nunes, *O dorso do tigre* (São Paulo: Editora Perspectiva, 1969), 185.

49 Nogueira Galvão, *As formas do falso*, 80. [He was citing passages from Guimarães Rosa, *The Devil to Pay in the Backlands*, 19, 154.—Tr.]

50 In the case of Rulfo's fiction, see Carlos Monsiváis, "Sí, tampoco los muertos retoñan. Desgraciadamente," in *Juan Rulfo: Homenaje nacional* (Mexico City: Instituto Nacional de Bellas Artes, 1980), 35–36.

Chapter Two: Regions, Cultures, and Literatures

1 See, for example, José Luis Martínez, *Unidad o divinidad de la literatura hispanoamericana* (Mexico City: Joaquín Mortiz, 1972).

2 See Julian H. Steward et al., *The People of Puerto Rico: A Study in Social Anthropology* (Urbana: University of Illinois Press, 1956).

3 João Guimarães Rosa, "Minas Gerais," in *Ave, palavra* (Río de Janeiro: José Olympio, 1970), 245–50.

4 Charles Wagley, *The Latin American Tradition: Essays on the Unity and the Diversity of Latin American Culture* (New York: Columbia University Press, 1963).

5 Darcy Ribeiro, *The Americas and Civilization*, trans. Linton Lomas Barrett and Marie McDavid Barrett (New York: Dutton, 1971); *As Américas e a civilização, estudos de antropologia da civilização*, 3rd ed. (Petrópolis: Editora Vozes, 1979).

6 Charles Wagley, "Regionalism and Cultural Unity in Brazil," *Social Forces* 26, no. 4 (1948): 457–64; reprinted in Dwight B. Heath and Richard N. Adams, eds., *Contemporary Cultures and Societies of Latin America* (New York: Random House, 1965), 124–36.

7 Manuel Diegues Júnior, *Etnias e culturas no Brasil*, 5th ed. (Rio de Janeiro: Civilização Brasileira, 1976).

8 Wagley, *Latin American Tradition*, 14.

9 Arnold Strickon, "Anthropology in Latín America," in *Social Science Research on Latin America*, ed. Charles Wagley (New York: Columbia University Press, 1965), 153.

10 Ibid.

11 Charles Wagley and Marvin Harris, "A Typology of Latin American Subcultures," *American Anthropologist* 57, no. 3 (June 1955): 428–51; reprinted in Wagley, *Latin American Tradition*, 81–117.

12 Cited in Wagley, "A Typology of Latin American Subcultures," 440.

13 José Luis Romero, *Latinoamérica: Las ciudades y las ideas* (Mexico City: Siglo XXI, 1976), 13.

14 Claudio Véliz, *The Centralist Tradition of Latin America* (Princeton: Princeton University Press, 1980).

15 Darcy Ribeiro, foreword to *Casa Grande y Senzala*, by Gilberto Freyre (Caracas: Biblioteca Ayacucho, 1977), xxvii.

16 [*Amauta*, a literary and political journal that combined literary modernism with socialist and indigenista politics, was founded in 1926 by Mariátegui, who edited it until his early death in 1930. Its indigenista cover was designed by Sabogal. — Tr.]

17 José María Arguedas, "José Sabogal y las artes populares en el Perú," in *Folklore Americano* 4 (Lima, 1956).

18 For data on regional economic inequality in Latin America, see Comisión Económica para América Latina, *La segunda década del desarrollo de las Naciones Unidas*, Session 13, Lima, Peru, April 1969. For a general consideration of the problem, see Walter B. Stöhr, *Regional Development: Experiences and Prospects in Latin America* (Paris: Mouton, 1975).

19 See his look back on his life's work in his introduction to the special issue of *Diogène* 43 (July–September 1963) on "Problemes d'Amérique Latine."

20 Claude Lévi-Strauss, *Tristes tropiques* (Paris: Plon, 1955); English translation by John and Doreen Weightman (New York: Penguin Books, 1992), 262.

21 Among the abundant bibliography on this point, see the outstanding work on the rediscovery of indigenous literature and philosophy by Mexican scholars Ángel María Garibay and Miguel León-Portilla, *The Broken Spears: The Aztec Account of the Conquest of Mexico*, trans. Lysander Kemp (London: Constable, 1962) as well as the contributions by Andean writers Jesús Lara

and José María Arguedas. An anthropologist, Laurette Séjourné, has provided evidence in favor of the Indians' allegations, *Antiguas culturas precolombinas* (Madrid: Siglo XXI de España), as does the book by Nathan Wachtel, *The Vision of the Vanquished: The Spanish Conquest of Peru through Indian Eyes, 1530–1570*, trans. Ben and Siân Reynolds (New York: Barnes & Noble, 1977). In his introduction, Wachtel observes: "Only recently, with the decline of European hegemony and the rise of anti-colonial movements, has the West begun to acknowledge the existence of other societies having histories of their own which do not necessarily conform to the European model. Present developments in anthropology, sociology and history have recognized the originality and complexity of those regions of the world which, by comparison with the West, we call 'under-developed.' The displacement of Europe from the centre of a mental universe has produced an upheaval in the social sciences" (1).

22 Ribeiro, *Americas and Civilization*, 34.

23 [Some relevant works by these ethnologists include Theodor Koch-Grünberg, *Zwei Jahre unter den Indianern: Reisen in Nordwest-Brasilien 1903–1905* (Stuttgart: Strecker & Schröder, 1910); Curt Nimuendajú, *The Tukuna*, ed. Robert Lowie, trans. William Hohenthal (Berkeley: University of California Press, 1952); Irving Goldman, *The Cubeo Indians of the Northwest Amazon* (Urbana: University of Illinois Press, 1963); and Julian H. Steward, "Western Tucanoan Tribes," in *Handbook of South American Indians*, vol. 3, ed. Julian H. Steward (Washington: Smithsonian Institution, 1948), 737–48.—Tr.]

24 Berta G. Ribeiro, "Introdução," in *Antes o mundo não existia: A mitologia heróica dos índios desâna*, by Umúsin Panlõn Kumu and Tolamãn Kenhíri (São Paulo: Livraria Cultura Editora, 1980), 9.

25 José Carlos Mariátegui, *Seven Interpretive Essays on Peruvian Reality*, trans. Marjory Urquidi (Austin: University of Texas Press, 1971), 274.

26 José María Arguedas, "*Taki Parwa* y la poesía quechua de la República," *Letras Peruanas* 4, no. 12 (August 1955): 73. [*Ollantay* is a drama written in classical Quechua. The earliest copy in existence was written down in the 1770s; its date and authorship is unknown.—Tr.]

27 Fausto Reinaga has paid a great deal of attention to the problems of the intellectual, beginning with his book *Alcides Arguedas* (La Paz, 1960). He has especially developed the theme in three books: *El indio y el cholaje: Proceso a Fernando Díez de Medina* (La Paz: PIAKK, 1964), *La "intelligentsia" del cholaje boliviano* (La Paz: PIB, 1967), and *El indio y los escritores de América* (La Paz: PIB, 1968). The polemical tone of these books and of his many doctrinal statements has drawn critiques. Among the latter, see Luis Antezana Ergueta, *El populismo criollo y la necesidad de combatirlo* (La Paz, 1970).

28 For the Colombian part of this region, Reichel-Dolmatoff states that the Comisaría del Vaupés, created in 1910, covers an area of 100,000 square kilometers and has a population of 14,000, whereas the Comisaría del Guainía, created in 1963, covers 78,000 square kilometers and has only 4,000 inhabi-

tants. See Gerardo Reichel-Dolmatoff, *Amazonian Cosmos: The Sexual and Religious Symbolism of the Tukâno Indians* (Chicago: University of Chicago Press, 1971), 9.

29 Márcio Souza, *A expressão amazonense: Do colonialismo ao neocolonialismo* (São Paulo: Editora Alfa-Omega, 1978), 17.

30 Ibid., 28.

31 Ibid., 34.

32 Ibid., 37.

33 Manuel Diegues, *Regiões culturais do Brasil* (Rio de Janeiro: Centro Brasileiro de Pesquisas Educacionais INEP, 1960), 221.

34 Irving Goldman, *The Cubeo Indians of the Northwest Amazon* (Urbana: University of Illinois Press, 1963).

35 Irving Goldman, "Tribes of the Uaupés-Caquetá Region," in *Handbook of South American Indians*, vol. 3 (1948), 763–64.

36 Reichel-Dolmatoff, *Amazonian Cosmos*.

37 Ibid., 249–52.

38 Berta G. Ribeiro, "Introdução," in *Antes o mundo não existía*, 10.

39 Ibid., 31.

40 [A line appears to be missing in the middle of this sentence in the published text. The translation "they layer their work beneath a series of social masks" is my effort to reconstruct the intended meaning.—Tr.]

41 See Reichel-Dolmatoff, *Amazonian Cosmos*, 159–66. Similar information is found in his other books, *The Shaman and the Jaguar: A Study of Narcotic Drugs among the Indians of Colombia* (Philadelphia: Temple University Press, 1975); *Beyond the Milky Way: Hallucinatory Imagery of the Tukano Indians* (Los Angeles: UCLA Latin American Center Publications, 1978); and some of the articles collected in his *Estudios antropológicos* (Bogotá: Instituto Colombiano de Cultura, 1977), especially the brilliant essay first published as "Cosmology as Ecological Analysis: A View from the Rain Forest," *Man* 11, no. 3 (1976): 307–18.

42 I have analyzed this in my book *Los gauchipolíticos rioplatenses: Literatura y sociedad* (Buenos Aires: Calicanto, 1976). [Juan Moreira was a nineteenth-century Argentine gaucho whose life and violent death inspired a biography, a serialized novel based on that biography (Eduardo Gutiérrez, 1880), a pantomime drama (also by Gutiérrez, 1884), a stage play (Juan José "Pepe" Podestá, 1886), and two movies (1948 and 1972).—Tr.]

43 See Basil Bernstein, *Class, Codes and Control*, 3 vols. (London: Routledge, 1971–74).

44 Márcio Souza, *Tem piranha no piraruco & As folias do látex* (Rio de Janeiro: Codecrí, 1978). See also his *Teatro indígena do Amazonas* (Rio de Janeiro: Codecrí, 1979).

45 [This statement cannot be verified, but among his many observations on myth, Roland Barthes wrote that "narrative is present in myth, legend, fable, tale, novella," and so on. Roland Barthes, *Image, Music, Text*, trans. Stephen Heath (New York: Hill and Wang, 1977), 79.—Tr.]

46 See Claude Lévi-Strauss, "The Structure of Myths," in *Structural Anthropology*, trans. Claire Jacobson and Brooke Grundfest Schoepf (New York: Basic Books, 1963), 202–28; and Claude Lévi-Strauss, *Mythologiques, Volume 1: The Raw and the Cooked*, trans. John and Doreen Weightman (Chicago: University of Chicago Press, 1969).

47 Reichel-Dolmatoff, *Amazonian Cosmos*, 93–97.

48 Berta Ribeiro, "Introdução," in *Antes o mundo não existía*, 33.

49 [The Bourbon and Pombaline reforms are remembered in Spanish and Portuguese America, respectively, as a series of modernizing measures taken by Spain and Portugal to consolidate and rationalize their rule over their American possessions, largely in response to the threat of British and French expansionism after 1750. Audiencias were the major civil and criminal courts of colonial Spanish America below the level of the Viceroyalties. The territories under their jurisdiction grew over time to reflect the actual economic and political relations among cities, towns, and regions. When mainland Spanish America gained independence (1810–25), they became the framework for forming the newly independent states. In Central and North America, the Audiencias of Guadalajara and Mexico joined to form the republic of Mexico, whereas the Audiencia of Guatemala broke apart after 1830 into the five countries of Central America. In South America, every independent Spanish American country that came into existence by 1830 was based on a former Audiencia, with the lone exceptions of Paraguay and Uruguay (both former districts in the Audiencia of Buenos Aires).—Tr.]

50 Juan Rulfo, "Los muertos no tienen tiempo ni espacio (un diálogo con Juan Rulfo)," in *La narrativa de Juan Rulfo: Interpretaciones críticas*, ed. Joseph Sommers (Mexico City: Sep-Setentas, 1974), 22.

51 Emile Benveniste, *Problemes de lingüistique générale* (Paris: Gallimard, 1966), 231.

52 See José López Portillo y Weber, *La conquista de la Nueva Galicia* (Mexico City: Talleres Gráficos de la Nación, 1935) and *La rebelión de la Nueva Galicia* (Tacubaya: Instituto Panamericano de Geografía e Historia, 1939).

53 See François Chevalier, *La formación de los grandes latifundios en México* (Mexico City: 1956); abridged English version, *Land and Society in Colonial Mexico: The Great Hacienda*, trans. Alvin Eustis, ed. Lesley Byrd Simpson (Berkeley: University of California Press, 1963).

54 Jean Meyer, "Pespectivas de un análisis sociohistórico de la influencia de Guadalajara sobre su región," in *Regiones y ciudades en América Latina*, trans. Enrique G. León López and Guillermo García Talavera, ed. Jean Piel et al. (Mexico City: Sep-Setentas, 1973), 156.

55 Luis González y González, *San Jose de Gracia: Mexican Village in Transition*, trans. John Upton (Austin: University of Texas Press, 1982), 26–27.

56 Joseph Sommers, ed., *La narrativa de Juan Rulfo: Interpretaciones críticas* (Mexico City: Sep-Setentas, 1974), 21.

57 Meyer, "Pespectivas," 149.

58 González y González, *San Jose de Gracia*, xxiv.

59 Meyer, "Pespectivas," 152.

60 Emmanuel Carballo, "Arreola y Rulfo, cuentistas," *Revista de la Universidad de México* 8, no. 7 (March 1954): 28–32; partially reprinted in Sommers, *La narrativa de Juan Rulfo*, 23–30.

61 Félix Luna, "Imagen de Juan Rulfo," *México en la Cultura* 540 (July 19, 1959): 3.

62 Sommers, *La narrativa de Juan Rulfo*, 17–18.

63 Luis Harss, *Los nuestros*, 7th ed. (Buenos Aires: Sudamericana, 1977), 335.

64 Alí Chumacero, "El *Pedro Páramo* de Juan Rulfo," *Revista de la Universidad de México* 9, no. 8 (April 1955): 25.

65 Hélene Riviere d'Arc, "Guadalajara y su región: influencias y dificultades de una metrópoli mexicana," in *Regiones y ciudades en América Latina*, 171.

66 Meyer, "Pespectivas," 157.

67 Jean Meyer, *La Cristiada*, 3 vols. (Mexico City: Siglo XXI, 1974); English translation of the one-volume French version, *The Cristero Rebellion: The Mexican People between Church and State, 1926–1929*, trans. Richard Southern (Cambridge: Cambridge University Press, 1976). In addition to *San José de Gracia*, see Luis González y González, *Sahuayo* (Morelia: Gobernación del Estado de Michoacán, 1979).

68 Harss, *Los nuestros*, 332.

69 [The quotations are from an interview with Rulfo in Reina Roffé, *Juan Rulfo: Autobiografía armada* (Buenos Aires: Ediciones Corregidor, 1973), 30, 24, and 31.—Tr.]

70 Jorge Ruffinelli, *El lugar de Rulfo* (Mexico City: Universidad Veracruzana, 1980), 18.

71 Meyer, "Pespectivas," 158.

72 Meyer, *La Cristiada*, 3:273.

73 Ibid.

74 [Reina Roffé, *Juan Rulfo: Autobiografía armada*, 31.—Tr.]

75 [Juan Rulfo, "They Gave Us the Land," in *The Burning Plain and Other Stories*, trans. George D. Schade (Austin: University of Texas Press, 1971), 13 and 9; translation modified here to emphasize the points made in the text.—Tr.]

Introduction to Part II

1 Quoted in Diógenes Vásquez, *Teoría regionalista y regionalismo peruano: Estudio económico, jurídico, político, ético* (Trujillo: Editorial Cordillera, 1932).

2 Among the books that show a change in perspective, see Carlos Iván Degregori et al., *Indigenismo, clases sociales y problema nacional* (Lima: Centro Latinoamericano de Trabajo Social, 1979).

Chapter Three: The Andean Cultural Area

1 Julian H. Steward, ed., *Handbook of South American Indians*, vol. 2, *The Andean Civilizations* (Washington: United States Government Printing Office, 1946).

Particularly useful are the following articles: George Kubler, "The Quechua in the Colonial World," 331–410; Bernard Mishkin, "The Contemporary Quechua," 411–70; John Murra, "The Historic Tribes of Ecuador," 785–821; A. L. Kroeber, "The Chibcha," 887–910; and Gregorio Hernández de Alba, "The Highland Tribes of Southern Colombia," 915–60.

2 See the essays on this topic by Pedro Henríquez Ureña in *Revista de Filología Española* 8 (1924): 358–61 and in *Biblioteca de Dialectología Hispanoamericana* 4 (1938): 334–35 and 5 (1940): 29.

3 On the problems of culture and dependence, see the essay by Aníbal Quijano, "Cultura y dominación: Notas sobre el problema de la participación cultural," in *Dos temas para el estudio de las teorías del subdesarrollo* (Caracas: La Enseñanza Viva, 1973). See also the interpretation of the cultural phenomenon among social groups in the lower social strata, in Paul-Henry Chombart de Lauwe, *Images de la culture* (Paris: Payot, 1970).

4 On the attitudes of the diverse dominant groups during the independence period, see Pierre Chaunu, *L'Amérique et les Amériques, de la préhistoire à nos jours* (Paris: Armand Colin, 1964); and Tulio Halperin Donghi, *The Contemporary History of Latin America*, ed. and trans. by John Charles Chasteen (Durham: Duke University Press, 1993), translation of *Historia contemporánea de América Latina* (Madrid: Alianza Editorial, 1969).

5 Darcy Ribeiro, in *As América e a civilização, estudos de antropologia da civilização*, 3rd ed. (Petrópolis: Editora Vozes, 1979), argues that the population of Gran Colombia formed a "new people," thanks to the acculturation offered by the very conditions of Chibcha culture, which had (he argues) served as a "sedan chair for carrying the lords." [The province of Cundinamarca is in the center of Colombia; Bogotá (ancient Bacatá) is the capital of both the province and the entire country. Gran Colombia was the first name of the republic, which also included the modern republics of Ecuador, Venezuela, and Panama.—Tr.]

6 [José Martí, "Nuestra América," *La Revista Ilustrada de Nueva York* (January 10, 1891).—Tr.]

7 [Juan Montalvo (1832–89) was an Ecuadorian writer who spent most of his adult life in exile in Colombia because of his political opposition to Ecuador's conservative dictators, against whom he wrote polemics. When the dictator Gabriel García Moreno was assassinated in 1875, Montalvo reportedly exclaimed, "It was not Rayo's machete, but my pen that has killed him."—Tr.]

8 ["Peru is a sick body: where a finger is pressed, pus bursts forth," quoted in José Carlos Mariátegui, *Seven Interpretive Essays on Peruvian Reality*, trans. Marjory Urquidi (Austin: University of Texas Press, 1971), 207.—Tr.]

9 [Jorge Basadre, "La promesa de la vida peruana," *Historia* 3 (1944): 27.—Tr.]

10 Luis Alberto Sánchez, *La literatura peruana: Derrotero para una histórica espiritual del Perú*, vol. 6 (Buenos Aires: Guaranía, 1951), 253.

11 Jorge Basadre, *Meditaciones sobre el destino histórico del Perú* (Lima: Ediciones Huascarán, 1947), 139.

12 [Between parentheses here, Rama mentions—by surname only—the nineteenth-century Spanish Romanticist writers Ramón de Mesonero Romanos (1803–82), José de Espronceda (1808–42), Angel María Saavedra, Duke of Rivas (1791–1865), Emilio Castelar y Ripoll (1832–99), and Spanish nationalist writer Marcelino Menéndez y Pelayo (1856–1912).—Tr.]

13 Manuel González Prada, "Nuestros indios," in *Horas de lucha* (Lima: Tipographía El Progreso Literario, 1908).

14 Mariátegui, *Seven Interpretive Essays*, 274.

15 Luis E. Valcárcel [Peruvian historian and anthropologist, 1891–1987] gives a summary of his rich output, including his thesis, in *Ruta cultural del Perú* (Mexico City: Fondo de Cultura Económica, 1945). In addition to his manifesto *Tempestad en los Andes* (Lima: Editorial Minerva, 1927) and *Mirador indio* (Series 1, Lima: Imprenta del Museo nacional, 1937; Series 2, Lima: Imprenta del Museo nacional, 1941), he has made an important contribution with his *Cuentos y leyendas inkas* (Lima: Imprenta del Museo Nacional, 1939).

16 Mariátegui, *Seven Interpretive Essays*; Víctor Raúl Haya de la Torre, *¿A dónde va Indoamérica?* 3rd ed. (Santiago: Ercilla, 1936) and *El antimperialismo y el Apra*, 2nd ed. (Santiago: Ercilla, 1936); Hildebrando Castro Pozo, *Nuestra comunidad indígena* (Lima: Editorial El Lucero, 1924), *Del ayllu al cooperativismo socialista* (Lima: P. Barrantes Castro, 1936), and "Social and Economic-Political Evolution of the Communities of Central Peru," in *Handbook of South American Indians*, 2:483–573.

17 [José Sabogal (1888–1956) was a Peruvian painter and muralist; Oswaldo Guayasamín (1919–99) was an Ecuadorian painter and sculptor; Enrique López Albújar (1872–1966) was a Peruvian writer whose collection *Cuentos Andinos* (1920) has been considered the first important work of indigenista fiction; Jorge Icaza (1906–78) was an Ecuadorian novelist best known for his indigenista novel *Huasipungo* (1934) (English version, *The Villagers*, trans. Bernard Dulsey, Carbondale: Southern Illinois University Press, 1964); Jesús Lara (1898–1980) was a Bolivian writer; Ciro Alegría (1909–67) was a Peruvian writer whose novel *El mundo es ancho y ajeno* won a prize for best Latin American novel of 1941 and was published simultaneously in English as *Broad and Alien Is the World*, trans. Harriet de Onís (New York, Farrar & Rinehart, 1941).—Tr.]

18 [The list includes novelists Rojas (Chile, 1896–1973), González Vera (Chile, 1897–1970), Rivera (Colombia, 1889–1928), and Gallegos (Venezuela, 1884–1969); poets Fernández Moreno (Argentina, 1886–1950), Storni (Argentina, 1892–1938), López Velarde (Mexico, 1888–1921), and Ibarbourou (Uruguay, 1892–1979); and story writers Bellan (Uruguay, 1889–1930) and Monteiro Lobato (Brazil, 1882–1948).—Tr.]

19 In his seminal essay, "Algunas características originales de la cultura mestiza en el Perú contemporáneo," *Revista del Museo Nacional* 23 (1954), 169, François Bourricaud perceptively notes: "The *indigenista* movement, which exalts the great pre-Columbian past of Peru with more passion than discernment, is a product of this mestizo mind, which expresses the protests of

educated, ambitious, discontented people whom the comfortable propertied class denies any opportunity for advancement."

20 [Francisco García Calderón Landa (1834–1905) and his son Francisco García Calderón Rey (1883–1953) were Chilean politicians and writers; José de la Riva-Agüero (1783–1858) and his great-grandson José de la Riva-Agüero y Osma (1885–1944) were Peruvian politicians and writers. Ricardo Palma (1833–1919) was a Peruvian writer in the regionalist mold, best known for his series of "Peruvian Traditions," published in ten volumes (1883–1908).—Tr.]

21 [Louis Baudin, *L'empire socialiste des Inka*, published in Spanish as *El imperio socialista de los incas*, trans. José Antonio Arze (Santiago de Chile: Zig-Zag, 1953) and in English as *A Socialist Empire: The Incas of Peru*, trans. Katherine Woods (Princeton: Van Nostrand, 1961).—Tr.]

22 Mariátegui, *Seven Interpretive Essays*, 202.

23 Ibid., 29.

24 Ibid., 22.

25 Ibid., 274–75.

26 Georg Lukács, *The Destruction of Reason*, trans. Peter Palmer (Atlantic Highlands, N.J.: Humanities Press, [1954] 1981).

27 José Carlos Mariátegui, "El hombre y el mito," *Mundial* (January 16, 1925); reprinted in José Carlos Mariátegui, *El alma matinal y otras estaciones del hombre de hoy* (Lima: Empresa Editora Amauta, 1950), 24.

28 Hildebrando Castro Pozo, *Renuevo de peruanidad: Novela, precedida de un prólogo polémico sobre cuestiones sociales* (Lima, 1934), 18.

29 Mariátegui, *Seven Interpretive Essays*, 275–76.

30 José María Arguedas and Alejandro Romualdo, "Poesía y prosa en el Perú contemporáneo," in *Casa de las Américas: Panorama de la actual literatura latinoamericana* (Madrid: Fundamentos, 1971), 187–206.

31 Alberto Escobar, *La narración en el Perú* (Lima: Editorial Letras, 1955).

32 Mariátegui, *Seven Interpretive Essays*, 165.

33 Arguedas and Romualdo, "Poesía y prosa en el Perú contemporáneo," 199.

34 [Clark Wissler, *The American Indian: An Introduction to the Anthropology of the New World* (New York: Douglas C. McMurtrie, 1917): 233.—Tr.]

35 José María Arguedas, *Canciones y cuentos del pueblo quechua* (Lima: Editorial Huascarán, 1949), 9.

36 José María Arguedas, "El complejo cultural en el Perú y el primer congreso de peruanistas: Lo indio, lo occidental y lo mestizo; los prejuicios culturales, la segregación social y la creación artística," *América indígena* 12 (April 2, 1952): 131–39.

37 José María Arguedas and Francisco Izquierdo Ríos, *Mitos, leyendas y cuentos peruanos* (Lima: Ediciones de la Dirección de Educación Artística y Extensión Cultural, 1947), 14.

38 For a discussion of various theories about the relationship between habitat and culture, see Melville Herskovits, *Man and His Works* (New York: Knopf, 1948).

39 Arguedas, *Canciones y cuentos del pueblo quechua*, 67–68.

40 José María Arguedas, *Deep Rivers*, trans. Frances Horning Barraclough (Austin: University of Texas Press, 1978), 60. [Here, I altered Barraclough's translation by adding Arguedas's exclamation points and semicolons and by changing *beloved* to *golden* in the final phrase to reflect the Spanish phrase *doradas* (not *adoradas*) *pampas*, as it appears in the edition of *Los ríos* that Rama used. — Tr.]

41 José María Arguedas, "Evolución de las comunidades indígenas: El valle del Mantaro y la ciudad de Huancayo, un caso de fusión de culturas no comprometida por la acción de las instituciones de origen colonial," *Revista del Museo Nacional* 26 (1957): 78–151; reprinted in José María Arguedas, *Formación de una cultura nacional indoamericana*, ed. Ángel Rama (Mexico City: Siglo XXI Editores, 1977), 80–147. José María Arguedas, "Folklore del Valle del Mantaro (provincias de Jauja y Concepción): Cuentos mágico-realistas y canciones de fiestas tradicionales," *Folklore Americano* 1 (1953): 101–298.

42 José María Arguedas, "Puquio: A Culture in Process of Change," in *Yawar Fiesta*, trans. Frances Barraclough (Austin: University of Texas Press, 1985), 149–92.

43 Arguedas, "Evolución de las comunidades indígenas," 105.

44 Ibid., 93.

45 Claude Lévi-Strauss, *Tristes tropiques* (Paris: Plon, 1955); English translation by John and Doreen Weightman (New York: Penguin Books, 1992), 109.

46 Arguedas, "El complejo cultural en el Perú," 136–37.

47 Arguedas, "José Sabogal y las artes populares," 241.

48 Arguedas, "Puquio," 192.

49 Ibid.

50 Ibid., 154–59. Arguedas recounts three versions of the myth that he and Josafat Roel Pineda collected. François Bourricaud republished these texts in the introduction to an article in which he analyzed them from a sociological point of view; "El mito de Inkarrí," *Folklore Americano* 4 (December 1956): 178–87. With the addition of more texts discovered by other researchers, including university students, Arguedas carried out a general study of the myth, drawing connections between each variation and the type of indigenous communities in which it was collected; "Mitos quechuas poshispánicos," *Amaru* 3 (July–September 1967): 14–18, reprinted in Arguedas, *Formación de una cultura nacional indoamericana*, 173–82.

Chapter Four: The Saga of the Mestizo

1 [This chapter originally appeared as the introduction to a collection of articles by José María Arguedas, *Formación de una cultura nacional indoamericana*, ed. Ángel Rama (Mexico City: Siglo XXI Editores, 1975). — Tr.]

2 [Stéphane Mallarmé, *Correspondance* (Paris: Gallimard, 1959), 233. — Tr.]

3 José María Arguedas, "I Am Not an Acculturated Man," in *The Fox from Up Above and the Fox from Down Below*, trans. Frances Barraclough (Pittsburgh: University of Pittsburgh Press, 2000), 268.

4 Arguedas, "I Am Not an Acculturated Man," 269–70.

5 The stories he published in *Agua* (Lima: CIP, 1935) as well as those collected later in *Cuentos olvidados*, ed. José Luis Rouillon (Lima: Ediciones Imágenes y Letras, 1973).

6 José María Arguedas, "The Novel and the Problem of Literary Expression in Peru," preface to *Yawar Fiesta*, trans. Frances Barraclough (Austin: University of Texas Press, 1985), xv.

7 François Bourricaud, "Sociología de una novela peruana," *El Comercio* (January 1, 1958).

8 On the problem of indigenismo as it relates to Arguedas, see Tomás G. Escajadillo, "Meditación preliminar acerca de José María Arguedas y el indigenismo," *Revista Peruana de Cultura* 13–14 (December 1970); Sebastián Salazar Bondy, "La evolución del llamado indigenismo," *Sur* (March 1965); Antonio Urcello, *José María Arguedas: El nuevo rostro del indio* (Lima: Librería Editorial Juan Mejía Baca, 1974), especially the chapter "'Indianismo' e 'Indigenismo'"; and the excellent revisionist take on the dualist thesis by Antonio Cornejo Polar, *Los universos narrativos de José María Arguedas* (Buenos Aires: Losada, 1974).

9 Among the first critical articles that emphasized this aspect of *Todas las sangres*, see Alberto Escobar, "La guerra silenciosa en 'Todas las sangres,'" *Revista Peruana de Cultura* (April 5, 1965) and José Miguel Oviedo, "Vasto cuadro del Perú feudal," *Marcha* (October 8–16, 1965). Later critical writing has further developed this point. See Gladys C. Marín, *La experiencia americana de José María Arguedas* (Buenos Aires: Fernando García Cambeiro, 1973) and Antonio Cornejo Polar, *Los universos narrativos*.

10 José María Arguedas, "Razón de ser del indigenismo en el Perú," in Juan Larco, ed., *Recopilación de textos sobre José María Arguedas* (Havana: Casa de las Américas, 1976), 419–20.

11 See Aníbal Quijano, "Naturaleza, situación y tendencia de la sociedad peruana contemporánea," *Pensamiento crítico* 16 (May 1968).

12 Arguedas, "Razón de ser del indigenismo en el Perú," 420.

13 Arguedas concludes his essay "The Novel and the Problem of Literary Expression in Peru," with the following question: "And why should the literature that shows us the disturbed and misty features of our people and of our own countenance in such a tormented fashion be called *indigenista?*" (xxi).

14 Arguedas, "Razón de ser del indigenismo en el Perú," 420.

15 [*Misti* is the Quechua word for "non-Indian," from the Spanish term *mestizo*. —Tr.]

16 Arguedas, "The Novel and the Problem of Literary Expression in Peru," xvi.

17 José María Arguedas, "El complejo cultural en el Perú y el Primer Congreso de Peruanistas," *América Indígena* 2 (1952), reprinted in Arguedas, *Formación de una cultura nacional indoamericana*, 3.

18 In an article published in the Sunday supplement to *El Comercio* (June 24, 1962), titled "El monstruoso contrasentido," Arguedas wrote, "The ancient arts of the indigenous people were admired, and the criollos and landlords

were dominated by their utter conviction that the continuity between the creators of those arts, universally honored as they were by foreign experts and critics, and the Indians and mestizos of today, had been broken absolutely. They took the transformations of style and in some techniques of indigenous art, imposed by servitude since the conquest, as a fundamental break between the spirit, the virtue, of ancient man and the contemporary 'degenerate' Indian. This conviction, which continues to govern the mentality of a large portion of criollos and landlords, constitutes the monstrous bit of nonsense. We shall attempt to show that for certain arts, such as music and dance, the postconquest forms are richer and more vast than the ancient ones, because they have assimilated and transformed excellent European expressive instruments, more perfect than their ancient counterparts."

19   [José María Arguedas, *Kachkaniraqmi! ¡Sigo siendo!: Textos esenciales* (Lima: Fondo Editorial del Congreso del Perú, 2004), 189. — Tr.]

20   See the series that Arguedas wrote for the Sunday supplement to *El Comercio* in 1962, including "Notas sobre el folklore peruano" (June 3) and "Apuntes sobre folklore peruano" (July 8); see also his "En defensa del folklore musical andino," *La Prensa* (November 19, 1944), "De lo mágico a lo popular, del vínculo local al nacional," *El Comercio* (June 30, 1968), and "Salvación del arte popular," *El Comercio* (December 7, 1969).

21   José María Arguedas, "José Sabogal y las artes populares en el Perú," in *Folklore Americano* 4 (1956), 242.

22   José María Arguedas, "La soledad cósmica en la poesía quechua," *Idea* 48–49 (1961), 4; reprinted in *Casa de las Américas* 15–16 (1962), 22; and in *Lectura crítica de la literatura americana, 4: Actualidades fundacionales*, ed. Saúl Sosnowski (Caracas: Biblioteca Ayacucho, 1997), 117.

23   His most serious studies on this subject are "Puquio: A Culture in Process of Change," which covers the research he carried out there in 1952 and 1956; his important article on the evolution of indigenous communities ["Evolución de las comunidades indígenas"], descriptively subtitled "The Valley of Mantaro and the City of Huancayo: A Case of Cultural Fusion Not Brought about by the Actions of Colonial Institutions"; and his perceptive study of religious art in Huamanga ["Notas elementales sobre el arte religioso y la cultura mestiza de Huamanga," *Revista del Museo Nacional* 27 (1958); reprinted in Arguedas, *Formación de una cultura nacional indoamericana*, 148–72]. A summary of his conclusions can be found in his paper "Cambio de cultura en las comunidades indígenas económicamente fuertes" [*Cuadernos de antropologia* 2 (1959); reprinted in Arguedas, *Formación de una cultura nacional indoamericana*, 28–34].

24   José María Arguedas, "La sierra en el proceso de la cultura peruana," *La Prensa* (September 23, 1953); reprinted in *Formación de una cultura nacional indoamericana*, 12.

25   [Claude Lévi-Strauss uses E. B. Tylor's phrase "if law is anywhere, it is everywhere" as an epigraph to *The Elementary Structures of Kinship* (Boston: Beacon Press, 1969), xxi. — Tr.]

26 José María Arguedas, "La cultura: Un patrimonio difícil de colonizar," *Formación de una cultura nacional indoamericana*, 183.

27 [Arguedas, "Notas elementales sobre el arte religioso y la cultura mestiza de Huamanga." *Retablos* from the Huamanga area, also known as *cajas de San Marcos* (Saint Mark boxes) or simply *San Marcos*, are religiously themed dioramas created inside small wooden boxes.—Tr.]

28 Arguedas also developed this theme in his article "Del retablo mágico al retablo mercantil," *El Comercio* (December 30, 1962); reprinted in Arguedas, *Señores e indios: Acerca de la cultura quechua*, ed. Ángel Rama (Buenos Aires: Calicanto, 1976), 248–54.

29 Ibid.

30 Arguedas, "I Am Not an Acculturated Man," 270.

Chapter Five: Mythic Intelligence

1 Claude Lévi-Strauss, *Mythologiques, Volume 1: The Raw and the Cooked*, trans. John and Doreen Weightman (Chicago: University of Chicago Press, 1969), 6.

2 Darcy Ribeiro, *The Americas and Civilization*, trans. Linton Lomas Barrett and Marie McDavid Barrett (New York: Dutton, 1971), 148.

3 José María Arguedas, "The Novel and the Problem of Literary Expression in Peru," preface to *Yawar Fiesta*, trans. Frances Barraclough (Austin: University of Texas Press, 1985), xv.

4 Ibid., xiii–xxi.

5 Ciro Alegría, "Notas sobre el personaje en la novela hispanoamericana," in *La novela iberoamericana: Memoria del Quinto Congreso del Instituto Internacional de Literatura Iberoamericana*, ed. Arturo Torres Rioseco (Albuquerque: University of New Mexico Press, 1952), 50. He says, "The Spanish American novel is an immense showcase of stories developed in a thousand panoramas and situations, which would have tremendous impact if only they did not lack the one thing that is the genre's essential element, its acid test: a real character."

6 Arguedas, "Novel and the Problem of Literary Expression in Peru," xiv.

7 [Chekhov expresses this opinion in an October 1888 letter to Suvorin; *Letters of Anton Chekhov*, ed. Avrahm Yarmolinsky (New York: Viking Press, 1973), 88.—Tr.]

8 José María Arguedas, "I Am Not an Acculturated Man," in *The Fox from Up Above and the Fox from Down Below*, trans. Frances Barraclough (Pittsburgh: University of Pittsburgh Press, 2000), 269.

9 Arguedas, "First Diary," in *Fox from Up Above and the Fox from Down Below*, 25.

10 Arguedas, "Algunos datos acerca de estas novelas," in *Diamantes y pedernales* (Lima: Juan Mejía Baca y P. L. Villanueva, 1954), 8.

11 Arguedas, "Novel and the Problem of Literary Expression in Peru," xix.

12 Ibid., xx.

13 Arguedas, "I Am Not an Acculturated Man," 269.

14 Roland Barthes, "Writing and Revolution," in *Writing Degree Zero and Elements of Semiology*, trans. Annette Lavers and Colin Smith (London: Jonathan Cape, 1967), 58.

15 François Bourricaud, "Algunas características originales de la cultura mestiza en el Perú," *Revista del Museo Nacional* 23 (1954): 162–73.

16 José María Arguedas, *Canciones y cuentos del pueblo quechua* (Lima: Editorial Huascarán, 1949), 11.

17 Arguedas, "Folklore del Valle del Mantaro (provincias de Jauja y Concepción): Cuentos mágico-realistas y canciones de fiestas tradicionales," *Folklore Americano* 1 (1953): 101–298.

18 [See the epigraph and first note to chapter 6.—Tr.]

19 [The title of the chapter, "Cal y canto" (Stone and Lime), is a pun: the Spanish phrase connotes "solidly built," but the word for stone, *canto*, doubles as the Spanish word for song, which is the actual subject of the chapter.—Tr.]

20 José María Arguedas, *Deep Rivers*, trans. Frances Horning Barraclough (Austin: University of Texas Press, 1978), 149.

21 [A collection of Quechua folktales compiled by a priest around 1589 (for the purpose of prosecuting his parishioners for idolatry), the Huarochirí Manuscript was translated into Spanish by Arguedas as *Dioses y hombres de Huarochirí: Narración quechua recogida por Francisco de Ávila* (Lima: Instituto de Estudios Peruanos, 1966).—Tr.]

22 José María Arguedas, "Cuentos religioso-mágicos quechuas de Lucanamarca," *Folklore Americano* 8 (1960–61): 142–216.

23 See Arguedas, "Novel and the Problem of Literary Expression in Peru" (a text that he republished as the prologue to the 1954 edition of *Agua*), xix: "It was necessary to discover subtle ways to disarrange the Spanish in order to make it into the fitting mold, the adequate instrument of expression. And since it was a case of an aesthetic discovery, it was made in an imprecise, dreamlike fashion. It was made naturally for me, the seeker. Six months later, I turned to the pages of the first story in *Agua*. There was no longer anything to complain about. That was the world! The small village burning beneath the fire of love and of hatred, of the great sun and of the silence; amid the singing of robins that had taken shelter in the bushes; beneath the highest and most avaricious of skies, beautiful but cruel."

24 Barthes, "Writing and the Novel," in *Writing Degree Zero*, 27.

25 [Arguedas, "Zumbayllu," in *Deep Rivers*, 64–86.—Tr.]

26 Adolf E. Jensen, *Myth and Cult among Primitive Peoples*, trans. Marianna Tax Choldin and Wolfgang Weissleder (Chicago: University of Chicago Press, 1963), 26.

27 Claude Lévi-Strauss, *La Pensée Sauvage* (Paris: Plon, 1962); translated as *The Savage Mind* (Chicago: University of Chicago Press, 1966).

28 Lévi-Strauss, *Raw and the Cooked*, 341.

Chapter Six: The Novel, a Beggar's Opera

[The chapter opening epigraph can be translated as "I became a fabulous opera." The quote is actually from Arthur Rimbaud's poem "Delirium II" from *A Season in Hell* (1893), and not from the later surrealist poet Guillaume Apollinaire. Rama probably cited it from memory, incidentally changing it to the present tense (he has "deviens" [I become]). — Tr.]

1 José María Arguedas and Alejandro Romualdo, "Poesía y prosa en el Perú contemporáneo," in *Casa de las Américas: Panorama de la actual literatura latinoamericana* (Madrid: Fundamentos, 1971), 187–206.

2 César Lévano, "El contenido feudal de la obra de Arguedas," *Tareas del pensamiento peruano* 1 (January–February 1960); reprinted in César Lévano, *Arguedas: Un sentimiento trágico de la vida* (Lima: Gráfica Labor, 1969), 64: "Would it be pushing the exegesis too far to see in this episode, in which a handful of former men return to life through their faith, a kind of anticipation of what the Indians—in this case, serfs of the haciendas—might be able to accomplish when they acquire the minimum level of consciousness and hope needed to defy bullets and take over a city?" See also José María Arguedas and Hugo Blanco, "Correspondencia entre Hugo Blanco y José María Arguedas," *Amaru* 11 (December 1969), 12–15.

3 See the discussion of this point in Tomás G. Escajadillo, "Meditación preliminar acerca de José María Arguedas y el indigenismo," *Revista Peruana de Cultura* 13–14 (December 1970): 84–126.

4 Carlos Iván Degregori et al., *Indigenismo, clases sociales y problema nacional* (Lima: Centro Latinoamericano de Trabajo Social, 1979).

5 See chapter 5.

6 For an overview of these "dismissive" interpretations, see Antonio Cornejo Polar, "José María Arguedas, revelador de una realidad cambiante," in *Literatura de la emancipación hispanoamericana y otros ensayos* (Lima: Universidad Mayor de San Marcos, 1971), 211–16. Mario Vargas Llosa, "Novela primitiva y novela de creación en América Latina," *Revista de la Universidad de México* 23 (June 1969): 29–36.

7 Mario Vargas Llosa, "José María Arguedas descubre al indio auténtico," *Visión del Perú* 1 (August 1964): 3–7.

8 The chronology of the creative process behind *Deep Rivers* can be followed in William Rowe, *Contribución a una bibliografía de José María Arguedas* (Lima: mimeographed paper, 1969).

9 Arguedas, "Algunos datos acerca de estas novelas," in *Diamantes y pedernales* (Lima: Juan Mejía Baca y P. L. Villanueva, 1954), 5–8.

10 See Jean Franco, "Modernización, resistencia y revolución: La producción literaria de los años sesenta," *Escritura* 2, no. 3 (January–June 1977): 3–19.

11 José María Arguedas, *Primer encuentro de narradores peruanos, Arequipa 1965* (Lima: Casa de la Cultura del Perú, 1969).

12 In his article "Guimarães Rosa: 'Yo no le tengo miedo a nadie'" [Guima-

rães Rosa: "I am not afraid of anyone"], in *El Comercio* (December 3, 1967), 34, Arguedas bore witness to his admiration: "It has been enough, majestic brother Guimarães—enough not to be afraid of anyone, to have lived in the countryside and in the cities, and to have written, fearlessly, what the world is like. And much more than enough to have written about the legs of ants, about the trunks and flowers of the great trees that drink up water from the very bowels of hell, about the voices of animals as diverse, as mysterious as those that wander the mountains and forests of Latin America, animals and flowers showered with dust from every land and every era—as you have been able to do."

13 See Sara Castro Klarén, "Realismo y retórica narrativa," chapter 2 of *El mundo mágico de José María Arguedas* (Lima: Instituto de Estudios Peruanos, 1973), 44–85.

14 [José María Arguedas, *Deep Rivers*, trans. Frances Horning Barraclough (Austin: University of Texas Press, 1978), 64. All other parenthetical citations within this chapter are from this edition of *Deep Rivers.*—Tr.]

15 José María Arguedas, "El *Ollantay*: Lo autóctono y lo occidental en el estilo de los dramas coloniales peruanos," *Letras Peruanas* 2, no. 8 (October 1952): 113–16, 139–40.

16 For an analysis of this problem, see William Rowe, *Mito e ideología en la obra de José María Arguedas* (Lima: Instituto Nacional de Cultura, 1979).

17 [*Vécu*, meaning "lived." André Breton wrote of "the conversion progressively more necessary . . . of the imagined to the lived (*vécu*) or, more exactly, to the ought-to-be-lived." *Communicating Vessels*, trans. Mary Ann Caws and Geoffrey T. Harris (Lincoln, University of Nebraska Press, 1990), 4.—Tr.]

18 José María Arguedas, "Folklore del Valle del Mantaro (provincias de Jauja y Concepción): Cuentos mágico-realistas y canciones de fiestas tradicionales," *Folklore Americano* 1 (1953): 239, 241.

19 José María Arguedas, "Canciones quechuas," in *Señores e indios: Acerca de la cultura quechua*, ed. Ángel Rama (Buenos Aires: Calicanto, 1976), 183.

20 Arguedas, "*Ollantay*," 130.

21 Arguedas, "Canciones quechuas," 178.

22 Arguedas, "Fiesta en tinta," in *Señores e indios*, 77–78.

23 Arguedas, "De lo mágico a lo popular: Del vínculo local al nacional," in *Señores e indios*, 243.

24 Arguedas, "Fiesta en tinta," 78.

25 Arguedas, "Los Wayak," in *Señores e indios*, 125.

26 Arguedas, "Carnaval en Namora," in *Señores e indios*, 91.

27 Arguedas, "La muerte y los funerales," in *Señores e indios*, 150.

28 Arguedas, "Taki Parwa y la poesía quechua de la República," *Letras peruanas* 4, no. 12 (August 1955): 73.

29 I first put this idea forward in my introduction to Arguedas, *Señores e indios*, 27–28.

30 Mario Vargas Llosa, "José María Arguedas entre sapos y halcones," in *Los ríos profundos* (Caracas: Biblioteca Ayacucho, 1978), 201; reprinted in Saúl Sos-

nowski, ed. *Lectura crítica de la literatura americana, 4: Actualidades fundacionales* (Caracas: Biblioteca Ayacucho, 1997), 134.

31 See Maurice Godelier, "Myth and History," *New Left Review* 69 (October 1971): 93–112; reprinted in Maurice Godelier, *Perspectives in Marxist Anthropology*, trans. Robert Brain (Cambridge: Cambridge University Press, 1977).

32 Ariel Dorfman, *Imaginación y violencia en América: Ensayos sobre Borges, Asturias, Carpentier, García Márquez, Rulfo, Arguedas y Vargas* (Santiago de Chile: Editorial Universitaria, 1970).

Chapter Seven: Crisscrossing Rivers of Myth and History

1 William E. Bull, *Time, Tense and the Verbs: A Study in Theoretical and Applied Linguistics, with Particular Attention to Spanish* (Berkeley: University of California Press, 1960).

2 [In the following discussion, the names of the Spanish and French verbal tenses and aspects are translated as their closest English equivalents, except in the case of the French *passé composé*, which seems to have no precise equivalent. — Tr.]

3 [The verbs that are highlighted in translated passages do not always correspond exactly to the verbs in the original, but Rama's point is to emphasize the verb tenses, which do match. José María Arguedas, *Deep Rivers*, trans. Frances Horning Barraclough (Austin: University of Texas Press, 1978), 25. All other parenthetical citations within this chapter are from this edition of *Deep Rivers*. — Tr.]

4 Arguedas, "Acerca del intenso significado de dos voces quechuas," *La Prensa* (June 6, 1948), reprinted in José María Arguedas, *Indios, mestizos y señores* (Lima: Editorial Horizonte, 1989), 193–6.

5 Émile Benveniste, "Les relations de temps dans le verse français," *Bulletin de la Société Linguistique de Paris* 54 (1959): 69–82.

6 Harald Weinrich, *Estructura y función de los tiempos en el lenguaje*, trans. Federico Latorre (Madrid: Gredos, 1974).

7 [I modified the translation here by changing "put" to "used to put," to make obvious the use of the imperfect tense in Spanish to which Rama draws our attention. — Tr.]

8 Antonio Cornejo Polar, *Los universos narrativos de José María Arguedas* (Buenos Aires: Losada, 1974).

9 Mario Vargas Llosa, "José María Arguedas entre sapos y halcones," in Saúl Sosnowski, ed. *Lectura crítica de la literatura americana, 4: Actualidades fundacionales* (Caracas: Biblioteca Ayacucho, 1997), 134.

10 [I have substituted my own translation here in order to reflect Rama's point. The published translation of *Deep Rivers* interprets "este es chico" as "it's a small matter," whereas Rama clearly understands "este" as referring to the narrator ("he," not "it") and "chico" as meaning "small boy," not "small thing." — Tr.]

11 [José Martí, "Odio la máscara y vicio," verse 3 of *Versos sencillos* (1891). — Tr.]

12 The other characters in the novel recognize Ernesto's curious knack for taking up critical issues. The director asks him, "Why is it that with you we always speak of such serious matters?" (137) Antero says, "You've made me talk. . . . I don't know why, when I'm with you I open my thoughts, my tongue is unloosened" (107).

13 [As noted above, this line was actually written by Rimbaud (1873), not Apollinaire.—Tr.]

14 Especially in Claude Lévi-Strauss, *The Savage Mind*; *Totemism*, trans. Rodney Needham (Boston: Beacon Press, 1963); and the four volumes of *Mythologiques*, trans. John and Doreen Weightman (New York: Harper & Row)— *The Raw and the Cooked* (1969), *From Honey to Ashes* (1973), *The Origin of Table Manners* (1978), and *The Naked Man* (1981).

15 Arguedas, "Mitos quechuas poshispánicos," in *Formación de una cultura nacional indoamericana*, by José María Arguedas (Mexico City: Siglo XXI Editores, 1975), 173–82.

16 Maurice Godelier, "Myth and History," *New Left Review* 69 (October 1971): 97.

17 Ibid., 102 (emphasis in original).

18 William Rowe, *Mito e ideología en la obra de José María Arguedas* (Lima: Instituto Nacional de Cultura, 1979).

19 Claude Lévi-Strauss, "The Structure of Myths," in *Structural Anthropology*, trans. Claire Jacobson and Brooke Grundfest Schoepf (New York: Basic Books, 1963).

20 José María Arguedas, "I Am Not an Acculturated Man," in *The Fox from Up Above and the Fox from Down Below*, trans. Frances Barraclough (Pittsburgh: University of Pittsburgh Press, 2000), 270. [A publishing error in Rama's Spanish text substitutes "Marx" for "Mariátegui" in this quotation.—Tr.]

21 José María Arguedas, *Primer encuentro de narradores peruanos, Arequipa, 1965* (Lima: Casa de la Cultura del Perú, 1969).

Index

Guatemala, 16, 50
Guimarães Rosa, João, 27–28, 33, 38, 63–66, 68, 81, 109, 163
Gutiérrez Nájera, Manuel, 6

Haya de la Torre, Víctor Raúl, 44, 82, 85, 90–91, 96
Henríquez Ureña, Pedro, 7, 8, 41, 86
Highland zones: of Andean region, 43; of Colombia, 20, 85; contrast with coastal zones, 95, 101, 109–10, 115–16, 124, 127–30, 212; of northern Peru, 110; of southern Peru, 44, 68, 82–83, 85, 113, 122, 125, 138, 169, 177, 184, 191
Huancayo, 113, 170
Huaynos, 172, 173, 186

Icaza, Jorge, 13, 96, 98, 99, 101, 104, 133, 137
Ideology, 13, 26, 29, 41–42, 47–48, 88, 145, 160–62, 166, 203–5, 209
Inca Empire (Tawantinsuyu), 82, 85–86, 101–3, 108, 112, 117, 127, 137, 171–72
Independence and originality in Latin American literature, 4–9, 12, 23
Indian, figure of, 95–96, 107
Indigenismo, xvi, 13, 44–45, 90, 103, 106, 110–11, 137, 144, 160, 178; as mestizo movement, 95–101, 108, 125, 146; revised by Arguedas, 114–15, 120–29
Indigenous culture, 38, 98; Arguedas's approach to, 112–17, 120, 128, 133, 136–48; idealized by indigenistas, 90, 95–96, 106, 125
Indigenous languages, 24, 43, 48, 51–61, 161, 164. *See also* Quechua
Inkarrí, myth of, 117, 131–32, 213

Jakobson, Roman, 60, 183
Jensen, Adolf, 154

Kautsky, Karl, 99, 210

Language diversity: cultural resistance through, 48, 75–76; indigenous, 24, 43, 51–61, 161, 164; literary use of, 23–26, 142, 145–52; regional dialects and, 24–

25, 29, 41, 75, 163, 165. *See also* American Spanish; Quechua
Lanternari, Vittorio, 17, 219 n. 21, 219 n. 24
Lara, Jesús, 96, 101
Latin America: colonial period, 3, 62, 86, 111, 128; common literary system of, 3–10, 35; conquest period, 46, 50, 58, 62–63, 85–86, 95, 164; independence period, 4, 46–47, 87, 95, 111; regional diversity of, 37–46; unity of, 5, 37–39, 49, 84–86
Lettered city, xi, 42–43, 59
Lévi-Strauss, Claude, 31, 45, 59–60, 112, 115, 130, 135–36, 148, 154, 203, 205
Lima, 82, 87, 89, 92, 100, 101, 109–10, 114–17, 122, 127–29, 141, 144, 179, 182
Literary structure, 26–29
López Albújar, Enrique, 13, 96, 101, 107–8, 124–25
Lukács, Georg, 30, 104, 145

Malinowski, Bronislaw, 220 n. 27
Mantaro Valley, 113, 130, 139
Mariátegui, José Carlos, xvi, 7, 82; indigenismo and regionalism redefined by, 12–13, 44, 51, 95–96, 98, 108–10, 124, 137, 142; influence on Arguedas of, 120, 122–125, 160, 209; myth and, 104; racial views of, 102–4, 107; social analysis of Peru by, 12–13, 90–92, 101–3, 115, 120; socialism of, 96, 99, 122, 209
Martí, José, 89, 92, 200
Marx, Karl, 97, 141, 203
Marxism, 22, 53, 99, 120, 127, 145, 211
Master-slave dialectic, 88, 90
Menéndez Pelayo, Marcelino, 8
Mestizos: in Arguedas's works, 83, 108, 113–16, 119, 122, 124–31, 133, 136–41, 165, 185, 197, 208–9; indigenismo (*mesticismo*) and, 95–108, 124–31, 146; transcultural status of, 38, 50–53, 86–89, 185
Metonymy, 60, 170
Mexico, 9, 31, 43, 50, 63–77, 82, 95, 100, 111, 123
Meyer, Jean, 69, 70, 73–76

Middle classes, emerging, 6–9, 43, 96–98, 100, 111, 123, 145–46, 179

Moderning periods: first (1870–1910), 4–6, 35, 62, 65; second (1918–40), 15, 23, 85, 97

Modernism, 64, 133, 137, 161; Andean, 13, 21, 92–93; Brazilian (*modernismo*), 11, 14, 17, 29; international (European), 15–16, 45, 70; nineteenth-century Spanish American, 6–7, 23–24, 92, 123, 163; regionalism, dialogue with, 34–35. *See also* Avant-garde

Modernization: impact on regional cultures, 17–18, 20–21, 25, 34, 42, 44–50, 63–66, 68, 84–85, 100, 123, 212; literary responses to, 25–26, 28–29, 70–77, 81, 144; Mariátegui and, 91–94; mestizo culture and, 104–7; resistance to, 28–29, 48, 50, 53, 114–17

Montevideo, xii

Myth, 30–34, 51–61, 83, 104, 112, 117, 131–32, 149, 155, 185–86, 195, 203–8, 212–14

Mythical thinking, 34, 53, 83, 104, 135–36, 152–55, 203–4

Narrator, role of the, 24–25, 28–29, 32–34, 66–67, 150–52, 154, 165, 172, 176, 180, 182, 184, 189–96, 205, 208, 214

Neoculturation, 19, 23, 26, 45, 48, 50, 64, 65, 68, 77, 143

Nogueira Galvão, Walnice, 29, 33

Novel, history of the, 153–54

Ollantay (classical Quechua drama), 51, 168–69, 223 n. 26

Onetti, Juan Carlos, 30, 196, 200

Ortiz, Fernando, xi, xv, 18–19, 21–23, 26, 45, 216 n. 6, 220 n. 28

Palma, Ricardo, 7, 91–92, 94, 99

Paraguay, 50, 88

Popular language and culture: Arguedas's analysis of, 131, 147, 195, 209; Arguedas's use of, 61, 145, 152, 172–73, 178–79, 182–83, 186, 189, 201; Catholicism in, 47; in Guimarães Rosa's works, 24, 27–28; in Rulfo's works, 69, 74–76; in

works by indigenistas, 103; in works by regionalists, 12, 17, 32, 47, 52

Puerto Rico, 38–39, 48

Puquio, 113, 116–17

Quechua, 22, 61, 85, 86, 103, 110, 128, 142, 145–52, 162–76; and Peru's hostile bilingualism, 163

Quiroga, Horacio, 11, 101, 107

Ramos, Graciliano, 18, 30, 81, 164

Realism, literary, 103, 123, 148, 151, 155, 176, 178, 183, 209

Regionalism, literary, 6–8, 101, 146–48, 152–53, 155, 196, 218 n. 11; Arguedas's dedication to, 109–10, 113; conflict with avant-garde, 10–17; conflict with modernization, 47, 63–64; indigenismo as a branch of, 43–45, 97, 100, 107, 123; innovation in, 52, 81, 138, 142, 151; language behavior in, 24–26, 164–65; literary structure in, 26–29; worldview in, 29–35

Regionalism, political, 62, 82

Regionalist novel, 14, 26, 30, 32, 145–46, 150, 161

Reichel-Dolmatoff, Gerardo, 51, 55, 58, 60

Ribeiro, Berta, 51, 55–56, 60–61

Ribeiro, Darcy, xv, 38, 43, 48, 130

Rio de Janeiro, 11–12, 56

Río de la Plata region, 92–94

Rivera, José Eustasio, 10–11, 30, 52, 97, 165

Romanticism, 4, 6, 7, 92, 121

Rowe, William, 205

Rulfo, Juan, 18, 25, 26, 27, 33, 34, 45, 63–77, 82, 109, 150, 161, 165, 166, 176; innovative use of language by, 74–77; Scandinavian writers' influence on, 45, 70–73

Sabogal, José, 44, 90, 96, 115, 124

Salazar Bondy, Sebastián, 109, 162

Sánchez, Luis Alberto, 44, 90–91, 161

São Paulo, 11, 17, 52

Sarmiento, Domingo Faustino, 7, 47, 92

Scorza, Manuel, 24, 100, 160

Silva, José Asunción, 93

Social novel, 13–14, 27, 30, 145–47, 153, 178–79, 211
Socialism, 73, 94, 99, 101–2, 105–6, 115, 120–21, 132, 145, 209–11, 213
Socialist realism, 13, 146
Souza, Márcio, 52–53, 58
Steward, Julian, 39, 40, 51

Todas las sangres (Arguedas), 43, 66, 115, 122, 126, 134, 139, 153, 155, 180, 184, 197, 209
Traba, Marta, xii, xvii–xviii
Transculturation: in Andean region, 88, 93, 128; Arguedas's works as models of, 50, 115, 138–39, 141–45, 175, 185; defined, xi, xv–xvi, 18–23, 216 n. 6, 220 n. 28; in hinterland and indigenous cultures, 46–49, 52, 57, 59, 106; novelists of (Guimarães Rosa, García Márquez, Rulfo), 63, 65–66, 68, 84–85, 153; regionalist writers and, 25, 29, 33–34; as viewed by Arguedas, 111, 118, 138–39, 141, 144
Tukâno (Amazonian people), 50–61

Unamuno, Miguel de, 28, 164

Valcárcel, Luis Eduardo, 13, 90, 96, 101, 125, 127
Vallejo, César, 13, 18, 44, 90, 122, 142, 144, 160, 169, 179
Vanguardismo. *See* Avant-garde
Vargas Llosa, Mario, 52, 90, 160–61, 179
Vaupés-Caquetá region, 50–61
Venezuela, 10, 38, 50, 85, 88

Wagley, Charles, 38–40, 45, 64
War of the Pacific, 89, 92
Weinrich, Harald, 193
Woolf, Virginia, 20, 26–27, 71
Worldview: indigenous, in conflict with modernization, 56, 95, 112, 116, 147; indigenous, represented in Arguedas's works, 113, 117, 133, 142, 150, 153, 209; of middle classes, represented in literature, 6, 96, 98, 104; reflected in aesthetics, 19, 131; of regional cultures, represented by regionalists, 26, 29, 34

Yáñez, Agustín, 69, 74
Yawar Fiesta (Arguedas), 121–22, 133, 137, 141, 165, 176, 197

Ángel Rama, one of Latin America's most distinguished
twentieth-century men of letters, was a noted literary critic,
journalist, editor, publisher, and educator. He left his native
Uruguay following the military takeover and taught at the
University of Venezuela and the University of Maryland.
Of Rama's many books, *The Lettered City* is available in an
English-language translation from Duke University Press.

David Frye teaches about Latin America at the University
of Michigan. His translations include *First New Chronicle and
Good Government* by Guaman Poma (Peru, 1615), *The Mangy
Parrot* by José Joaquín Fernandez de Lizardi (Mexico, 1816),
and several Cuban and Spanish novels and poems.

Library of Congress Cataloging-in-Publication Data
Rama, Ángel.
[Transculturación narrativa en América Latina. English]
Writing across cultures : narrative transculturation in Latin
America / Ángel Rama ; edited and translated by David Frye.
p. cm. — (Latin america otherwise)
"A John Hope Franklin Center Book."
ISBN 978-0-8223-5285-3 (cloth : alk. paper)
ISBN 978-0-8223-5293-8 (pbk. : alk. paper)
1. Latin American fiction—20th century—History and
criticism. 2. Latin America—Civilization. 3. Literature
and society—Latin America. I. Frye, David L. II. Title.
III. Series: Latin America otherwise.
PQ7082.N7R34313 2012
863'.609—dc23   2011053342